Balancing East-West

Selected Works by
Paramhansa Yogananda

Alight Publications
2011

Balancing East-West
(Volume 3 from the Collected Works of Yogananada)

by Paramhansa Yogananda

First Edition Published in March 2011

Alight Publications
PO Box 930
Union City, CA 94587
http://www.alightbooks.com

ISBN 978-1-931833-36-3

Original Painting on Front Cover by Jeeti Singh

Printed in the United States of America

Dedicated
to
All Admirers
of
Paramhansa Yogananda

Contents
Balancing East-West

Introduction	1
A Balanced Life	7
Cosmic Consciousness	15
Affirmations	20
Life's Dream	21
My Native Land	23
Fixing Habits In The Brain At Will	24
Bits Of Wisdom	28
Spiritual Interpretation Of A Biblical Passage	30
Who Is A Yogi?	31
Reincarnation	32
The Doctrine Of Rebirth	36
Objects To Reincarnation Answered	37
The Needle's Eye	45
World Appeal For Recruiting A Spiritual Army	47
Message To My Los Angeles Yogoda Students	49
Christian Science And Hindu Philosophy	52
Luther Burbank: An Appreciation	64
Hart Of Heaven	68
Three Recipes - April 1926	71
Ethnologists vs The "Common Man"	72
At "Sul Monte"	80
Occidental Christianity And Yogoda	83
Doors Everywhere	92
Sympathy For Aimee Semple McPherson	93
Three Recipe Message - August 1926	94
Thoughts On The Florida Disaster	96
Message To Los Angeles Students	97
Spiritualizing Business	98
What I Mean By The Word "Hindu"	105
Christmas Message 1926	108
Three Recipes - December 1926	109

Vibratory Healing	112
Ocean Of Intuition	116
Four Recipes - May 1927	118
A Visit To Mt. Vernon	121
Overcoming Nervousness	124
There Is No Stranger Now	129
Three Recipes - July 1927	130
The Fire	133
Reforming Religion By Science	134
Samadhi	139
The Ramakrishna Swamis	143
Three Recipes - October 1927	144
Hamid Bey, "Miracle Man"	148
Sayings (In Washington Herald)	150
The Rose	154
Realization Versus Book Learning	155
Nicholas Roerich	161
To The Aurora Borealis	162
Three Recipes - December 1927	165
Miracles Of Raja Yoga	168
Your Most Important Engagement	174
Washing Sorrows With Moonbeams	177
Recipes - February 1927	179
Yellow Journalism versus Truth	181
The Righteous Battle	192
Shadows	194
Spiritualizing The Newspapers	195
Mother's Eyes	202
The Screen Of Life	203
Book Review	205
Prayer For Table Blessing	205
Two Recipes - April 1928	206
Watching The Motion Picture Of Life	208
Book Review of "The Creative East"	212
Two Recipes - June 1928	214

After This	220
Overcoming Pain And Sorrow	222
In The Endless Land	230
Four Recipes - August 1928	232
The Mystery Of Life And Death	235
Christmas Message - 1928	245
Ode To My Master	246
Quickening Human Evolution	248
Fountain Of Smiles	258
The Meaning Of Lent	261
Recipes Messages - January 1929	262
Resurrection	265
Recipes Message - February 1929	277
Vision Of India	283
My Mother India	284
Ode To Lake Chapala	292
Recipe Message - March 1929	295
What Is Love?	297
Oriental Christ	299
How To Acquire Initiative	306
Recipes - April 1930	311
Echoes	313
Guests: Good or Bad	315
Lessons On Spirituality	318

Introduction

by Runbir Singh

Paramhansa Yogananda, a Master of Kriya Yoga, devoted his life to introducing and spreading the science of Self-Realization to the West. In the process, he inspired millions and even sixty years after his passing in Los Angeles, his writings and his teachings continue to influence spiritual seekers all over the world.

I was introduced to the great spiritual tradition that he represents in 1969 and have been thankful ever since.

It is my intention that the original writings of this great spiritual Master be made available to a wider readership. The present volume is the third in the series of his collected works. It represents a selection of the articles he wrote for the magazine called "East West Magazine" during 1925-1930, especially from 1926.

The following is an article from 1926 that gives a glimpse of Yoganandaji's activities in 1923-1925:

> "Swami Yogananda came to this country in 1920 as the delegate from India to the Seventh Congress of Religious Liberals in Boston, Mass.
>
> Before leaving India, the Swami was asked by his father (who had undertaken to bear the expenses of Swami's journey to America) when he expected to return. "In about four months—if the Americans don't need me," Swami replied. Due to the "if", we have kept him with us, for we have needed him greatly and have appreciated his efforts for America's spiritual welfare for the last five years.
>
> Thru the financial assistance of his father, and the enthusiasm of a few devout students, the Swami started a small Sat-Sanga (Fellowship with Truth) Center in Boston. He lectured before many clubs, colleges and associations. A small summer-school was established near Waltham for students —mainly thru the cooperation of Sister Yogmata. The work grew and Swami sent

for his beloved associate, Swami Dhirananda, to come to America and help in the spread of the message of Yogoda and all-round human education. Mrs. J. Southwick helped greatly in the work of the Center.

In 1924, the call of God, for which the Swami had been patiently waiting, came for the further extension of the work.

Swami came to New York in 1923, aided by Dr. M. W. Lewis of Boston, and in one lecture at the New York Town Hall sowed the seeds of interest in his work. He was invited by the management of the Pennsylvania Hotel to become their guest, and he gave lectures and weekly classes there.

In early 1924 Swami visited Philadelphia and spoke there in the Public Library to a capacity house from which several hundred were turned away. He left a large enthusiastic class in Philadelphia, including Mr. Leopold Stokowski, the internationally-known Conductor of the Philadelphia Orchestra.

Swami felt every city to be like a big human mind that vibrated differently. New York said, "How much have you got?" Boston said, "How much do you know?" Philadelphia said "Who are you?" One Philadelphian did actually ask this question of Swami and he replied: "I come from a very high family headed by the Almighty Father." And Philadelphia was well satisfied, if the thunderous applause of the audience was any indication, and asked no further questions of lineage.

About this time Swami felt an inner call to further extend the work, and saw in his mind's eye the West of America and especially Los Angeles, swept by his teachings. Accordingly, he started out to cross the continent in a Maxwell automobile, accompanied by three students who alternated at driving the car. The little party of four was very harmonious, and the three boys did all in their power to make Swami comfortable through-out the long transcontinental journey. By leisurely travelling and camping, Swami managed to see and study America and Americans very closely and enjoyed each minute of the trip.

Finally Denver was reached and the good Maxwell took Swami up the famous Pike's Peak road and Swami wrote his poem about

Balancing East-West

the ride, beginning :

> "Ne'er did I expect to roam,
>
> On wheels four,
>
> Where thousand clouds do soar."

Swami spoke to a cultured audience of 3,000 people in the Denver City Auditorium, where the city organist played "The Song of India" when Swami entered for the lecture. A large class of Yogoda students was formed. The city of Denver vibrated to Swami the love for Nature and health-giving life.

Swami then proceeded to beautiful Colorado Springs, and thence to Yellowstone Park, which he considers "the greatest Nature-made, man-protected Park in the world." "All scenic marvels are here," the Swami wrote. "Lakes, rivers, mountains and the hot springs—heaving, smoking, hissing, boiling everywhere. The Turquoise Springs, as blue as their name, and the Old Faithful Geyser, shooting its hot waters several feet into the air at regular intervals —have deeply enthralled me with their beauty. I am reminded of our Indian forests when I see here the wild bears, bison and deer roaming about freely. A little greedy wild bear came up to the Maxwell and put its two little front paws against the car and ate from my hands."

From Yellowstone, Swami went to the Coast and boarded a ship for Alaska, about whose beauty he had often heard. Swami said of Alaska, "If it were possible to hold a beauty contest of all Nature's grandeurs and scenes of loveliness, it would be difficult to choose between Alaska and her Hindu sister, Kashmir, for the Queen's throne. If regal Kashmir with her floating gardens and lotus lakes, guarded all around by snow-crowned kingly ranges of the Himalayas, is the epitome of the world, as the geographers say, then Alaska alone is worthy to vie with her for beauty and diversity of scenic glory."

Swami described the journey to Alaska by steamer as

> "A voyage thru the garden-valley
>
> Laid on the barren sea,
>
> Surrounded by snow-capped island hills,

And draped with the lace of ever-green ferns."

After seeing Ketchecan, Anchorage and other Alaskan towns, and collecting specimens of walrus ivory, a gold nugget and a polar bear skin for his museum collection, Swami departed for Seattle, where he spoke to two thousand people each night. Devoted students cooperated to get together a large and enthusiastic class for Yogoda.

Proceeding to Portland, Swami lectured to huge crowds at the Multnomah Hotel and had a large class of students. In Portland for the first time Swami gave his public divine healing meeting and prayer affirmations which have proved so popular everywhere. In late October, 1924, Swami and his staff of three young men reached San Francisco, and lectures were given to packed houses in the Scottish Rite Auditorium. Classes of several hundred students were given in San Francisco and Oakland.

Finally, in January, 1925, Swami arrived at his goal and final destination of Los Angeles. The Great Divine Power seemed to have roused the whole city to receive the message of Yogoda, for truly Los Angeles gave Swami a royal and hearty welcome. Clubs, colleges, societies, educational centers, churches and newspapers extended him every courtesy and Swami's days were filled to overflowing with engagements to speak, write and be interviewed everywhere. Then, when the free lectures began at the Philharmonic Auditorium, which seats 3,000, the whole city turned out to hear Swami speak, and thousands were turned away each night. Swami gave several classes and had about 1500 students, and also a Special Advanced Course which Swami gave in Los Angeles for the first time in America.

One day during his Los Angeles stay, one of his students casually mentioned Mount Washington. Swami's soul was strangely stirred at the mention of this place and suggested that they drive up there on the following day. When he entered the grounds of the Mount Washington Hotel site, he strolled about, and then touching the bars surrounding the tennis court, he exclaimed to his companions. "This place feels like ours!" Today it is "ours," for thru the kind and willing cooperation and donations of his thousands of students throughout America, this property was purchased for

Balancing East-West

the American Headquarters of Sat-Sanga and Yogoda. On Easter morning, Swami gave a beautiful and impressive Easter Sunrise Service on Mount Washington.

After Los Angeles, Swami took a short vacation to view the unrivalled grandeur of the Grand Canyon of the Colorado, and then proceeded to Long Beach and San Diego where he met with great response, then on to Fresno, and then a second series of lectures and classes in San Francisco, Portland and Seattle. He spent September, 1925 in Spokane, Washington, who gave him a royal welcome. Everywhere the message of Yogoda has aroused spontaneous attention and has been supported by leading citizens of each city where the Swami has lectured."

Paramhansa Yogananda had come to USA on the behest of this own Master Swami Shri Yukteswar and under the ultimate direction of the immortal and ineffable Mahavatar Babaji. The following is part of a letter that was written by Shri Yukteswar to Yogananda. The translation is rather formal but the relationship between the two was closer than between father and son. It is translated from Bangali:

"11th August, 1926.

Child of my heart, O Yogananda!

Seeing the photos of your School and students, what joy comes in my life I cannot express in words. . . . I am melting in joy to see your Yogoda students of different cities. Beholding your methods in Chant Affirmations, Healing Vibrations and Divine Healing Prayers, I cannot refrain from thanking you from my heart.

Seeing the gate, the winding hilly way upward and the beautiful scenery spread out beneath the Mount Washington Educational Center, I yearn to behold it with my own eyes. . . .

Through the Guru's grace, everything here is going well. Through the grace of God, may you ever be in Bliss.

Your well-wisher,

(Signed)

SRI YUKTESWAR GIRI."

It is our hope that the articles in this volume will provide guidance to all sincere seekers. It has been over 59 years since the passing of Yoganandaji from this earthly plane but his spiritual presence is still very strong for all those who tune into his teachings.

It is fortunate that much of this Master's writings have been preserved and published for the guidance of future generations. However, there has been an unfortunate tendency to edit or even alter them to suit the expectatons of devotees or serve the purpose of the organization that he founded. It is our hope that publishing his unaltered original works would serve his legacy better by providing sincere seekers the pristine voice of Paramhansa Yogananda.

A Balanced Life

Imagine the misproportioned figures about to be described —the first one with a peanut-sized head and a body as fat as a balloon, the second figure with one arm developed like that of a Sandow, but with the physique of a dwarf, and the third one with a top-heavy head fitted to a frail Lilliputian body. Would it not be very amusing or pathetic spectacle (according to your mood) if you suddenly beheld a crowd of such people?

Behold the group on the right side of the picture. These people are normal so far as their outward physical form and appearance is concerned. But they are mentally unsound and deformed. As clothing hides scars, sores and some deformities, so also the neat-looking garb of human flesh often covers serious mental maladies.

If you were confronted with a vast crowd of average people, well-dressed and physically healthy, and if you were gifted with the power to see their mental bodies, what a surprise and heartache you would have. Their mental bodies ...with reason as the head, feeling and senses as the trunk, and Will as the feet —you would observe to be abnormal, diseased and deformed. You would see some people with a tiny head of small sense, attached to a bulging trunk of sense-appetites. Some would possess a withered body of feeling and pep, with the arm of business faculty very much over-developed in proportion. Another perhaps has a large Socratic brain but his trunk of sympathy and feeling is shrunken and dried-up. Still another, normal in head and body, would be seen to possess a pair of impotent paralytic feet of will and self-control. And so on.

Such multitudinous psychological deformities and pathological mental bodies, under-developed in some directions and over-developed in others, lie concealed within man, causing suffering to his soul and hampering his expression on the material plane.

It would not be out of place here to name a few such psychological diseases, so that ...invisible and supreme cause of all havoc in human life though they are —they may yet be detected and brought into the distinct consiciousness of the unconscious sufferers— who may learn their —nature, silent growth and symptoms ...and thus guard against their secret onslaughts and all-destroying powers.

One disease is prevalent among those that are mentally and physically idle under the pretext of being too busy with spiritual things. These sufferers neglect the great and small duties of material life, in the name of serving God, and thus invite the devil of mischief to dwell in them. They suffer from pessimism and lack of appreciation for all things good and beautiful in the material life. This is a contagious disease and all spiritual aspirants must guard themselves against it ...by keeping their blood of energy warm and immune —with constant healthful worthwhile activity.

Spiritual Indigestion

This results from indiscriminately swallowing a lot of mental patented medicines in the form of pseudo-spiritual books and lessons by quack spiritual doctors. This disease kills not only the real hunger for Truth but also destroys the power to discriminate between good and bad teachings. He who eats all the time and eats anything that he can get, will not only over-eat but will eat poisonous food along with the good, thus inviting: first —spiritual indigestion—and finally ...spiritual death. The long-continued over-study of all sorts of philosophical principles and treatise without ever trying to assimilate them and test them out in one's own practical experience ...results in doubt, indifference and disbelief in all spiritual laws.

Spiritual Melancoly

Those afflicted with this disease lead a purposeless life, through having too much time or money on their hands and lacking a true aim or understanding of life. They are whim-led, doing anything that comes into their heads, filling life with cheap novels, exciting movies, or other unproductive pastimes. They do not realize their malady until some terrible shock or nervous breakdown overtakes them. You don't know when you are going to catch it, and suffer from its outbursts of despondency, intolerance and impatience.

Chronic Worrier

This disease consists in harboring constant chronic worldly worries which are usually neglected and passively yielded to, instead of being fought and routed.

Psychological Insanity

It causes its victims to be one-sided in the pursuit of happiness. They begin to think that money is happiness, or fame is happiness, or health, or power. They sacrifice everything else, youth, reputation, peace of mind, etc., on the altar of their all-consuming ambition and learn too late that the balanced life alone —observing all the laws of nature and of God and combining activity with calmness— can bring happiness and fulfill man's natural destiny. The sufferers of Psychological Insanity become "money-mad" or obsessed with some one ambition ...until their perspective on life is warped and distorted. One man, for instance, was very successful in his business and amassed a million dollars, but before he could use it, he died of a complete nervous breakdown and excessive worry. Others, to gain fame, sacrifice their self-respect and sincerity. Sufferers from this disease of one-sidedness— miss their true goal and can never derive real satisfaction from the possession of their longed-for object, since man's nature is many-sided and demands all-round development.

Spiritual Fanaticism

This Ism-fanaticism among so-called spiritual people results from the clinging to some untested dogma or opinion of man without putting it to the test of experience, and causes paroxysms of anger and hatred against the laws of tested Truth and liberal rational thought. This religious madness leads to disobedience of God's simple laws of mental efficiency, material prosperity and physical health.

Physical diseases, being tangible, painful and repugnant, arouse our active resistance, and we seek to remedy them by exercise, diet, medicine or some definite method of cure. But psychological diseases, though the root cause of all human woes, are not prevented or attended to promptly and are allowed to devastate and wreck the life.

Educators, physical culturists, preachers, reformers, doctors and law-makers will hasten the progress of true civilization only when they themselves first learn and then teach others—how to harmoniously develop all the factors of life and of man's nature. This is the true education and all-round human culture that all the world is seeking.

Educational authorities deem it impossible to teach spiritual principles in public schools because they confuse them with the variety of conflicting forms of religious faiths. But if they concentrate on the universal principles of peace, love, service, tolerance and faith— that govern the spiritual life, and devise methods of practically growing such seeds in the fertile soil of the child's mind, then the imaginary difficulty is dissolved. It is the greatest mistake to ignore this problem just because it is seemingly difficult.

Many college graduates after leaving their universities are often found with a top-heavy, book-inflated head ...and are unable to walk straight in the path of life due to their legs of Will and Self-control being almost paralyzed through disuse. They tumble headlong into the pit of wrong marriage, sex-misuse, inordinate dollar-craving and business failure. They had not been taught any other use of their college-sharpened mental blades of smartness except to hurt themselves. Many young men seem to take pleasure in doing those things which react to their own disadvantage and suffering in the end. Last year in America young men ranging in years from 15 to 30 stole one billion dollars by the "hold-up" method. Who was responsible? We, all of us. They also are vicious who do not prevent the spread of vice, and teach others to be virtuous through their example. Schools, colleges, and society have not scientifically tried to prevent crime ...by eliminating its true mental cause.

Why not take the proper educational steps to avoid this annual theft of one billion dollars, and use some of those millions for creating "How-To-Live-Schools," where the art of living and a balanced development of all human faculties would be taught? We hope to have such a "How-To-Live-School" for all-round development, at our Mount Washington Educational Center in Los Angeles, as soon as funds are available and proper interest has been aroused for the work. In the meantime, we plan to work along such lines as far as possible.

I consider properly organized schools as *gardens* where infant souls are grown and nurtured. The gardeners should be well-selected and co-operated with by parents and the public. The teachers should never be neglected for they are *soul-molders*. The care and spiritual nourishment of the early life of a human plant usually determines its later development.

I sincerely praise the modern school system of America and its constantly improving methods of intellectual and to a certain extent physical training. But I cannot fail to point out its main shortcoming. *It lacks spiritual background*, and very badly needs to be supplemented by *moral and spiritual training*. The boy who belongs intellectually to Class "A", or is a great baseball or football player, often attracts notice and is encouraged by the professors and students, but very few observe or warn him rightly if he is leading a dark Class "D" moral or spiritual life.

But where is such a school which adopts definite measures for developing the whole nature of man, teaching him the true art of life and fitting him to go through the various minor and ultimately the final examination of life? Such schools are urgently needed, to teach the following arts and sciences of all-round growth.

Recharging Technique

- Technique of *recharging* the body-battery from the Cosmic Current by Will. Scientific *relaxation* of energy from the body parts for perfect rest. Conservation of vital energy. Bodily suppleness and agility. Physical endurance (of cold, heat, strain,

etc.)
- Knowledge of what and how much to eat daily, and the value of partial fasting. Regular habits of eating and sleeping.
- Value of sitting erect and thus keeping the cerebro-spinal axis, diaphragm and lungs in proper position and action. Moderation in some sport, such as swimming, tennis, baseball, etc.
- Cleanliness—daily bath for keeping the body pores open.
- Sex Hygiene—Relation of sex-control to good memory, long life, mental inspiration and matrimonial happiness.
- Art of building bridges over the river of difficulties between failure and success. Psycho-physical methods of keeping the sense employees of sight, hearing, taste, touch and smell ...well trained, regulated, reliable, busy and free from rebellion.
- Art of keeping the mental life free from the bacteria of fear, despondency, melancholia, greed, lack of initiative, anger, worry, idleness and boredom.
- Art of injecting the tonic of cheerfulness into the body.
- Knowledge of the superiority of the mind over the body, obtained thru practical experience.
- Developing **Will-power** for carrying out plans made by noble ideas and for resisting the lure of temptations.
- Art of training the Will so that it makes it ...its own business to be better without the necessity of being goaded by commands.
- Understanding of the fundamental importance of the Will through-out life.
- Art of choosing the right life-companion and of keeping the matrimonial life smooth thru *consideration, tact, love and fidelity*.
- Art of creating spiritual children and of rearing them beautifully.
- Art of Concentration (positive and negative).
- Art of training the Sub-conscious mind and of learning during sleep.
- Art of keeping the mind strong and immune from diseases.

- Art of regulating self-ambition so it does not conflict with the interests and requirements of society.
- Art of converting the greed to possess ...into the desire to share.

Methods of fostering social service.

- Art of inventive ability to serve mankind and lighten labor or improve on existing conditions.
- Art of working towards better laws thru right education and intelligent understanding and cooperation.
- Art of graciousness, noble bearing, and genuine interest in the problems of others.
- Art of cooperation, and knowledge of the absolute *interdependence* of man's destiny and universal laws of being.
- Value of self-sacrifice and good-will for all. Law of individual life as related to social life.

National and international interest and patriotism.

- Law of sincerity in *thought, word and deed*.
- Art of seeking personal happiness thru the happiness of others.

Relation of man to God.

- Art of converting self-ambition into ambition for All.
- Art of merging the little self into the Self of All.
- Law of protecting the wealth of inward peace from the robbers of worry, unfavorable circumstance, disease, etc.
- Art of being supremely happy always and of making others so.
- *Freedom from all habits*, and performance of right actions thru discrimination and free-will.

The preceding Arts and Sciences are those which should be taught in a "How-To-Live-School" ...to children whose minds are still plastic and their forces as yet unguided into any definite channel. Adults too may master the subjects, if they will exercise *willingness* and *patience* while the good habits are displacing the undesirable ones.

After a thorough training, the students of such a School will undergo ceaseless examinations through-out life, and the various diplomas won will be ...*health, fame, efficiency, wealth and happiness.*

The issue of the Final Examination at the end of this Earthly sojourn ...will only be determined by the sum-total acquirements of the mental and spiritual diplomas won at the various examinations through-out life. And those successful in this Last Great Examination receive a Diploma of ...lasting efficiency, free conscience and blessings—engraved eternally on the parchment of the Soul. This rare reward is incorruptible by moths, beyond the reach of thieves and the eraser of Time, and is awarded for honorable entry into the Fellowship of Truth.

Cosmic Consciousness

I sat on the mound with eyes closed,
Watching the inky darkness
That enveloped me.
There was naught within me but darkness,
But I seemed to seek something unknown
Yet familiar.
I opened my eyes
And the gay world of splendor
Richly decorated with the measureless sheet
Of twinkling moonbeams,
Sublime stars
Teeming with mysteries unspoken,
Myriads of flowers, green velvet grass,
Chains of shining peaks,
Light-bejewelled waves of the heaving seas,
Mighty Power of cities,
These mocked at me and called me dreamer.
The voice of the proud world
Seemed to laugh and say:
"Foolish dreamer! Why shut your eyes
And banish my beauty from your sight
And live in empty darkness?"
I silently said within myself,
"Audacious Intruder, thy beauty
Would forever remain unappreciated
Without the invisible inmates

Of my dark mental chamber."
Even as I thought this,
I felt the thrilling call
Of some mysterious charm within.
I closed the doors of my eyes.
There again, I was confronted
With the same abysmal darkness.
I watched with steady vision
Looking and seeking in all directions
—Sometimes bewildered,
I felt I caught glimpses of opaque thought
Which became half-visible
In that deep mystic chamber.
I steadily watched in the dim
But growing light of my concentration.
The gloom became softer
And revealed its hidden glory.
I found I could see there
Without my eyes,
See each glimmering thought
.....Like dream-lightning,
Flash and disappear
Or come bursting like star-shells,
With revealing showers of light,
And vanish in the mental sky.
I could count each flash, each outburst,
Recognize their intensity, their duration,
And meaningful splendors.
I found I could hear there
Without my ears,

Balancing East-West

The muffled chafing roars
Of loud powerful thoughts,
Softer sweet suggestions of conscience,
And the quiet voice of reason.
I heard distinctly all they said
As I had never heard before.
Thus for the first time I felt the presence
Of these living inner invisible
Blood-relations,
Their warmth
And their indifference toward me.
These, my own,
Long had lived so near in this dark chamber,
Planning, organizing, moulding my destiny,
Yet unassuming, unnoticed, unseen, Unheeded.
What charm you cast around,
What stupendous work you do,
Invisible Friends!
Are you afraid to plainly appear
In the crude scorching gaze of human minds?
Do you fear to be hurt
By the twilight of pale
Unthinking mentalities,
Or choked by the gross vibrations
Of noisy matter?
Yet how stealthily you go out
Of the dark chamber
To build the huge sky-scrapers,
The mighty bridges
And all material achievements,

Paramhansa Yogananda

Then slip away, unknown,
Unthanked, unhonored, unsought.
The coursing train in the nightly gloom,
The whirling airplane,
The floating steel village with small cabins,
The triumphs of art,
The Parthenon and Taj Mahal,
All man-made miracles,
All remind me of you only and your powers,
O Mighty Thoughts!
But when I see the sparkling lake
Welcoming me to quench my thirst,
And the dark clouds bursting with eagerness
To pour its rivers of rain
To fill our life-giving paddy fields
And nectar fruit-trees,
And the moon's light
Switched on at the approach of darkness,
And the changing round of the seasons,
And the hall of the world
Beautifully carpeted with soft green grass,
And the sunlight-painted clouds
On the canvas of the sky,
All these matchless scenic pictures,
I begin to question
Whose is the Cosmic Hand
That works so wisely-powerful everywhere!
I wonder whose all-pervading voice
Commands the sun, moon, planets,
Earth, nature, the seasons,

Balancing East-West

All blind forces, the ebbing and flowing seas,
Man, life and death,
And receives their obedience!
Is there an inifinite chamber of mystery
In which one Limitless Luminous Mind hides
And secretly reaches forth
To decorate the Universe
With endless charms?
Down thru the windows of Memory I looked.
I recalled the early hour of my childhood,
When the sun of my consciousness
First began gradually to appear.
As it slowly
Rose out of the darkness of the unconscious Mind,
It dimly lighted only one part
Of my little mental horizon
That lay encompassing my mother,
Playthings and few multi-colored candies.
Later, as my consciousness grew brighter,
I found a great part of my mental horizon
Became illumined.
I saw in it many other things,
My friends, relations, neighbors, my country,
These were revealed and included.
Now,
As I look within,
On the mental sky,
The sun of my consciousness
Seems to be shinning
Brighter than ever

In its supreme power.
It no longer lights one direction
Or only a portion of my mental horizon,
Or only a few friends or one nation
—But all nations,
Nay, all creatures and nature, all planets,
All stars, all shining electrons,
All Universes, all Space.
I did not know
That out of the inky darkness of my mind
I would discover
The Sun of Cosmic Consciousness!

Affirmations

(Repeat whisperingly and forcefully with all Sincerity before beginning an enterprise).

"Oh Supreme Director, I will ...will.
I will reason,
But lead my will and reason
To the right things that I should do."
"I am Will for Thou art in me."

Life's Dream

Dedicated to Mount Washington Educational Center

The Summer-East and the Wintry-West
They say—but Mount Washington
Named rightly after that pioneer
Of Freedom's great career, Thou dost stand,
The snowless guardian Himalaya
Of the Angel Land—
In perpetual green regalia.
Nippon's camphor trees and
Perfumed wisteria and smiling roses,
Palm, date and well-beloved
Spicy bay leaves of Hind —stand close,
With endless scenic beauties
Of ocean, canyon, setting sun,
Moon-studded sky
And nightly twinkling cities
To declare Thy ever-changing beauty.
On Thy crown Thou shalt newly wear
A priceless starry-school
Which in all future near
Shall draw the lost travellers
Of the East and West
To find their goal and one place of rest.
Here one path shall merge
With all other paths.

Paramhansa Yogananda

Here the love
Of Earthly Freedom's paradise, America,
Shall blend fore'er
With Spiritual Freedom's paradise, India.
Here church in deepest friendliness
Shall all other churches meet.
Here the temple, the mosque, shall greet.
Here the long-divorced matter-laws
Will wed again —in peace— the Spirit laws.
Here all minds will learn
That —True Art of living life.
And the way to start straight
To the One great place
Where all must meet at last.
Jehovah! This is the land of solace
Where my Life's Dream
—In truth—reappears!

My Native Land

The friendly sky,
Inviting shades of banyan tree,
The holy Ganges flowing by—
How can I forget thee!
I love the waving corn
Of India's fields so bright,
Oh, better than those Heav'nly grown
By deathless gods of might!
My soul's broad love so grand
Was born here first below—
In my own native land,
On India's sunny soil aglow.
I love thy breeze,
I love thy moon,
I love thy hills and seas,
In thee I wish to cease.
Thou taught'st me first
To love thy sky, the stars, the God above;
So my first homage meets,
Oh India, at thy feet!
From thee I now have learn'd to see,
To love all lands alike as thee;
I bow to thee, my native land,
The Mother of my love so grand.

FIXING HABITS IN THE BRAIN AT WILL

Who lives in this marvelous Hall of living walls of mortared osseous tissues fitted with the various ocular, tactual, auditory, olfactory and gustatory doors? This hall of life, the human skull, presents a veritable epitome of a huge State. It includes the range of hilly convolutions of the cerebrum, inlaid with the arterial streamlets and dark rivers of veins. Is this exquisite territory vacant, unoccupied? Is this hall filled just with a senseless mass of physical cells? Is there a book without an author, a child without parents, a clock without a maker, a rose without a designer? Nay—and similarly there are wondrous Ruling Agencies *behind* this Kingdom of Mystic Beauty. Beneath the dome of the human skull is enacted scenes of intense activity, pulsating life and intelligence. The strange colony of myriads of little brainy cells are guided and controlled by a mixed host of good and impish ...invisible —sprites, pixies and fairies of Unseen Habits.

There ....the little blood corpuscles are paddling their tiny boats laden with various vital commodities in the arterial stream. There is buying and selling—absorption and elimination ...going on here. The little intelligent cells are engaged in banqueting or introspecting ....or receiving the guests of sensations from the outer sensory doors. Some, are creating mischief by inviting sprites of invisible Disorderly Habits into the Great Common-Wealth.

The Habit Lords, and the Commoners—the brain-cells— are gathered together and are furiously debating ....who should assume the responsibility of the Bodily Government. These United States of Flesh have been the scenes of many wars and revolutions. At certain election times, the whole State is in disorder and confusion. Who is going to be President? How many votes will the various candidates receive? Every human Action, mentally or physically performed, is a voter. When a particular Action is repeated, it swells the number of its votes and a huge number of such Actions ...elects a certain Habit-Candidate. Then a collective vote of All Human Action —determines at different periods of life, which Habit is going to be the predominant one and rule supreme.

Balancing East-West

Election by *numerical superiority* often ignores the *qualitative standard*. If the majority of voters are morons or criminals, they are bound to blunder and elect the wrong Habit-Candidate. Unless the Voting Human Actions are guided by the *supreme law of discrimination*, they enslave themselves anew under an Undesirable Ruler.

A true Spiritual Democracy in this Bodily Kingdom —necessitates the thorough education of the Voting Human Activities. They should not only depend on their *numerical power of repetition*, but also on the *quality of attentive performance*. Above all, they should be trained to be guided by Ideal Rationalism —and warned against the bribing effects of Sentimental Environment, leading to the misuse of their voting powers. The power of *reason* should select the candidates. Habits of *anger, greed, envy, drinking, excessive smoking, coffee or tea drinking, sloth, failure* ....result from their being elected to office by unwise hordes of *little Actions,* whose numerical strength alone elected them ....without thought of the after-effects of enslavement. Habit-Slaves are not born, they *make* themselves so, unknowingly or knowingly thru their <u>constantly repeated actions</u>. The first drink never made a drunkard; the first act of sensuality ...never made a sensual slave; the first use of dope ...never made a dope-fiend. *A series of mechanical or thoughtless repetitions <u>of the wrong action</u> elected the Gripping Habit as Ruler.* Quantitative <u>strength</u> won against the weak qualitative voice of <u>reason</u> ...that had no votes because it had *not* been exercising its powers.

Guard yourself against the *first* performance of Evil Actions. What you will do once ...you are liable to do again. Like a rolling snowball, Habit grows stronger and bigger by repetition. Use your reason in all your Actions —otherwise you become converted into helpless slaves of Undesirable Habits.

A strong Bad-Habit —presiding for a long time in the Bodily State, brings chaos and misery. Spiritual famine, mental fevers, universal poverty of body and brain ...exist in a Kingdom thus misruled. A strong Bad-Habit should be impeached before a tribunal of Daily Introspective and Conscience Judges, who should inform the Daily-Offending-Actions that the inevitable outcome of their persistence will be a *nervous breakdown, wasted youth and exploded happiness.* This constant note of warning ...may serve gradually to awaken the enslaved *reason and will* of the Habit-Bound Victim.

Many excessive smokers, drunkards, sex-slaves are not free because they do not think they are doing wrong and because they don't die immediately. But though the shovels of Habit dig slowly, yet they dig surely ....a yawning untimely grave, preceded by the <u>scorching flames of suffering</u>.

Convince your Actions of the tyranny of the Undesirable Ruling Habit first, then begin the work of *constitutional agitation* and actual *impeachment*. A whining or sorrowing attitude, remonstrance, or even violent but spasmodic rebellion ...is of little avail. You are the maker of your Habits and you must undo them by regular effort.

Relate your Actions to new ...better ways. Keep them continuously —busy, interested, attentive— in serving and fraternizing with Good Actions. If the Actions begin to revert back to their old dangerous associations ...don't get discouraged. Persist, give sufficient time and attention ...and the voting strength of the New Actions will increase and finally get power enough to overthrow the worthless Ruler and elect in his place, their own Good-Candidate Habit.

A Bad Habit takes time to attain supremacy, so why be impatient about the growth of its rivalling Good Habit? Do not despair about your Undesirable Habits, simply stop feeding them by repetition.

The time used in the formation of Habits ...varies with the individual kind of nervous system and brain cells, and is chiefly determined by the *quality of attention*. But any Habit can be installed in the brain, almost instantaneously at will, by creating <u>brain-grooves</u> ...thru the power of *deep trained attention.*

True Democracy presupposes rational, willing obedience to good laws —ungoaded by Higher Authority or any other external influences whatsoever. Similarly, a Wise Man —one who is really free ...avoids error and performs good —not compelled by Habit—but from free reasonable choice.

"To him who hath ...shall be given; but from him who hath not ...shall be taken away —even that which he hath." This Biblical statement is very true of Habits. A man of Good Actions increases in virtue, but a slave of Bad Habits —loses all power of will and reason.

All national tastes, human customs —are results of Habits— and are environmental in nature. Love of Americanism or Hinduism is the outcome of Habit and familiarity. When I was a baby —if I had a choice— I would have preferred to be a human chameleon ...free to embrace the desirable aspects of all nations and creeds.

Government of Actions by *internal self-evolved discrimination* —unguided by Good or Bad Habits— imparts unbounded power of will. A man with such power can instantly fix a New Habit in his brain, or stop one at will, without feeling the compulsion of a Habit-President. One must not be dominated by a Good Habit either, because the Habit may be in power ...simply because there has never been any temptation of Evil. Such a Good Habit is not permanently fixed in the nature, because it is born —not from choice and reason, but thru circumstance.

One way we can test our power over our Habits is to command the mind to like or dislike a certain food at will. When I first arrived in America, I was served at a dinner —some Roquefort cheese and crackers. No sooner had Mr. Roquefort touched the palate and its arrival become known to the cerebral cells ...than the Habit Lords rebelled and were about to upset the Honored Guests in my stomach. I didn't enjoy this sudden embarrassment, and saw that everyone else at the table was greatly enjoying this particular cheese. I strongly urged my senses to immediately elect the Roquefort-cheese-enjoying Habit. I liked the taste at once and do so to this day.

Why do things happen contrary to your desires? Because ...your Habits are also contrary to your desires, and —your Actions *flatter* your Habits. Your Habits must cater to your True Ideals.

Habit is an automatic mental mechanism for performing Actions ...... without the labor involved in initiating New Actions. Wrongly used, this mechanism becomes man's arch-enemy. Be practical. Try from today to overcome the hidden Enemy-Habits within you —garbed with your environmental likings—and be free to act from reason alone. Your Habits are not you. Be yourself ... and you will remember the lost image of God within you.

BITS OF WISDOM

The following sayings are taken from the Lectures

"Loyalty to a spiritual custom ...without sincerity and conviction ...is hypocrisy. Loyalty to the spirit of a custom even without clinging to the form —is wisdom. Loyalty both to the form and the spirit is the greatest wisdom. But loyalty neither to spiritual custom, principle or teacher ...is spiritual degeneration.

"How can you nourish yourself by only listening to a talk on food? You must apply your knowledge. To know food only theoretically, is to always remain hungry. So he who seeks new doctrines continuously —but does not put them into practice in his own life— is in continual spiritual starvation."

"A good habit is your greatest friend—a bad habit ...your mortal enemy. Be careful about the repetition of an action. It will become a habit before you realize it. Habit is second nature. But it can be changed by persistent good action."

"When we serve others ...we serve ourselves. Do not think, 'I will help others'—think rather, 'I will help my own, my world ...because I cannot otherwise be happy.'"

"Praise does not make you better, nor blame worse ...than what you are. Then why heed these two? Don't pay attention when they praise you, but survey yourself carefully when they blame you. If you are in fault, free yourself from error quickly, but if you are not guilty ...laugh and forget it. Truth will speak for you. Spiritual action talks louder than the utterance of many sacred words.

"No disease is incurable. Some diseases are beyond the reach of medicines, which are by their nature limited. When a disease is persistent and long-continued, and medical aid and other ordinary methods fail to cure it, it is then called chronic or incurable.

"The fault or deficiency in the medicine, and its inability to cure, are illogically transferred to the disease. The medicine is uncurative—so doctors call the disease incurable! But the power of the Infinite is unlimited and can heal all disease.

"Medicine has its uses ...why deny facts? But it is strictly confined to certain limits. If a disease is beyond medical aid, that is not the time to despair, but rather the time to put your faith ...on the Infinite power who is Omnipotent.

"Medicine cannot help you if you just talk about it and do not use it ...similarly, faith cannot cure —unless you use it and not simply talk of it.

"In mental or spiritual healing, one must have faith to 'burn the boat ...to walk on the sea.' Would you not rather doubt ...the aid of limited material forces —than the power of the Infinite Spirit?"

SPIRITUAL INTERPRETATION OF A BIBLICAL PASSAGE

John 6:27—
"Labor not for the meat which perisheth,
But for that meat
Which endureth unto everlasting life,
Which the son of man shall give unto you:
For Him hath God the Father sealed."

Labor not for the meat which perisheth (do not devote all your energies simply to the maintenance of the physical body, for even the most scientifically balanced diet ...can nourish the body only for a limited time) but for that meat (but seek the infinite source, the cosmic energy and life current) which endureth unto everlasting life, (which can spiritualize the material forces into deathless or changeless energy, serviceable to the soul eternally) which the son of man (the human body which comes from another human body) shall give unto you: (because it contains divine possibilities within it) for Him hath God the Father sealed (God the creator has stored His immortal energy in man and has labelled or marked It as the storage battery of His own cosmic design. One can recharge his body-cells from within ...by knowing the mechanism of the body-battery and its secret storehouse of cosmic current)

WHO IS A YOGI?

"Not a sword-swallower, crystal gazer or snake charmer, but one who knows the scientific psycho-physical technique of uniting the matter-bound body and soul with their source of origin, the Blessed Spirit. He is a Yogi who says:

> "I shall go within
>
> To bring Thee without
>
> Where I am ....Thou must come."

Such an Enlightened One ...dives deep within the Soul thru meditation, and brings God-realization ...without, to apply it in worldly life. He is a Yogi who acts for all, and not he who shirks activity or is a fugitive from the battle of life. If we all go to the forest, we will have to build a city there and face the problems of life just the same.

A business man, literary man, artist, musician, laborer or king; all can be Yogis, if they so choose. A Yogi aspires to know the Spirit thru living according to the spiritual laws of life, thru renunciation of all material fruits of success and by devoting such fruits to the good of all. Such a man as the Hershey chocolate king, who has given his entire fortune of eighty millions to a school, and now works in his own factory, has accomplished a renunciation equal to that of great saints.

We must struggle to attain success and have the broadening experiences of life. Many would-be Yogis say, 'My wife died, I lost my wealth; hence I will forsake everything and become a hermit.' Why, they have nothing to forsake! Such sacrifice is not real. It is the renunciation of the fruits of successful action, the translation of selfish ambition into selfless service for all ...that is true sacrifice.'

REINCARNATION
HOW CAN IT BE SCIENTIFICALLY PROVED?

If one believes in the existence of a just God, then a belief in reincarnation can follow very readily, as the two beliefs are really dependent, one on the other. But what about the skeptics and the atheists? Can the truth of reincarnation be scientifically proven to their satisfaction? Can the theory of reincarnation be in any way scientifically experimented upon so as to furnish not only hope but actual proof of its reality?

Material scientists claim they have not found any actual proof of the existence of a God, and hence ...cannot offer any proof of the existence of His just law —giving equal opportunity to all life to improve through reincarnation. To such scientists, the sufferings of innocent babies and other inequalities of life, seem inexplicable and point to the absence of any just God.

On the other hand, most of those who do believe in a just God, base their faith on belief only, and have no scientific proof to offer to unbelievers. They do not dare, for the most part, to scrutinize or deeply question their faith, for fear of losing it or of starting some social inharmony. They are not aware, in other words, of the existence of a scientific spiritual law which can prove their beliefs to be truth.

But why should not the methods of experimentation used by the material scientist to discover physical truths, be applied in investigating spiritual law? This question was asked centuries ago by the Hindu savants, and they set about the task of answering it. Their experiments resulted in scientific methods which can be followed by anyone to discover the reality of spiritual law, and hence of reincarnation and many other of the great cosmic truths.

Since this method does exist, no one has the right to say reincarnation and other spiritual laws do not operate, until he has tried the method and seen the result for himself. A scientist is, of course, privileged to express his opinion, but it remains an opinion only, not a fact. In physical science, certain methods must be adopted and followed in order to prove the truth of any given theory. To the naked eye, certain germs are not visible. One must use a microscope to detect the presence of the germs. If a person refuses to look through the microscope, he cannot be said to have scientifically tested the theory that germs were present. His opinion is, therefore, valueless, since he had not followed the prescribed rules for arriving at the truth of the theory. So it is in spiritual things. The method has been discovered, the rules laid down, and the result is open to anyone who is interested enough to experiment. In the Western world, due to the lack of this scientific approach to spiritual law, the value of religion has been greatly diminished as a living factor in the life of man. Spiritual doctrines are believed in or rejected ...simply on the ground of personal bias, rather than as a result of scientific investigation.

How did the master minds of ancient India discover these unalterable cosmic laws! Through experiments on the life and thought of man, in the laboratories of their hermitages. To find the truth of physical things, we must experiment upon physical substances. So to find the truth of reincarnation, of the passage of an identical soul through many bodies, it is necessary to experiment upon the consciousness of man. These scientists of old found that the human ego outlasts all the changes of experience and thought during the state of wakefulness ...of dream ...and of deep sleep—during the life-time. The experience changed, the environment, sensations, thoughts and bodily states changed, but the sense of identity, of "I", did not change, from birth to death. Hence the Hindu experimenters argued that through concentration on the ego, through a constant, conscious, aloof, unidentified introspection ...or watching of the various changing states of life—of wakefulness, dreaming or deep sleep— that one could perceive the changeless and eternal nature of the ego. Ordinarily, one is conscious of his waking state and even sometimes of his dreaming state. Often, people are aware that they are dreaming. Even in their dream, they know they are dreaming. So, through certain methods and practices, one can come to be aware of every state—of sleep, dream, or dreamless "deep sleep."

During sleep, there is involuntary relaxation of energy from the motor and sensory nerves. Through practice, one can produce this relaxation during the waking state also, at will. In the Big Sleep of death, there is still further relaxation—the retirement of energy from the heart and cerebro-spinal axis. But by certain practices, this further relaxation may be produced consciously in the waking state. In other words, every involuntary function may be accomplished ...voluntarily and consciously by practice.

These ancient Hindus found that death was the withdrawal of the electricity of life ...from the bulb of human flesh —containing the wires of sensory and motor nerves— to the different channels of outward expression. Just as electricity does not die when it is withdrawn from a broken bulb, so life-energy is not annihilated ...when it retires from the involuntary nerves. Energy cannot die. It withdraws, upon the occasion of death, to the Cosmic Energy.

In sleep, the conscious mind ceases to operate—the current is temporarily withdrawn from the nerves; and in death, the human consciousness ceases to express through the body permanently. It is as though one had a paralyzed arm—one is mentally conscious of that arm, but cannot function through it. Medical records tell of the case of a clergyman who once fell into a state of coma (suspended animation). He heard everyone around bewailing his apparent death, but could not express his awareness through his physical organs. His body motor had "stalled" and refused to respond to his mental commands. At last, when his friends were about to take him to be embalmed, he made a supreme effort, and was able to move, after 24 hours of complete apparent death. This instance illustrates the constancy of awareness of "I-ness" or personal identity, even though the body is seemingly dead.

The Hindu teachers stated, that one must learn to separate the energy and consciousness from the body, consciously. One must consciously watch the state of sleep, and must practice the voluntary withdrawal of energy consciously from the heart and spinal regions. Thus he learns to do consciously, what death will otherwise force on him unconsciously and unwillingly.

There is a case on record, in the files of French and other European doctors, of a man named Sadhu Haridas, in the court of Emperor Ranjit Singh of India, who was able to separate his energy and consciousness from his body, and then connect the two together again after several months. His body was buried underground and watch was kept over the spot, day and night, for months. At the end of this time, his body was dug up, and examined by the European doctors, who made an examination and pronounced him dead. But after a few minutes, he opened his eyes and regained all the control over all the functions of his body, and lived for many years more. He had simply learned, by practice, how to control all the involuntary functions of his body and mind. He was a spiritual scientist who experimented with prescribed methods for learning the truth of cosmic law, and as a result, he was in a position to demonstrate the truth of the theory of the changelessness of personal identity and the eternal nature of the life-principle.

Those who would know the scientific truth of the doctrine of reincarnation, must follow the rules laid down many centuries ago by Hindu savants, and must learn to

(1) be conscious during sleep,

(2) be able to produce dreams at will,

(3) to disconnect themselves consciously, not passively as during sleep, from the five senses, and

(4) to control the action of the heart, i.e., experience conscious death or suspended animation. This is the art of separating the soul from the body.

By following the practices which lead to the above results, we can follow the ego in all states of existence—follow it consciously through death, through space, to other bodies or other worlds. But those who do not learn these things, cannot retain their sense of personal identity, of awareness or consciousness, during the big sleep of death, and hence cannot remember any previous state, or even the "deep sleep" states during one life.

But by adopting the methods of the ancient Hindu scientists who experimented with such laws, and who thereby gave the world a knowledge that is priceless and demonstrable, one may come to know the scientific truth of reincarnation and all other eternal verities.

THE DOCTRINE OF REBIRTH

"Nay, but as when
One layeth his worn-out robes away,
And, taking new ones, sayeth,
"These will I wear today!"
So putteth by the Spirit lightly
Its garb of flesh
And passeth to inherit a residence afresh.
"Never the Spirit was born;
The Spirit shall cease to be never;
Never was time It was not;
End and Beginning are dreams!
Birthless and deathless and changeless
Remaineth the Spirit forever;
Death hath not touched It at all,
Dead though the house of It seems!"
From "The Bhagavad Gita," Translated by Sir Edwin Arnold.

OBJECTIONS TO REINCARNATION ANSWERED

(The following article is a summary of the arguments presented by various writers to show the truth of the theory of Reincarnation.)

The doctrine of Reincarnation, or Rebirth, is as old as history, and older. All nations, either wholly or in part, have believed in it ...in some form. All the older religions firmly maintained its truth. It is part of the basic religion of the Hindus, who wove it into their philosophy and theology. Its details were systematically elaborated in the earliest Upanishads and Sanskrit literature. It continues to be the inspiration and conviction today not only of the Hindus, but also of the Buddhists of Ceylon, India, Japan and China, who accept it as the only solution to life's mysteries and the only logical road to salvation. The earliest Egyptians and Hermetic philosophers believed in it. The old Persian Magi faith, Zoroaster's followers, and the Greek mystics firmly upheld it. Aristotle and Plato, both of whom have contributed very largely to Western thought, very decidedly believed in Reincarnation, and so did Socrates. The Jewish faith thoroughly approved this belief. The early Gnostics and practically all the Christian fathers, up to the fifth century, accepted it and wrote elaborately about it. The doctrines slipped out of the European mind during the Dark Ages.

Surely a belief that has been —and still is the accepted doctrine of uncounted millions of both past and present time, and which has inspired and moulded the thoughts of many of the greatest thinkers and philosophers for thousands of years,—should not be rejected by present-day Western minds ...without due investigation and reason. As a matter of fact, the theory of Reincarnation is today slowly but surely gaining a foothold again in Western thought, and many of the most advanced thinkers are realizing that this doctrine holds the key to the solution of life's otherwise insoluble problems. Some of the great Western minds that believed in it were: Kant, Swendenborg, Schopenhauer, Goethe, Lessing, Boehme, Schelling, Emerson and Shelley. Many of our best progressive minds of today, including Henry Ford, accept the doctrine of Reincarnation.

The popular belief in Reincarnation in Jesus' time is shown by the passage in the Bible (John 9:2) where the disciples ask Jesus: "Master, who did sin, this man or his parents, that he was born blind?" In as much as the man was born blind, the disciples could not think he became blind from sin in this life, hence they could only have been referring to a possible sin committed by the man in one of his former lives. The same thought is expressed in the passage from John 5:5-14, where Jesus healed a man of an infirmity which he had had for 38 years, and whom Jesus told, "Sin no more, lest a worse thing come unto thee." He meant the man had sinned in a past life. Jesus speaks several times unmistakably of the reincarnation of Elias into the body of John the Baptist. He says, (Matthew 17:12-13), "But I say unto you, that Elias is come already, and they knew him not, but have done unto him whatsoever they listed. . . . Then the disciples understood that he spake unto them of John the Baptist." And again Jesus says, (Matthew 11:13-15), "For all the prophets and the law .....prophesied until John. And if ye will receive it, this is Elias, which was for to come. He that hath ears to hear, let him hear." Again, in Revelation 3:12, the Lord reveals to John, "Him that overcometh, will I make a pillar in the temple of my God, and he shall go no more out." This passage makes it clear that he who conquers himself, shall be no longer forced to "go out"—to be reincarnated and die time and time again. Those who "overcometh" are henceforth free from this cosmic necessity.

It would be of no importance whether people believed in the doctrine of Reincarnation or not, if the theory had no practical and ethical bearing on life. But its value lies in the fact that it does have a very close and significant relation with all our actions. The doctrine of Reincarnation is only one-half of a theory. The other half is Karma. Reincarnation means rebirth, or the passage of the soul from one body to another, until salvation or freedom is finally won through merit. Karma means the chain of action committed in present or past lives that must be expiated, rewarded or burned into nothingness by the fire of meditation. The "karma" of a man are the seeds of potential action within him, awaiting only the proper environment or opportunity to become an active manifestation in the outer world. The Law of Karma, then, means that whatever we do in thought, word or deed, leaves traces or effects in our sub-conscious mind and subtle body, and that they must —in present or future time— inevitably express themselves in further thought, word or deed. These thoughts, words and deeds, being freshly reinforced by environmental influences and fresh actions, will again be the cause of still further thoughts, words and deeds, and so on. Hence we see that this Law of Karma is nothing but an application of the Law of Causation, scientifically applied to human activities, even as it is applied to every other science, whether it be Astronomy, Physics or Geometry.

Hence the doctrines of Reincarnation and Karma are an attempt to solve the riddles of life, death and final liberation. The test of a theory is whether or not it can cover all the facts. Let us apply this test to the theory of Reincarnation.

> 1. THE JUSTICE OF GOD. The theory of rebirth ...alone can account for the justice of God, by attributing the evils of life ...not to an Omnipotent caprice, but to our own action. Practically all atheists lose their faith in a God ...because of the terrible injustice that seems to prevail in the world. Thinking they have but one life to live on this earth, these atheists argue that they would rather believe in no God, than in a God who would thus show such favor and disfavor to innocent babes. But a belief in Karma and Reincarnation dispels these erroneous ideas of an unjust God, and gives one a basis for belief in eternal justice and impartial opportunity. Furthermore, to believe that every good action will beget another good action, and every evil act fathers another evil effect, is to watch our actions more carefully and to think more of our future state, since we alone will be responsible for it. The moral effect that a belief in Reincarnation causes, cannot help but be strengthening, uplifting and practical. It supports the theory of Free-Will by indication that our future and present life are not caused by an inscrutable fate, but by our own actions and our use of forces that are or can be within our own control. It helps us to center our attention on the "kingdom within," of which all religions speak as being the only true heaven, and relieves us of a slavish dependence on, and ignorance of, the seemingly causative external forces. It reveals us to ourself as the cause of all things, instead of the puppets of chance.
>
> 2. REVEALS EXISTENCE OF SCIENTIFIC LAW. The first law of Science is, that nothing happens by chance; that everything in nature has some cause, and that only ignorance of the cause makes us think of accidental occurrences. A is the cause of B, which is its effect, B is the cause of C which is its effect, C of D, and

so on. The universe is a network of events interrelated as cause and effect. The whole equilibrium of the world is changed every moment at the occurrence of the minutest phenomena. So Science tells us, basing its judgment not on belief, but on demonstrated fact. The body and mind of man are subject to this universal Law of Causation. Science knows this, and attributes every detail of man's body and mind to heredity and environment. But a belief in eternal justice would account for it by reincarnation and environment, since the latter theory visits, not the father's sin upon the child (at least not as a cause) but the sins of the child upon himself. Hence, a belief in Reincarnation is supported by scientific law, proving the body and mind to be the outcome, not of a whimsical Creator, but of our own deeds and thoughts in past and present lives. Furthermore, matter being indestructible, the mortal energy cannot be destroyed. It must express itself through reincarnation. "And it is easier for heaven and earth to pass, than one tittle of the law to fail"—Luke 16:17. St. Paul says, "Work out thy own salvation. Whatsoever a man soweth, that shall he also reap."

3. IMMORTALITY. If the Soul is immortal and eternal, it must have exited before living in this body. If it is changeless, why should it suddenly occupy a human body for one life and then never again? Hence a belief in the immortality of the Soul leads to a belief in reincarnation. If one says, with the materialists, that the Soul rises with the birth of the body, and dies with the death of the body, then no further argument is possible. But we possess an instinctive belief in immortality, and reason also supports it. The orthodox idea of the creation of a Soul at birth, must inevitably mean the annihilation of such a Soul at death. For what begins in time must end in time. Something cannot come out of nothing, nor can something be reduced to nothing. If immortality of the Soul, and its eternal nature, is granted, then the pre-existence, the present existence, and the future existence of the Soul are settled beyond doubt.

4. SENSUOUS INSTINCTS OF MAN. All desire leaves seeds in the mind, which cannot die until fulfillment is reached. After death, the soul of the man cannot rest indefinitely in the spirit world, because it has brought with it the unexpressed and unsatisfied

longings of the ego, which boil and bubble, so to speak, until they return again to become manifest. Souls having no material desires attached to them, may live in the spirit world ...in its different spheres, for evolution, and work out their redemption there. But the scientific law of causation requires the working out of the sensuous tendencies of man in the sensuous world, and not anywhere else.

5. DIFFERENCES OF HUMAN NATURE AND CAPACITY. The vast differences in disposition, ability, morality and achievement that sometimes occur between two members of the same family, cannot possibly be accounted for on any reasonable ground ...except reincarnation. The difference in twins, having the same birth, training and environment, must ever remain a total mystery ...unless the karma from past lives is accepted as the cause. To say that God meant them to be different, is to refuse to see the immediate and personal cause.

6. INEQUALITIES OF FORTUNE. The sufferings of the virtuous man, and the pleasures of the vicious, make us believe in reincarnation, since it explains that the past good actions of a man will bring him joy in this life, even though by his present evil actions he is storing up future suffering for himself. Similarly, the good man is laying away future treasures for himself, even though he may at present be suffering from the effects of evil deeds done in lives gone by.

7. EVOLUTION. Everything in this world changes, and Science proves that physically, the change has been for the better, by evolution. Man's physical body, the Biologist proves, is the outcome of a long series of changes and gradual improvement. We know we improve morally and spiritually by slow degrees after passing through distinct stages. We do not improve all at once or without opportunities being given us. Many births give us such opportunities to grow perfect. Evolution holds good in all spheres.

8. THE CONSTANT UNIVERSE. The scientific principle of causation, and expenditure of energy, requires constancy in the universe. The force or energy of the world is constant—no decrease, no increase. There is only passing from one form to another. So the force or energy brought by the soul into human

life, can neither be created or destroyed. It is neither born nor does it die, but it does pass from one form to another. The conservation of energy is as true in the subtle immaterial world ...as in the physical world.

9. SOLVES THE ORTHODOX ENIGMAS. If our present-day deeds are responsible for our rewards and punishments, why does a mere child ...die, who, has done no wrong? Further, if Heaven or Hell —for eternity— is the result of actions done in this short span of one earth-life ...is not the scale unbalanced? Seventy years, say, on the one side, and eternity on the other! Such a supposition is entirely at variance with both reason and our experience of Just Cosmic Law. Further, if such a view be true, what will be the reward or punishment of a man who has been partly good and partly bad in this life, so that they are equal? Will he go to Heaven or to Hell?

10. TESTIMONY OF SAINTS. Great spiritual seers and saints have affirmed the truth of reincarnation and have had glimpses ...of their own earlier incarnations. Ordinary men, too, sometimes experience flashes of pre-natal memory.

Some of the objections offered to the truth of the theory of Reincarnation are

(1) we do not remember past lives,

(2) we should not be held responsible for forgotten deeds,

(3) the theory of Reincarnation conflicts with the evidence of heredity, and

(4) Orientals, and people who believe in Reincarnation, are not progressive.

The answer to the first two objections is, that ...memory is not the test of existence. You do not remember your birth and early babyhood, but you experience them just the same. There is a merciful provision in nature. If we remembered all the past events of countless lives, with their sorrows, sins, sufferings and ignorance, the mind would be overburdened and miserable. Further, if we remembered all these past lives, there would be no point in reincarnation at all, since the object of reincarnation is to give the ego a new chance, a new body and brain, a new start, a new environment. No matter how black our past may have been, we are wisely spared that memory and can begin life anew ...every century or so. For most of us, each life is an advance, an improvement over the past. We are growing toward perfection. It is not necessary or desirable that we should remember all the details of ancient ages. The experiences of past lives, however, are not lost, but remain with us in the form of tendencies, abilities and moral perception.

Even in one life, a man may completely forget his identity and imagine himself to be someone else. Many such cases, well-authenticated, are on record, especially since the war.

People wrongly imagine that reincarnation and heredity are conflicting theories. Due to the presence of unchanging cosmic law for everything in nature, heredity is the law through which the reincarnating soul works. A son is not like his father ...simply because he was born of him, but because the soul of the son ...had chosen to reincarnate in that family ...because the material and mental qualities of the ego ...would find it most convenient and harmonious ...to manifest through just such a family. The "path of least resistance," or "like attracts like," accounts for the possible entrance of an ego into an undesirable body. Cosmic law compels the ego to become incarnate through a body and mind which most suitably express the karma and experience of the evolving ego.

It is true that many Orientals have misunderstood the doctrine of Karma and Reincarnation, and have suffered for it. Their mistake lay in stressing one angle of the theory and forgetting other angles. The masses degenerated the theory into a doctrine of Fatalism, feeling that the present life was inevitably the outcome of past deeds and hence there could be no hope to change it. But such a view is not true. Some of our present fate, such as our birth and family ties, are indeed changeless so far as this life is concerned, but besides past karma, there are also present actions, or karma ...in the making, to be considered, which in turn determines our future. We must work out the effects of past actions, it is true, but not only our future, but even some of our present, is wholly dependent on present action. The future is ours to make or mar, according to present action. This is the view of karma and reincarnation that has escaped the attention of many Orientals, but it is the true view. Furthermore, even if and when the Western nations accept the truth of reincarnation, they will never fall into the same lethargic habits that afflict many Oriental nations. The West has a different karma, a different outlook and temperament, not to mention differences of climate and of natural environment. Japan is Buddhist and believes in reincarnation, yet she is as energetic as any Western nation. No nation of today will fall into the same mistakes as to Fatalism that older and more easy-going nations have done. The conditions of the age and the civilization forbid it. But the truth of reincarnation, hidden now from Western eyes as a whole, for many centuries, is again claiming the attention and adherence of larger and larger numbers in the West, and satisfying the soul-hunger for knowledge of life's problems and mysteries.

One more point—even though we are tied to this wheel of cosmic birth and death, even though no end is in sight ...yet there is a way of escape for us. All religions point the path. Through knowledge, through non-attachment, through selflessness, through the fire of meditation on spiritual reality ...the seeds of all karma may be roasted, may be reduced to ashes, and thus the soul may be liberated from the otherwise eternal Wheel of Necessity.

THE NEEDLE'S EYE

> Children ...how hard is it
> For them that trust in riches
> To enter into the kingdom of God.
> It is easier for a camel
> To go through the eye of a needle,
> Than for a rich man
> To enter into the kingdom of God."
> —St. Mark, 10:24,25.

To his followers the loving Master Jesus always made His teaching as clear and simple as possible, using the things with which they were familiar ...to illustrate his lessons.

Sometimes it was the growing grass of the fields, the sheep and the good shepherd, the birds, the lilies,—always something the people knew about.

On this memorable occasion the Master had looked upon the man who had kept the commandments from his "youth up," and had loved Him; then, the Master had sorrowfully watched the man go away because he put his faith in material possessions.

How the loving heart of the Master must have yearned over the people gathered there under the blue skies by the murmuring waters of the Jordan! They had come to him to be taught spiritual truth they could not find elsewhere; they were ready to be taught. And to make clear the lesson He would teach them about not placing their trust in material possessions, He spoke of the Needle's Eye, a gate that led into the city of Jerusalem. All the people there knew about this gate, and many of them, no doubt, had passed through it. The Needle's Eye was so small the merchants and travelers who came to pass through it had to dismount and unpack the loaded camels before they could enter. Even then the camels had to crawl through in a kneeling posture. None of the costly wares, none of the fine silks and linens, none of the precious perfumes could the camels carry through this gate upon their backs.

Thus the Master made the lesson clear to them, if they would enter the kingdom of God they must put their trust in something higher than material possessions; they must learn to put their trust in the Creator of the substance of all things.

And after nineteen centuries the Needle's Eye still stands, and we still must learn this lesson!

WORLD APPEAL FOR RECRUITING A SPIRITUAL ARMY

It is noon-time! Dear ones, sleeping yet? The Divine Trumpet is calling! Everything may seem peaceful and quiet to you, perhaps, because you are asleep, enjoying partial health and prosperity. But wake, watch, listen! Ignorance, disease, poverty, crime and death, fully equipped with a million missiles of misery, are swarming in hordes to invade your souls, cities, homes, your dear ones. We want recruits, to train themselves first, and others afterward, to fight these universal enemies.

It is not enough to praise God, who is unmoved by human flattery or disbelief. It is the time, in this world of universal war. He loves God best ...who serves His children. Our world is in a state of terrible siege, fighting Delusion and its vast army. The cry of the diseased, dying and mentally wounded ...rend the air. Our toll is heavier than ever. Only last year, right here in Enlightened America, the records of crime show that unknowing youths from the ages of fifteen to thirty ...stole one billion dollars by hold-ups. Who is responsible? We, who did not train them how to fight temptation and crime.

Ignorance of —right laws of living and health rules— is untimely slaughtering the human family at the rate of 305 individuals per second. Disease with its various machine guns ...has wounded almost 90% of the total population. Death gets almost 100% of our harassed brothers and sisters to a premature grave. Are we immovable, insentient, less even than stones? Rocks, trees and animals lead a happier and more certain existence than we do. Are we not better equipped, more powerful than anything in Nature? Then why should we suffer at the hands of weaker agencies? Let us seek the remedy.

Let us, forgetting —race, creed, dogma, and caste— gather together and make a world-wide united organized attempt ...to train our fifteen hundred million members of the human family to fight —disease, death, misery and ignorance. We must have Spiritual Military Schools for all-round human training ..in every city of the globe. One such is started on Mount Washington, Los Angeles. Won't you enlist? Why spend your finances and energy indirectly to support luxury, crime and disease, or leave your money behind you without having put it to a good use while living? Join us. Every dollar you give will go to save a soul, to fight the enemies of right living. Let us unite for real liberty and freedom—freedom from bad habits, uncontrolled whims and ignorance. Let us learn to be ruled —only by right discrimination.

How many of the world's million are healthy? Only 5%. How many are free from poverty? Only 1%. How many die prematurely? Almost 99%. How many have never suffered disease? Less than 1%. How many are spiritual and have a sound scientific spiritual training ...so that no circumstances could ever overcome them? Less than 1%. What is the cause of this terrible situation? It is because we have slept so long, and let the army of Ignorance ...swarm everywhere.

I am not asking for myself, but for the American Spiritual Army Headquarters on Mount Washington, where we are recruiting to start this world fight against our common enemy, Delusion. Come on, join us, donate your energy, good-will or purse. Do your share, do what you can, that is all we ask of you. Won't you do something while you are still unscathed? Anything that you do is sincerely welcome. Save a soul from ignorance, and you have saved his body and mind as well. Do good while you are living, and have the fruits of noble actions in this life.

What can you do for your human family?

> 1. Send whatever you can, with your good-will, to help establish a big general educational fund for starting schools all over America and the world.

> 2. Help us establish a big library of good books by sending books.

Applications for Teachers

> 3. Help us recruit a Spiritual Army. We want real workers, robust in body and mind, of calm disposition, mental shock-absorbers who will allow nothing to upset or anger them, who will join us for life, or who can receive at least one year's training to be teachers, according to the rules of the institution. These rules will be printed in the near future in this magazine. Make your application now, telling your occupation, education, age, marital status, and sending a recent photograph of yourself.

Let us all be eager to serve in the best way we can, for this world-wide fight against ignorance and suffering.

MESSAGE TO MY LOS ANGELES YOGODA STUDENTS

America, India and the world expect a great deal from you. I have called Los Angeles ...the Spiritual World Army Headquarters (see my article on "World Appeal for Recruiting A Spiritual Army" in this issue.) You must live up to that title. Never mind how good you have been—think always you can be better. Make yourself ideal by observing the following rules. I especially require every one connected with the Center to follow the routine outlined here:

Let half of your diet be raw food. Eat more ground nuts, rather than too much meat. Don't indulge in very hot or cold drinks. Thus you will avoid colds. Drink more orange juice. Omit lunch or dinner as often as you can (whenever you are not hungry). Fast one day a week. Run every day (the Center members can run, in a body, around the tennis court for several rounds) or take a very brisk walk. Help in hospital and prison and other welfare work.

Preach the gospel of Yogoda

—health and concentration—

everywhere.

Do your daily work cheerfully, intensely, seeking more opportunities and prosperity ...that you may serve more and more members of the human family.

Read the Bible, the Bhagavad Gita, and Scientific Healing Affirmations every night before retiring, after meditation. Reverse wrong thoughts in others by kindness, not criticism. Don't criticize anyone except yourself. Make it a rule to bring a friend with you whenever you visit the Center, especially to Sunday School and Sunday meetings, and thus spiritually help a Soul. Be loyal to Yogoda, spread the message, and grow. Practice kindness and sweetness in word and deed. Keep your minds engaged by reading good books. This will keep the bad habits of fear, worry and gossip ...out of your minds. Let God and His work alone reign there. Know that I constantly think of you all and want to see you growing in every way.

Paramhansa Yogananda

MESSAGE TO MY STUDENTS

Dear ones!

The power of Truth
Is secretly spreading
In different lands.
Like the rising dawn
It is creeping all over,
Pushing the darkness away.
Hold on to

Love,

Truth,

Meditation

And Service.

Think of nothing but Light —
And ignorance shall disappear.
Ignorance must first go
From within us;
Then it disappears without.
The power of truth
Has been proved to you.

Hold on.
Faith everlasting

To the Teacher,

Teaching and God.
You shall see the goal;
Lo! it is there,

Right before you!

Paramhansa Yogananda

CHRISTIAN SCIENCE AND HINDU PHILOSOPHY

It may be a matter of much interest to many Christian Scientists to learn that the great founder of their faith, Mrs. Mary Baker Eddy, was a student of the Hindu Scriptures. This fact is shown by her quotations from them in her "Science and Health," up to the 33rd edition. We find in this edition the following excerpt from Sir Edwin Arnold's translation of "Bhagavad-Gita":

> "Never the Spirit was born;
>
> The Spirit shall cease to be —never;
>
> Never was time it was not:
>
> End and Beginning are dreams!
>
> Birthless, deathless and changeless
>
> Remaineth the Spirit forever;
>
> Death hath not touched It at all,
>
> Dead though the house of It seems!

Again, Mrs. Eddy makes reference in the same chapter to another translation of the Bhagavad-Gita. On page 259 of the 33rd edition, she says:

"The ancient Hindu philosophers understood something of this Principle, when they said in their Celestial Song, according to an old prose translation:

> 'The wise ...neither grieve for the dead
>
> Nor for the living.
>
> I myself never was not, nor thou,
>
> Nor all the princes of the earth;
>
> Nor shall we ever hereafter cease to be.
>
> As the Soul, in this mortal frame,
>
> Findeth infancy, youth, and old age,

So in some future frame
Will it find the like.
One who is confirmed in this belief
Is not disturbed by anything
That may come to pass.
The sensibility of the faculties
Giveth heat and cold, pleasure and pain,
Which come and go
And are transient and inconstant.
Bear them with patience;
For the wise man,
Whom these disturb not,
And to whom pain and pleasure are the same,
Is formed for immortality.'"

Both these quotations from the Bhagavad-Gita or Song Celestial, which contains the essence of the Vedas, or the Hindu Bible, are to be found in Mrs. Eddy's 7th chapter on "Imposition and Demonstration." This whole chapter has been omitted from later editions of "Science and Health"; that is why many Christian Scientists are not aware that their great leader, Mrs. Eddy, was familiar with Hindu thought, and in her bigness did not hesitate to acknowledge it in print.

Impartial investigation will show all the world's great religions to be based on the same universal truths, that do not conflict ...but reinforce one another. The great religious teachers of history would be in perfect accord if they met face to face today. It is only some of their followers that are at war with one another, thru ignorance of their own true religion.

The great triumphant power of Christian Science over disease and distress is due to the imperishable principle of truth —upon which it is founded—the truth of God's love and man's immortal nature. Hence it is not strange to know that the Vedanta philosophy of Hinduism bears out the conclusions of Christian Science. "The Truth is one; men call it by various names."

The similarity or mutual influence of the Hindu Vedanta and Christian

Science and other religions should bring fresh hope to mankind by suggesting to it that religious principles have an inner scientific unity ...and can, like the discoveries of physical science, be universally used with benefit by all mankind in practical life. The material scientist uses the forces of the body and of nature to make the environment of man better and more comfortable, and the spiritual scientist, who uses mind-power to enlighten the soul of man, can be of even greater service.

In this article my purpose is to show not only that the doctrine of "mind over matter" had been worked out by the Hindus prior to the birth of Christian Science, and that the similarity of the message of Mrs. Mary Baker Eddy and the principles of Hindu Vedanta is quite evident, but that the Hindus and Christian Scientists will find mutual benefit and will add to their knowledge of the power of mind by a combined study of the Bhagavad-Gita and the Vedanta of the Hindus, and Mary Baker Eddy's "Science and Health."

No matter what great similarity may exist between Christian Science and certain Hindu spiritual doctrines, still, both being different presentations of the principles of a specific truth, and laying emphasis on its certain points differently, are both differently serviceable to the different mental needs of the people in general. Christian Science is no doubt a new presentation of the truth which the Hindus preached long ago, and as such is really needed in this age. Christian Science, by its sole emphasis on mind-power and complete denial of matter and medicine, has greatly helped to free many matter-bound, materially-minded people. A strong, quick jump from one extremity of faith in matter and in the regular use of drugs, to the other extremity of believing in mind alone, and a complete abandonment of medicine, if successfully accomplished by strong-minded people, will certainly bring results in healing the body. Christian Science in the West has succeeded in turning the thoughts of people from matter to mind.

The Hindu Scriptures point out that the belief in the non-existence of matter and the disuse of medicine, in order to fit in with practical human necessity, must not be abrupt, dogmatic, illogical, unintelligible, or inexplicable, but must be scientifically founded, proved and understood.

The Hindu philosopher does not deny the miraculous healings wrought by Christian Science practitioners, but humbly asks them," Do you know exactly what law operates in order to effect a physical healing by mind-power, and the exact causes which prevent the operation of the power of mental healing in certain cases?" Then, again, while the Hindu savant thoroughly believes in the power of the mind for healing physical sickness, he does not disbelieve the miraculous healings also wrought by certain doctors. Only he says, "The mind-power is superior to drug-power. Mental cure, if scientifically applied, is more powerful than drug cure." The Hindu healer says, however, that great mental preparation is necessary to understand the relation of mind and matter, or to change the material habits of thinking into spiritual habits of thinking —in an individual wholly living on the material plane.

When a man thinks he cannot exist a day without munching a big piece of beef steak, and at the same time talks about the non-existence of matter and the uselessness of medicine, he contradicts himself. If one believes in food, one believes in medicine also, for food is nothing but certain chemicals taken to heal the decaying tissues, which purpose medicine also serves. The Hindu healer says that when your consciousness is on the material plane, you have to obey material laws no matter how much you mentally deny them. Material and mental laws both come from the Divine source, and as such —both are true differently. But in order to see the work of the Divine Mind one must know how to lift the consciousness from the physical to the superphysical plane. That requires training and concentration. The aspiring Christian Scientist who wants to live by mind-power alone will do well to go thru the following preparation:

First, one ought to practice fasting under expert advice, not to reduce or for any other material benefit, but for the sole object of getting the soul accustomed to living without being conditioned by food. Hindu saints who have preached about the non-existence of matter have demonstrated their statements by indefinitely living without food (without losing weight or strength). I knew of a lady in 1920 in India, who lived a few miles from my school at Ranchi, who remained forty years without eating. Her case had been several times tested by authorities and found to be genuine. She had been locked up several times for months, in a room in the palaces of certain princes, without food and drink, and at the end of the period, she showed no sign of physical deterioration or loss of weight.

Shankara, one of the greatest of Hindu saints, who lived in the 6th century AD., and was the foremost exponent of the Vedanta philosophy in India, taught the illusion of matter and the eternal reality of man's true nature.

A story is told of a conversation between Shankara and a certain black magician. The latter used to acquire magical powers thru human sacrifice. While Shankara was preaching the non-existence of matter, the black magician approached him and said, "If matter is illusion, then what is this I see before me?" pointing to Shankara's body. "That is illusion." Shankara replied. The magician was quick to seize this opportunity and said, "If then your body is non-existent to you, let me use this illusion to some practical purpose and acquire some more powers for myself."

"Take it," the great Shankara replied and was ready to ignore his body as if it were an image in a forgotten dream.

Thus Shankara, the "Swami of Swamis," founder of the Swami order, and full of practical realization of his own inner imperishable nature, agreed to accompany the black magician, who led him to a forest, bathed him as though he were a goat for sacrifice, and began to sharpen his long knife for the slaughter in accordance with the rites of black magic. Even then Shankara did not lose his knowledge that the body was illusion. He was not a fanatic —but knew exactly what he was doing.

Just then one of Shankara's disciples happened to sit in deep meditation—and on opening his spiritual eye he saw to his great horror a vision of his master Shankara about to be sacrificed at the hands of the wicked magician. Thru his great devotion and psychical power —the disciple quickly dematerialized his own body and appeared at once at the scene in the forest. There he saw the knife about to fall on his master's neck and he looked at the magician with his eyes burning with spiritual electricity. The necromancer's whole body was electrocuted and he gave up the ghost with a loud voice.

"Why did you kill the man?" Lord Shankara asked his disciple.

"Sir, he was going to kill you." answered the disciple.

To which the teacher replied, "Foolish one! Didn't I teach you —all is illusion? How could he kill me, who have no body?"

The disciple smilingly replied, "Dear Master, if the attempt to kill you was illusion, then the act of Divine Law killing the magician thru me, was illusion too."

In this connection, it is interesting to recall the biblical story of how Peter rebuked Ananias and his wife for greed, and the immediate subsequent death of the two, in answer to their transgression against Divine Law.

The above illustrations of the lady fasting forty years, and Lord Shankara's great mental composure when threatened with immediate death, go to show how the Hindus are practical in their knowledge of the superiority of mind-power over the material consciousness. Man's body is like a wet battery. It depends partially on carbohydrates, liquids, oxygen, and certain chemicals taken into the body, and internally it depends on the vibratory cosmic life-current which flows thru the medulla into the body of man." Man shall not live by bread alone, but by every word that falleth out of the mouth of God."

So man's life is not dependent on bread alone, (solids, liquids or gaseous material food substances), but on every word (unit of vibratory energy) of God (cosmic energy).

Being mentally identified with food and body, man forgets that if the inner life-energy fails him, no amount of dieting or oxygenating the body can enable him to live. If the stomach of a dead man is stuffed with good food and his lungs are inflated with oxygen, he does not revive. Outwardly, food helps to keep life in the body, but life-force is maintained from within, and when the Cosmic Current fails to supply from within, no outward aid is of any avail.

Those who never fast—do not know that man can live by the word of God, or energy flowing from God. Jesus fasted forty days in order to convince himself that his soul had risen above the bodily conditions. That's why he uttered—when he was tempted by the material hunger-consciousness "Man shall not live by bread alone," etc.

Hence the earlier stages of a weeks' fasting are marked by hunger, but as the days of fasting multiply, less hunger and more freedom from food are distinctly felt. Why? Because the soul is unconsciously made to depend on the inner source of supply by a forced denial of the external source of supply of food. But this method of fasting is only one of the physical methods of rising above the consciousness of matter. No spiritual aspirant should indiscriminately indulge in long fasts without expert advice. Partial fasting, by omitting one or two meals a day, or by a day's fasting every week, done with the sole purpose of forgetting food, and followed by deep meditation, is helpful in spiritual realization.

The Christian Scientist generally employs strong imagination, developed by study of "Science and Health," in order to heal his physical diseases and convince himself of the non-existence of matter. But there is a more powerful element in man, says the Hindu teacher—the Will—by development of which, man can convert his body into a dry battery, charging his body with life-current from within by the Cosmic Source, and living without food, chemicals, or medicine. This requires long practice, and is difficult, but the easiest way is to learn to treat the body like a wet battery and live more by the Vital Force charged by the Will from within, and less by material food.

The Will is the great inner generator of energy into the body. When one is unwilling to do his daily work —one feels a lack of energy in the system. Whereas when one works incessantly but willingly, he feels full of energy within the body. Imagine if a man lying down quietly on a sofa, does not will to move his limbs or muscles or does not will to imagine or think or feel, and goes on remaining in that passive state, can he live? No.

Hence the body movements and physical processes are initiated by Will, consciously or unconsciously. Therefore, when one learns the higher metaphysical method, living by Conscious Energy and Will, he can then know that mind-power is self-contained and may live without being conditioned by the requirements of the body.

Then comes the method of learning the art of concentration by which one can transfer the attention —at will— from the body —to the soul in order to destroy the gross identification of the soul with the body—for this identification is the sole cause of the soul's ascribing to itself all the frailties and diseases of the body.

In order to fix a broken bone, the doctor, a child of God, with the help of God's material laws, has developed an almost perfect method of bone fixture. Then why ask a suffering layman to wait for a mental method of bone fixture, which only the highly developed ones, acquainted with the law of materialization and dematerialization of atomic vibration and body tissue, can perform. Until belief in mind-power is converted into exact knowledge, the layman is in danger of disillusionment. Merely ignoring a disease by belief in health would not prevent the progress of a disease, for the operation of God's physical laws are just as true as His mental laws. That's why many have died of disease —though they believed in mental healing. In order to be absolutely sure of mental healing, one must regularly develop his powers. Jesus was always sure of His healing because He had studied and knew what He was doing.

The inspired Hindu teachers are thoroughly in accord with the basic principles of Christian Science. But they express themselves differently. Instead of saying, as the Christian Scientist does, that matter does not exist, they say —matter is materialized mind-force, and scientifically prove this statement by their power of materialization and dematerialization of matter.

Science has demonstrated that all matter is composed of vibration. The ninety-two elements of matter, which enter into the composition of all the universe, from stars to human beings, are nothing but different forms of electronic vibration. For example, in ice —we find coldness, weight, form; it is visible. Melt the ice; it becomes water. Pass electricity thru it; it becomes invisible H2O, which, analyzed further, is a form of electronic vibration. Hence, one may scientifically say that ice does not exist, even though it is perceptible to our senses of sight, taste, feeling and so forth. In reality its essence is invisible electrons or forms of energy. In other words, that which can be dissolved into invisibility cannot be said to have valid existence. In this sense, matter can be said not to exist, but only in this sense, because matter does have relative existence, i.e., matter exists in relation to our mind and as an expression of the invisible electronic forces which do exist, because they are unchangeable and immortal. Just as the child could not be born without the parents, so matter is dependent on mind for its existence. It is born out of Divine Mind, and is perceptible to mortal mind; in itself and of itself, it has no reality and no existence. Hinduism supplies the missing link between Matter and Mind as being energy, just as the missing link between invisible H2O gas and ice —is water. Water and ice are both manifestations of invisible H2O, with only formal existence ...transitory appearance. Similarly, conscious mortal mind and matter are the formal manifestations of Divine Consciousness, with formal existence; but essentially, only Divine Mind exists.

In a very interesting booklet by Swami Abhedananda on "Christian Science and Vedanta," the following observations are made: "Christian Science, by denying the existence of matter and mortal mind, denies the existence of the phenomenal world and reduces it to nothingness. This difficulty does not arise in Vedanta philosophy, because it does not deny the existence of matter, mind, and everything that is on the phenomenal plane. Altho it tells us that the world is unreal, that matter is unreal, mind unreal; still it recognizes their existence, but adds that that existence cannot be separated from the absolute existence. If Brahman, or the absolute existence, be all in all, then everything that exists on the phenomenal plane is in reality Brahman, or the absolute Truth. The reality of the chair, the table, the earth, the sun, moon, and stars, is the absolute existence, is divinity itself. The reality in you, in me, and in all living creatures is the same as the absolute reality of the universe; only, on account of names and forms, the One Reality appears to be many. As, for instance, the one substance clay, appears thru diverse names and forms in numberless varieties, such as pots, jars, bricks, etc., so the One Absolute Reality, when clothed with varying names and forms, appears to be sun, moon, stars, animals, vegetables, etc. . . .

"The names and forms have of course no Absolute Reality, but they have Conditional Reality; or, in other words, they exist in relation to our minds. The world is real, according to Vedanta, but at the same time it is not as it seems to be; it is not that which appears to us at the present moment. This is what is meant by 'illusion' in Vedanta. For example, here is a chair; the substance of this chair is the Absolute Reality, because the Absolute Reality is All-Pervading and One. It is in you, in me, in the table, and in everything, and that which gives reality to the chair ...is one with the Absolute Reality. But the chair appears as chair only so long as it is clothed with the name and form of chair. If we can mentally separate the name and form from the substance of the chair, that which will be left —will be common wood; take away the name and form of wood —atoms and molecules will remain; take away the name and form of atoms and molecules —there will be nothing but Eternal Energy, and that is inseparable from the Absolute Substance. In this way, if we can mentally separate the names and forms from the substance, all phenomenal objects can be reduced to one substance which is the Absolute Reality of the universe. . . .

"In this age of agnosticism and materialism, Christian Science has done an admirable work, in making people realize that this phenomenal world of ours is like a dreamland, and that all objects of sense are nothing more than objects seen in a dream. This is no small gain for Western minds;

because the more we realize that this world is like a dream —the nearer we approach to Absolute Truth. In this respect, what Christian Science is at present trying to do in this country, has been done by Vedanta in India for centuries. Furthermore, Christian Science has rendered a great service to humanity by demonstrating the power of the mind over the body, the power of Spirit over matter. Altho this fact was in no way new to the spiritual teachers, sages and best thinkers of every country, still in no other country and at no other time had there ever been so well organized a movement as that started recently by Mrs. Eddy under the name of Christian Science. Like Vedanta, it has brought health to many diseased bodies and rest to may diseased minds.

"The power of healing is the property of every individual soul. There have been many remarkable healers in every country—among the Hindus, the Buddhists, the Mohammedans, and those of other religious creeds. It is a great mistake to think that the power of healing comes from any outside source or from belief in this or that. It is developed by living a right life in accordance with the moral and spiritual laws of nature. . . . If we read the religious history of the world carefully, we find that long before the birth of Christ, the same healing Power of the Mind or Spirit was practiced by the followers of Buddha —with marvellous success. Wherever Buddhist missionaries travelled, they healed the sick without using drugs. The yogis in India also use no drugs in curing disease, but rely entirely upon the spiritual power which they acquire thru right living and the practice of Yoga. . . . The power of healing is universal and cannot be confined within the boundaries of any one creed, sect, religion or book."

Resuming our discussion of mind and matter: We find that the blind or non-intelligent electronic forces of creation, in order to be Creative Teleological Agents, contain within themselves the vibrations of the Universal Conscious Life-Force, which in its turn —came from the vibrations of God's Divine Cosmic Consciousness. God said, "Let there be light," i.e., the Creator vibrated in His consciousness and It produced light or energy, and flowing conscious light of life-current and electrons, which further vibrated more grossly and became the diverse subtle forces of Nature, which in their turn became the gross ninety-two elements of matter that constitute the material universe.

To the human consciousness —matter is both real and perceptible. But man has discovered thru theoretical investigation, thru logic and thru certain experiments (such as being able to convert a visible piece of ice into an invisible force) that there is a permanent and unalterable creative force behind all the transitory and illusive forms of material creation. This truth may be grasped just as we grasp the fact that the ocean exists ....though its waves have no permanent existence, being just the passing formal manifestations of one great substance. The waves cannot exist without the ocean, but the ocean can exist without the waves. So matter cannot exist without Divine Mind-Power, but Divine Mind-Power can exist without matter. These concepts can be intellectually grasped, but they cannot be realized until one has learned the conscious method of converting matter into conscious energy and conscious energy into Cosmic Consciousness, as Jesus could and as many Hindu Saints have been able to do. To such Enlightened Ones, mater does not exist because They can see the whole unchangeable ocean of Spirit beneath the slight rippling waves of creation.

The Universe has been spoken of in Vedanta and Yoga philosophies as God's dream. Matter and mind, with the universe, planets, and the human powers of feeling, will and consciousness, the states of life and death, disease and health, the gross surface waves and the subtle under-currents of material creation, are realities according to the Law of Relativity governing this dream of God's. All the dualities perceived thru the Law of Relativity are real to the dreamer, to the ordinary man in the world who plays his little part in the great dream of God. To escape from these dualities, one must awaken from this dream into eternal God-wakefulness. We cannot change God's dream just by imagination or denying matter, or by accepting life but rejecting death, or by seeking health and fleeing sickness. One state is as much a part of its opposite state as the two sides of the same cloth. The dualities are part and parcel of each other. The man who sees his body different from mind, who cannot dematerialize his body into Electronic Energy, who cannot see the inconsistency of rejecting medicine but accepting food, or denying sickness but affirming health, is a man still under the delusion of the dream-world. Just as the ordinary man has dreams which seem real for a time, but lose their reality when the man emerges into the ordinary waking state, so it is possible for every one to awaken some day from the seeming reality of the present world-dream, and live in the eternal Cosmic Consciousness of God.

The super-man, He who has consciously awakened in God by transferring and expanding His consciousness into the world of unchangeable reality, He alone can realize this creation as a dream of God; He alone can say matter has no existence. Thru a long series of self-disciplinary steps, thru the different paths of Yoga, or thru any method of spiritual perfection, thru service, love, wisdom and self-effacement, the Aspirant climbs beyond the clutch of dualities and the impermanence of all created things, into the incomprehensible grandeur of His true Being.

LUTHER BURBANK: AN APPRECIATION

My friend Luther Burbank has passed on. His body lies under a Lebanon cedar that he planted years ago in his own little garden, but his spirit smiles at us today from every sweet flower that blooms by the wayside. He, who was so close to nature, so confidential and so understanding to her, is now part of her great spirit, whispering in her winds, shining in her stars, walking the dawn with her.

I loved him very dearly. He was one of the saintliest men I have ever met. To look at his sensitive face with its compassionate eyes and kindly smile —was to see a man bathed in a great spiritual radiance. I would not mind walking all the way from New York to Santa Rosa to meet him and discuss humanity and spiritual subjects with him once again. His vast learning and genuine modesty repeatedly reminded me of the trees that are bent low with the burden of ripening fruits. It is always the fruitless trees that lift their heads high in the sky in empty boastfulness.

His love of the voiceless plants, creepers and flowers intensified his love for mankind. He had a burning desire to be of service, to help to bear as much as possible of the world's burden. He was well-acquainted with humility, patience, sacrifice. His life was simplicity itself. He knew the worthlessness of luxury, and the joy of few possessions.

The keynote to his whole personality was love, great love. His heart especially went out to children, yearning to see them given an opportunity to express the infinite goodness within them. "But the educational system of today is afraid to experiment." he said to me. "Nothing worth while is possible without fearless experiments. At times the most daring experiments are needed to bring out the best in fruits and flowers. The human body, human mind and human soul are much more complex, and important, than those of the vegetable world, so the experiments should likewise be more daring, more numerous. . . . The experiments you are carrying on in your schools in India are of much value to humanity."

Balancing East-West

I like to remember that Luther Burbank was open-minded to the spiritual message of the East. "In spite of the Western knowledge of science," he told me repeatedly, "we have much to learn from the East. There they have great stores of truth that the Western mind as yet scarcely knows the existence of."

Just before his death, Burbank dramatically martyred himself by calling himself an infidel so that people might wake up from their sleep of superstition, and seek God rationally. As Jesus offered himself for love, so Burbank was willing to be crucified by public opinion for the sake of truth and the destruction of ignorance. Many newspapers actually called Burbank an "atheist," considering him as one more scientist without faith in God.

An atheist denies the existence of God. But an infidel is simply a disbeliever in the established religion. To a Turk, a Christian is an infidel. Yet both believe in God. But the public does not realize the fundamental difference between the two terms. To most of them, Burbank has denied God. But how far that is from the truth! His faith in the great power that rules the mighty forces of nature was the deepest chord in his being. He himself declared to his interviewer that he was an infidel only in the sense that Jesus was an infidel—because they both rebelled against prevailing systems. But let us read Burbank's actual words as recorded by the interviewer, Mr. Edgar Waite, and first published by the S. F. Bulletin in a copyrighted article:

"Religion grows with the intelligence of man, but all religions of the past and probably all of the future will sooner or later become petrified forms instead of living helps to mankind. Until that time comes, however, if religion of any name or nature makes man more happy, comfortable, and able to live peaceably with his brothers, it is good. . . .

"The idea that a good God would send people to a burning hell is utterly damnable to me. I don't want to have anything to do with such a God. But while I cannot conceive of such a God, I do recognize the existence of a great universal power which we cannot even begin to comprehend. . . .

"As for Christ—well, He has been most outrageously belied. His followers, like those of many scientists and literary men who produce no real thoughts of their own, have so garbled His words and conduct that many of them no longer apply to present life. Christ was a wonderful psychologist. He was an infidel of his day, because He rebelled against the prevailing religions and government. I am a lover of Christ as a man, and His work and all things that help humanity, but nevertheless, just as He was an infidel then, I am an infidel today."

In reference to the theory of Reincarnation, in which his friend Henry Ford has recently declared his belief, Burbank told the interviewer: "The theory of Reincarnation, which originated in India, has been welcomed in other countries. Without doubt, it is one of the most sensible and satisfying of all religions that mankind has conceived. This, like the others, comes from the best qualities of human nature, even if in this, as in the others, its adherents sometimes fail to carry out the principles in their lives."

Burbank, when asked to state his position more clearly, said later: "Euripides long ago said, 'Who dares not speak his free thought is a slave.' I nominated myself as an 'infidel,' as a challenge to thought for those who are asleep. The word is harmless if properly used. Its stigma has been heaped upon it by unthinking people who associate it with the bogey devil and his malicious works. If my words have awakened thoughts in narrow bigots and petrified hypocrites, they will have done their appointed work. . . .

"Most of us possess discriminating reasoning powers—can we use them or must we be fed by others like babies? What does the Bible mean when it distinctly says, By their works ye shall know them? Works count far more than words with those who think clearly. . . .

"I love everybody. I love everything. I love humanity—it has been a constant delight during all my seventy-seven years of life, and I love all the works of nature. . . . All plants, animals, and man are already in eternity travelling across the face of time. . . ."

The urge toward infinite realization is in every human soul. But in some, as in Burbank, that urge is keenly felt, tirelessly probing, actively seeking fulfillment. The stupendous power that guides all creation came very close to Burbank in the course of his chosen work. He felt its overwhelming grandeur, its incomprehensible goodness and beauty. And he knew that he, as a man, could not define It or know It completely. On all subjects, he kept an open mind, sure that the truth could not be so small as to be exhausted and contained in one religion, one age, one mind. . . . We should honor him for that.

Henry Ford writes of Burbank: "There was in him a beautiful and abiding faith in the permanence of that which now lives, whatever form it may take, here or hereafter, and whatever function it may perform in what we call the 'world of matter.' He believed that no life was ever lost. . . . His faith was so great and firm that he did not feel the need of being over-positive about things he could not scientifically prove."

Hail and farewell! It is the law of life. I am happy to remember the fragrance of his life, and that it blew across my way. I like to think of him now, in every flower and tree, and in the faces of little children.

Paramhansa Yogananda

THE HART OF HEAVEN

(Inspired by "The Hound of Heaven," by Francis Thompson.)

Like a wild, cruel hunter
Sure of my prey,
I chased for the Heavenly Hart
Thru forests of dark desires,
Maizes of my passing pleasures.
Thru corridors of ignorance
I raced for Him,
The Hart of Heaven.
Farther, farther He fled,
Driven— afraid of me,
(Equipped with spears keen of selfishness.)
As He fled ...the Earth echoed,
"I am more fleet
Swifter than thy feet
Of fiery passion's greeds
Which vainly rush at Me.
None reach Me
Who frighten Me
And thus make Me wise."
Then I flew on the planes of heavenly prayer
In pursuit of the Deer.
But crashed to Earth;
—Of restlessness I fell.
The Deer yet flies,

Balancing East-West

The echo replies:
"I am fleeter
Than thy noisy plane of prayer.
Thy loud-tongued noise of hollow prayer
In the earliest hour of the chase
Startled Me.
I fly beyond thy sight."
My spears, my dogs, my plane ...I left;
Stealthily I crept,
Holding my dart of concentration.
Ah, all sudden
Lo! There I spied the Hart of Heaven
Grazing peacefully,
Fearlessly, before me.
I took aim ...and shot—
But, my hand shook with unsteadiness.
Look! The Deer bounded
And the Earth resounded:
"Without devotion
Thou art a poor, poor marksman!"
Though I shot again and again
At the Heavenly Hart,
It fled, crying:
"I am beyond the range of thy mental dart.
I am beyond!"
In despair I gave up the chase
And finding a secret lair of Love ...in me
By strange intuition and in curiosity led
I strolled ...deeply within.
Lo! There came my Hart of Heaven

Paramhansa Yogananda

Willingly walking in.
Eager, devoted,
Steadily I shot ...again and again
With my concentration-dart;
Afraid It might again fly.
I missed many times, yet
It stirred not, moved not, fled not.
There my Heavenly Hart
Wounded by devotion's dart
Lay gasping, dying in me.
And Its vanishing breath
Sang thru the silent Earth
Echoing within me:
"None can seize Me
Save with the help of Mine.
Save only Mine!
I am thine! Receive Me!"

THREE RECIPES

Spiritual Recipe

1. Read the EAST-WEST well and try to practically follow the best in it, using your own judgment.
2. Lead a balanced life. Be neither too Oriental nor too Occidental. Let not calmness develop into laziness, nor let activity convert you into a business automaton. Be calmly active, actively calm.
3. Polish your feelings. Exercise them by practical sympathy, and say to yourself, "I can only be happy by making others so."
4. Try to consciously contact God. Will to know Him, persevere in the effort to know Him, and be dissatisfied until you do know Him.

Intellectual Recipe

1. Read a few lines from Shakespeare every day.
2. Read the "Imitation of Christ," by Thomas Kempis.
3. Read "In Tune with the Infinite," by Ralph Waldo Trine.
4. Read "The Man Nobody Knows," by Bruce Barton. It is the best modern book on Jesus.

Health Recipe

Fast one day a week, or at least a half-day. If you feel unable to do that, live for one day on nothing but orange juice. This plan will give needed rest to the body-machine which overworks incessantly thru over-eating or wrong eating. Do not think that satisfied hunger means satisfied body needs. Learn the laws of rational, scientific diet, and live on simple and wholesome food.

ETHNOLOGISTS

vs.

THE "COMMON MAN"

(All lovers of justice and international brotherhood will find the following facts of vital interest to them; and it is specially asked that they read each word carefully and then act on the suggestions offered.)

Up until recently, a Hindu of Aryan stock has always been free to become an American citizen, if he so desired. This right was granted him in accordance with an early American statute which declared all "white persons" to be eligible to American citizenship. For 133 years this phrase "white persons" has been interpreted in all courts of law to include the Hindus as a branch of the Aryan race. According to the Dictionary of races and peoples which has been approved and used by Congress in the past, the "white race" includes "the dark Hindus and other peoples of India, still more emphatically because of their possessing an Aryan speech, relating them still more closely to the white race, as well as because of their physical type."

The decisions of the American courts for almost a century and a half have interpreted the words "white persons" to mean those belonging to the Caucasian race. Hindus belong to the Caucasian race and as such have always been eligible to American citizenship. Webster's Dictionary defines "Aryan" to mean "a member of that Caucasic race of which one branch early occupied the Iranian plateau, and another entered India." Every ethnologist acknowledges that the Hindus are Caucasians and Aryans. The skull and other bone formations and the hair texture, as well as historical records and the possession of a common root language, all point to the fact that the Europeans and the Hindus came from the same stock, and they still maintain the same common racial characteristics.

So for 133 years Hindus have occasionally availed themselves, as members of the Caucasian race, of the privilege of becoming American citizens. But on February 19, 1923, when a high-caste Hindu, Mr. B. S. Thind, applied for American citizenship, he was refused this right by Justice Sutherland, who, in an attempt to explain why he was reversing the decisions of his predecessors on the bench for the last 133 years, said:

"What we now hold is that the words 'free white persons' are words of common speech, to be interpreted in accordance with the understanding of the common man, synonymous with the word 'Caucasian' only as the word is popularly understood and used, whatever may be the speculations of the ethnologists."

What Justice Sutherland means by these extraordinary words is that he believes that only those persons should be admitted to American citizenship whose skin is so white that even the most ignorant "common man" would know he belonged to the white race. In thus interpreting the words "white persons," Justice Sutherland takes the stand that he prefers the judgment of ignorance to the judgment of science. He would rather let the "common man" interpret what "white persons" means, regardless of what the ethnologist thinks, not withstanding the fact that the former may be an ignoramus on the subject and the latter a learned specialist who has studied the matter and is in a position to give a true impartial decision.

Further, the most remarkable complications may logically result from the decision of Justice Sutherland. If, then, the interpretation of what a "white person" is, is going to be left to the "common man" rather than the ethnologist, and if the words are going to be interpreted so literally that one must have a certain degree of whiteness in the skin in order to qualify for American citizenship, then we may logically expect that not only Hindus but also great numbers of southeastern Europeans will be barred. Certainly many Spanish, Italian, Greek and other Latin peoples have dark skins. Even fair English and other blond types often become very dark thru long association with tropical suns. Many English officials in India return to their native land after years of service in India, so dark that their own mothers would scarcely know them. Such is the power of the fiery sun. So perhaps it is well to warn naturalized Americans who intend traveling in tropical countries that, if Justice Sutherland's ruling is going to stand as a law in this country, they had better extract a solemn promise from their own American government that they will be allowed to return to America and retain all their rights as American citizens, regardless of how dark they may appear on their return. Such a precautionary step is certainly advisable in the present state of affairs!

Then, reflect that many Hindus of Kashmere and other north India provinces within the cold climatic belt of the snowy Himalayas, are very fair and white in complexion and often have blue eyes. The "common man" whose interpretation is so dear to Justice Sutherland, would certainly consider these Kashmiris to be "white persons." The State Department has since ruled that such persons would be ineligible to American citizenship on account of their race, but, so far as Justice Sutherland's decision is concerned (because his ruling makes citizenship dependent not on race, but on skin color), it would not have been impossible for a Kashmiri Hindu to have become an American citizen, while another naturalized American, visiting foreign parts, and who had rashly sunned himself into a shade of brown too deep for political recognition, would find on his return to America that he could not satisfy the "common man" that he was a "white person," since obviously he is not, and hence his citizenship might be lost to him! Nor is this example too far-fetched, since the State Department has since used Justice Sutherland's ruling with what practically amounts to unconstitutional retro-active application.

The situation is not without its humorous aspects. It is most unusual, fortunately, to find a judge who is willing to waive the opinion of experts in favor of the "understanding of the common man." For example, imagine a judge who, in a murder case, would rather accept the opinion of the ordinary layman, and who set at naught the findings of a chemist, in reference to whether or not a certain spot on a vital piece of evidence, was a spot of blood! So, when ethnological advice is obtainable as to the meaning of the words "white persons," it is inexcusable to prefer the judgment of the "common man."

Consider, too, other complications that are bound to arise. Justice Sutherland refused citizenship to Mr. Thind solely because his skin was not white. But in thus refusing to interpret "white persons" to mean Caucasians, and in agreeing to interpret the phrase as referring only to the color of the skin, Justice Sutherland leaves room for a host of new difficulties, some of them of the most humorous "complexion." Who is going to decide just where "white" leaves off, and "brown" begins in the skin pigment? And who will decide just where powder and other cosmetics leave off and true skin color begins? Assuredly, the learned Justice must have realized that he was treading on very delicate ground here!

Jesus Christ, according to Justice Sutherland, was not a "white person" and would be ineligible to American citizenship were he present today. All thru the ages, the spiritual contribution of India to the world has been boundless. But Justice Sutherland is not interested in the quality of the candidate for American citizenship. He thinks that the color of the skin is more important. But it is difficult to believe that the American people agree with him or think as he thinks. The American people realize that their national greatness lies in the contributions of diverse races and minds. "The Melting Pot!" The land of equal opportunity! America would not be America without her cosmopolitan spirit, her racial admixtures, her diverse representatives. When Justice Sutherland expressed his willingness to accept the interpretation of the "common man" in the belief that the "common man" would base his judgment of what a "white person" was, solely on the color of the person's skin, I do not think that the Justice gave much credit to the intelligence and the fair-mindedness of the average American.

What has been the result of this decision of Justice Sutherland's? It has not only prevented any Hindu from becoming an American citizen since 1923, but it has even been used to deprive all Hindus in this country who had become citizens prior to 1923, of their citizenship. The injustice of this simply cannot be overstated. It rendered such Hindus absolutely stateless. They automatically ceased to be British subjects when they took the oath of American allegiance. By British law, they rendered themselves for all time to come, aliens in the eyes of the British. Hence, though they were considered "white persons" at the time they were granted citizenship, and had no reason to suppose the United States would ever retract its pledge of protection, yet they are now in the sorry plight of the "man without a country." The retro-active application of Justice Sutherland's decision has worked the utmost hardship upon those Hindus who had previously been granted citizenship. As stateless persons, neither their liberty nor their property is secured to them. It is hard for them even to make a living as professional men, for few people would wish to employ stateless persons. The American Government will not issue them a passport to travel abroad, and there is no other government to whom they may apply. They cannot enter any other country with proper credentials, nor can they secure citizenship in any other country while staying in America. The wives of these stateless Hindus are also rendered stateless, even when these women are American-born. The sudden change of political fortune forced many Hindus to give up their property under the Alien Land Laws, and wrought the utmost economic injustice and even ruin upon them.

Race distinction by the color standard has in it the dynamite of violent racial passion, which once roused fully would work havoc in the world. America needs statesmen who can design laws to bring out international good will, not racial animosity for pointless purposes.

One such statesman is Senator Royal S. Copeland of New York. On June 23rd, 1926, he introduced into Congress a bill designed to give a legal definition to the words "white person" and to include Hindus within the scope of this definition. For 133 years it has not been necessary to thus specifically define "white persons," because all judicial authority during that period of time has agreed to interpret the words "white persons" in their ethnological and true sense. It was left to Justice Sutherland to discover that all his predecessors for 133 years had been mistaken and that he alone had at last discovered the proper and literal meaning of the word "white." Senator Copeland, in an effort to legally define the words "white persons," has introduced a bill, which, if passed, will effectively prevent any more literal rulings by individual judges to whom white is white, and brown is a crime. The new bill aims to include all Caucasian peoples within the scope of the words "white persons."

One authority sums up the situation thus: "The Hindus affected by this ruling (of Justice Sutherland's) number from three to five thousand, most of them farmers on the Pacific Coast. They had made an important contribution to the economic life of the country in developing cultivation of cotton in the Imperial Valley, and were in many cases well-to-do. The opinion of Judge Sutherland placed them in the class of those ineligible for citizenship, who under California law are ineligible to hold or lease land. They were enabled to remain on the farms which they had developed on what was thought to be sterile and arid land, only by virtue of transferring title or leasehold to American citizens, by whom they were mulcted of the fruits of their industry, and in some cases reduced to peonage. The present bill, which should be promptly passed, will have no effect on the immigration of Hindus from the barred zone. It will merely make impossible the economic exploitation of a group of extraordinarily able farmers and artisans. It will rescue the Hindus already admitted to citizenship from their stateless condition, and in cases where Hindus not citizens have married American women, it will allow their wives to retain United States citizenship. It will save the United States from the meanness and dishonor of retracting a pledge already given. A man who renounces one government and swears allegiance to another in good faith has a right to expect good faith on the part of the nation to which he is admitted, particularly if he is ready to shed his blood in its defense."

Senator Copeland's bill is worthy of the support of all right-thinking and justice-loving Americans. It was introduced into the last session of the 69th Congress on June 23, 1926, and is Bill Number S. 4505. It was read twice and referred to the Committee on Immigration. The bill reads as follows: "A BILL: To amend section 2169 of the Revised Statutes as amended, in respect to the definition of a white person. Be it enacted by the Senate and House of Representatives of the United States of America in Congress assembled, that section 2169 of the Revised Statutes, as amended, is amended by adding at the end thereof the following new sentence: 'A person shall be deemed to be a white person within the meaning of this section if such person is of any one of the following peoples; Scandinavian (Danish, Norwegian, Swedish), German, Dutch, English, Flemish, Lithuanian, Scotch, Irish, Welsh, Russian, Polish, Czech (Bohemian, Moravian), Servian, Croatian, Montenegrin, Slovak, Slovenian, Ruthenian, Dalmation, Herzegovinian, Bosnian, Albanian, Armenian, French, Italian, Romanian, Spanish, Spanish-American, Mexican, Portuguese, Greek, Hindu, Gypsy, Arabian, Hebrew, Syrian, Caucasus, Basque,'"

Thus it will be seen that Senator Copeland's bill does not have any reference to immigration of Hindus from the barred zone. Nor is it my wish or intention in this article, to give the United States Government any advice or suggestions about handling its immigration situation or other political problems. It is my desire simply to protest against the injustice that the Hindus in this country have suffered thru an interpretation of the words "white persons" from a standpoint of color rather than from the proper standpoint of race. Color is a most unnatural and arbitrary standard to use. The Hindu Aryans and the European Aryans are brothers, not only in the wide and beautiful sense that all men are brothers, claiming the same Divine Father as their Creator, but also in a narrow historical sense. Because one branch of the Aryans settled in the warm regions of India and acquired a darker skin, and the other branch settled in the colder European countries and remained lighter in color, is surely no argument in favor of their denying their common blood and heritage.

I specially request all my students to write to the Senators who compose the Immigration Committee, to which Senator Copeland's bill has been referred, urging the passing of the bill. The name of the Senators comprising the Committee, are as follows:

1.--Hon. Hiram Johnson, of California.

2.--Hon. Henry W. Keyes, of New Hampshire.

3.--Hon. Frank B. Willis, of Ohio.

4.--Hon. David A. Reed, of Pennsylvania.

5.--Hon. Rice W. Means, of Colorado.

6.--Hon. Gerald P. Nye, of North Dakota.

7.--Hon. William H. King, of Utah.

8.--Hon. William J. Harris, of Georgia.

9.--Hon. Pat. Harrison, of Mississippi.

10.--Hon. Royal S. Copeland, of New York.

11.--Hon. Cole L. Blease, of South Carolina.

These gentlemen should all be addressed as above, in care of the Senate Office Building, Washington, D. C.

If you have not time to write to all of them individually, then write to Hon. Hiram Johnson, who is Chairman of the Committee; to Hon. Royal S. Copeland, thanking him for introducing the Bill; and to President Coolidge, asking for his support.

In your letters, please stress the following points:

1—Senator's Copeland's Bill (Number S. 4505; please mention this) does not have any bearing on the immigration problem.

2—The passage of the bill will prevent the economic exploitation of those Hindus who now have had to dispose of their property under the Alien Land laws.

3—It will rescue those Hindus, admitted to citizenship prior to

1923, from their present stateless condition of men without a country.

4—It will enable American women who have married Hindus to retain their American citizenship. An American man does not lose his citizenship thru marriage with a foreigner. The same privilege should be granted to American women.

5—It will prevent racial bitterness and the raising of a new color barrier. The Hindus are now discriminated against, not as members of the Caucasian race, but as the possessors of a dark skin. This is manifestly unjust and unwise.

6—India has ever been the great giver of spiritual gifts to the world. America has ever been the land of political freedom. To cultivate friendship between the two countries is to foster a constructive and mutually advantageous relationship.

Please write up the above points in your own words. Try to interest all your friends in this struggle against injustice and untruth, and ask them to write to Senator Copeland and Senator Johnson. If you have time, besides writing to President Coolidge and to the eleven Senators of the Immigration Committee, mentioned above, write also to the two Senators in the National Senate who represent your own state.

My object in writing this article, is not merely to aid in securing simple justice for the Hindus in America, however desirable that object might be. For the Hindus have their own great and spiritual land, and Americans should deem it at least as high an honor to welcome a son of India to American citizenship, as the Hindu should feel in assuming that position.

But my object is also to point out to all truth-loving, Christian Americans that their high and sacred duty is to uphold the beautiful standards of Christianity, whose Founder said, "All ye are brethren" (Matthew 23:8). If Christianity is to remain a vital and redeeming faith in the world, it must inspire its followers with courage to maintain its principles. Mental sloth is spiritual stagnation. We must fight for the right, and be willing to actively bestir ourselves in a spiritual cause against injustice.

Paramhansa Yogananda

AT "SUL MONTE"

(Dedicated to Amelita Galli-Curci and Homer Samuels.)

They say He's far remote, unseen,
Too austere and beyond our vision keen.
Ah, yet when I passed thru the tunnel of leaves
An saw the hill-top green grassy orchid-vase
(Adorned with a doll temple
Little, artistic, grand and simple)
Hanging from the big skiey roof
High amidst the clouds, aloof
From din and uproars loud
Of aimless rushing crowds,
I asked myself this and that—
Who made this, Who made that?
And I found my answer
From His servitors, O everywhere,
O everywhere;
The painted screens of varying light and shade
Did drop, go up or fade.
And the changing charming scenic players
Did speak of Him, entertain and disappear.
Rows of motley costumed leaves did stand
And dance in tune with the playing breeze
Or fitful thunder-band.
The turbaned soldier trees.
Serious, mystic, grim,
Merging from colossal castle of mounts

Balancing East-West

Stood in the distant dim to declare
"Hark! He's very near; Wake, He's very near."
And soon with the nightly curtain fall
They'd vanish all.
By the flower-fringed lawn strolling
A song came wafting—
"Is it a nightingale or a fairy voice?"
Nay, coloratura of celestial choice!
I listened and listened and listened
And when I thought the song was best
And the voice reached the supreme test,
Came whistling a deeper, deepest mystic note
Straight from her soul, from the Spirit remote.
Around the tiny temple
Oft the listening breeze long drank
The sweet music of Homer,
And her soul-solacing song.
And in wild joy would call
The wren, the whippoorwill and all
To this peace-bathed pure God-altar,
Where man's beauty-touches rare
Did soften Nature's scenic painting bare.
Of all the august guests
A few forget-me-nots
From unknown somewhere
Came peeping thru the little temple door
To remind us, said she,
"Love not My things, more than Me.
Thru little forget-me-nots thy Father
Will speak to thee ever, ever.

Paramhansa Yogananda

No never forget Me, O never, never,
Amelita de Sul Monte and Homer.
Remember Me ever, ever."

OCCIDENTAL CHRISTIANITY AND YOGODA

The Spirit is the infinite reservoir of Wisdom. Each human life is a channel thru which His wisdom flows steadily. There are wide and narrow channels. The larger the channel, the greater the flow of God-power.

We are peculiar channels. It lies in our power to make ourselves narrower or wider. We have been gifted with the freedom of Will and the power of choice. Some choke the channel of their lives with the mud of accumulated Ignorance, never allowing themselves to be cleansed by the dredge of Knowledge. The Ocean of Truth fruitlessly attempts to flood thru such narrow openings in greater volume.

There are others who keep on digging, widening, deepening the channels of their lives by self-discipline and culture, thus inviting bigger and bigger volumes of God-wisdom to pass thru them. Jesus the Christ was one of the greatest channels thru which the Cosmic Wisdom flowed. We must remember each channel is finite and has its limitations. I daresay there shall never be born a Prophet who can contain or exhaust the whole Ocean of Truth in His short span of life. Newer Prophets shall always come to express the Infinite Truth anew. Thus, though the Infinite Truth must suffer measurement even at the hands of Prophets, yet these Great Souls serve to widen the channels of smaller lives and inundate their shores with their Wisdom.

True Christianity

True Christianity must not be confounded with some of the forms that cloak it. True Christianity is neither Oriental nor Occidental, nor does it belong to Jesus and His Saints alone. It is the property of every truth-seeking soul. Jesus the son of man lifted himself to the state of being a Son of God. From human consciousness, he grew into Cosmic or Christ Consciousness. When Jesus said that all those who received Him, should become the Sons of God, he meant that all those who could receive (i.e., increase their capacity to hold) the infinite ocean of truth, such could be Sons of God. For there is no use in following the life of Jesus if he were the only Son of God and we could not be like Him. He was not given to us to symbolize an unattainable goal, but came as a living inspiration of what we all may successfully seek and achieve. If God created all men in His image, then He could not have made Jesus any different from the rest of us. We are all His children, created by the power of His being. He could not give to one —more than he gives to all. He cannot be accused of partiality and still be Divine.

Nor did God ...alone make Jesus the spiritual giant that He was, for if He creates Prophets in a spiritual factory, then we might rightly think it is needless to struggle and would wait for Him to remould us and do our spiritual thinking for us. The gift of reason and choice, the power to exercise free will, is peculiar to man and is sufficient to demonstrate to him that he must acquire his own spiritual growth by struggle and individual achievement. Jesus struggled, fasted, disciplined Himself in every way. If He were born a Son of God, then He would not have required such training. We admire Jesus more, that, being human, he became Divine.

Spiritual Truth is One; interpreted by Christians it is called Christianity; by Hindus, Hinduism, and so forth. Narrow-minded Christians and Hindus think true Christianity and Hinduism is church or temple worship, thus mistaking the form for the spirit. Truth has suffered measurement at the hands of all narrow and even all liberal interpretations. We must choose the ever-widening interpretations until we reach the goal where man-made interpretations no longer limit us. In order to do that, we must study Truth as it has expressed itself as Oriental Christianity, Occidental Christianity, and Yogoda.

What Yogoda (SRF) Does

Yogoda is a combination of both, plus everything contained in Transcendental Truth. Yogoda is not a new religion, nor a new cult, nor a new interpretation; it aims to teach the practical methods, the exact technique of widening the channel of human consciousness, so that Truth might flow in ceaselessly, endlessly, without obstructions of dogma or unproved beliefs. Yogoda points out the path of concentrating on the practical system and not only on the words and personality of Saints and Prophets. Yogoda teaches the step-by-step progress to individual personal realization and attainment of divinity.

"Sell all ye have and give to the poor." "Take no heed for the morrow, what ye shall eat, what ye shall put on," and other beautiful sayings of Jesus, would not admit of strict practical application in the Occident today.

What Jesus preached can be understood only by developing the inner consciousness. Oriental Christianity originally placed less emphasis on the forms of religion. Jesus taught in a Oriental setting and atmosphere, to an Oriental people. The truths He spoke were interpreted by the Oriental mentalities which surrounded Him. If the Bible had been written by Jesus and not by His disciples, it would have been much different. The spiritual experiences of the Biblical characters, however transcendental, or intuitional, when expressed thru Oriental mentality and terminology, took on an Oriental hue. Soul experiences cannot be expressed thru words, and when language tries to half-lisp them, they take on a distinguishing individual stamp.

Oriental Conditions of Life were Different

The above teachings of Jesus were especially applicable and possible to Oriental conditions at that time. If Jesus were preaching today to Americans, His message would be differently expressed from the message He gave 2000 years ago to an Oriental people in a land where living conditions and climatic and social factors made it possible to live much more simply than it is generally possible to do today. Then, a little labor would suffice to gain the necessities of life. Warm climate made the clothing and housing problem very simple. Less attention was needed for the physical side of life. Oriental Christianity taught plain living, outdoors living, meditating on the lap of Mother Nature. Jesus did not preach a mode of living far removed from the customary life of that day. Nor would He today advocate a radical change in our customary routine of life. This is a different age; the purposes of the Creator demand that the World's evolution proceed thru ever-new and varied conditions. So Jesus would not concentrate today on a radical change in the forms and conditions of our life; now, as then, He would point out that forms of life are secondary, that the only worth-while change, the only permanent advance, is the inner evolution of the man toward spiritual perfection. The outer conditions of life will never be perfect till the inner is perfect. The effect cannot precede the cause. Christ's teaching, interpreted by and adapted to Occidentals, is different, and is Occidental Christianity.

Thru a misunderstanding of Christ's teachings, His followers conceived a contempt for, and disregard of, the progress of the material life. They did not attempt to translate inner growth to outer achievement. This has been the case thru-out the Orient generally. But God's laws do not respect any man-made interpretation. Whenever and wherever Christians or Hindus or any race breaks God's physical or mental or spiritual laws which govern the spiritual, mental, social, industrial and materially progressive conditions of life ...he is punished with —war, plague, famine, material poverty and spiritual ignorance. History teaches us that man must develop his life in an all-round manner, neglecting neither the physical, mental nor spiritual sides —if he would achieve perfection.

Why Christianity Changed in the West

However, we must admit that the Orient generally and India in particular, has always been the breeding-ground of the world's greatest prophets and saints —Jesus, Buddha, Shankara, Krishna, Chaitanya, Lahiri Mahasaya, my Master and many others. Strangely, we do not find in the West any prophet of such eminence. If we could take statistics of the world's mentalities, we would find that the Orientals are more spiritually inclined, and the Westerners more materially and industrially-minded. One of the most important reasons for this difference between Occident and Orient lies in the difference of environment and climatic conditions. The Orient has more natural advantages, warmer climate, less difficulty in providing for its material wants. The colder climate of the West stimulated the industrial consciousness of man and led to keener struggle for a living. That is why Oriental Christianity, as taught by Jesus and His disciples, underwent a distinct change in form when arriving in the Occident. Jesus' exhortation to the Oriental multitude, "Seek ye first the kingdom of God" was changed to all practical purposes in the West to "Seek ye bread first and the kingdom of God later." "Sell all ye have and give to the poor" became, "Buy all ye can at cost price, then sell at top price and invest wisely the surplus."

But even if Occidentals desired to carry out literally the instructions given by Jesus to His Oriental listeners, the Occidentals would not be able to do so with a good conscience. Family responsibilities in most cases would prevent a man from selling all his goods and giving the money to the poor. If he took "no heed for the morrow, what ye shall eat, what ye shall put on", he would not be acting rightly by those dependent on him —who have a right to expect his support and protection. But because Occidentals cannot always follow literally the precepts given by Jesus to an Oriental people, that does not prevent Occidentals from being in every respect true Christians, following faithfully the inner teachings and true essence of Christianity. They can avoid luxury, and satisfy only their real needs.

Jesus was able to preach to the multitudes on mountain-tops and other outdoor places. News of his meeting spread by word of mouth, for the people of his day did not depend on newspapers for their news, nor do the people of the Orient generally to this day. But such delightful freedom form hall-rents and advertising expenditure is not possible today in the Occident. The preacher may be willing to preach on the mountain-top covered with snow, or inaccessible by subway or streetcar, but the audience is not willing to come to him there. They want large steam-heated and centrally located meeting-places. So the teacher who is sincerely wiling to sow the seeds of spirituality in the hearts of the multitude, ought to be willing also to accept the conditions of life in the country and age in which he finds himself. As Bruce Barton has pointed out, in his wonderful book on Jesus, "The Man Nobody Knows", Jesus would employ all the methods of the successful business man and be a large user of the newspaper columns as a means of communication if He were preaching today in America. The means do not greatly matter; putting the message "over" is the main thing.

Big costly churches have to be erected today to house the religious multitudes, with consequent concentration on the financial problems. Once a man came to me after my first lecture in that city, and said, "Swami, many times I have come to different lectures here and sat on one of those hard, uncomfortable chairs of the auditorium and was forced to leave after a half-hour of discomfort. But tonight, I am glad to tell you, your lecture completely erased the hard chair-consciousness from my mind during the whole two hours. But just the same, you should arrange always to provide your audience with comfortable seats, as otherwise an American audience will not stay!"

Churches in the Occident have done untold good by their efforts to remind people of their spiritual relationships and of God's laws. But the churches have become form-bound, lacking in the spirit of meditation and real God-communion which Jesus and his disciples so plainly manifested in their own lives. Today, the congregation at church are there in body, but in mind —most of them are somewhere else. At the time of prayer, often they are thinking of the chicken dinner awaiting them, or of a business deal. Such mental waywardness is not the fault of the church-goer, for he has never been taught the art of directing his mind, focusing it on God and of withdrawing the mind from the realm of sense-distraction. Indeed, the average man does not even know that it is possible for him to communicate personally with God, to contact Him thru cosmic vibration and a definite technique of concentration and meditation, until He is as real and near as one's own thoughts and body. So Yogoda (SRF) has arrived to teach this art of communion, of personal God-contact, of coming into conscious touch with the Source of all light, all power, all bliss.

The Occidentals and Orientals have limited truth by claiming to monopolize it, each calling the other "heathen". The Christian thinks the Hindu and Buddhist to be a "heathen"—the Hindu and Buddhist return the compliment as a matter of bigoted religious courtesy. But true religion is neither Occidental nor Oriental. The essence of religion is two-fold. First and most important, it consists of certain inner principles which make life progressive, permanently happy, and beautiful in every way. Secondly, it has material and mental forms of routine and discipline which are required to bring those inner principles into manifestation in man's material life. Religious customs and forms are like husks, necessary to cover the kernel of truth. But if the husk is without its seed of life, it is useless, barren. So the sacraments, conch shells, temple bells, the cross and crescent, have been necessary to symbolize certain spiritual truths. But as time went on, people's minds became concentrated on the form of service, method of delivery, personality of the preacher, shape and size of the church or temple, and the number of followers and their possessions. The symbols of religion thus began to act as red rags to excite the bull of religious fanaticism.

But on the other hand, those with iconoclastic ideas want to destroy all forms. Their error is that in their zeal to destroy forms, they have concentrated too much on form. Yogoda offers a remedy, a solution. It asks the different religionists to concentrate not on forms but on the one Reality behind form, the Truth that is the kernel of every religion. Yogoda has come, not to unite all churches and religions into one church and one form, or to destroy individual expressions of religion, but to show the scientific methods by which the utility and truth of the church and creed may be proven and demonstrated. Change of religious customs, or fusion of all forms into one common form, would not change the essential religious attitude. Nothing but proven truth, religious truth that can be tested and experienced individually, will ever satisfy the mind of man and do away with religious bigotry and ignorance.

Real God-Communion is Needed

In the West, because of this lack of scientific methods for directly perceiving truth, there is not any overwhelming interest in religion or spiritual problems. Whereas, in the East, where thousands of Saints and Men of Realization testify to the truth that all men may know God thru a definite series of steps and methods of concentration and meditation, we find that religion plays the most prominent part in the daily life of the multitude. But East and West alike suffer from over-development of one phase of life and under-development of other phases. India in her religious one-sidedness broke God's laws governing the material part of life, and as a consequence has had to suffer from famine and plague. In the West, worship of the god of wealth, and ignorance of God's spiritual laws —have produced nations without inward peace, manifesting outwardly in the horrors of the World War(s). Thus East and West have failed in one respect, and succeeded in another respect. Orientals have a wealth of spiritual insight and peace that no outward circumstances of suffering can destroy. And the West has conquered the plague and famine. So each needs the other's help to achieve perfection. Westerners need not blow up their factories, give up their banks and business, and go to the jungle, in order to be spiritual. But they can accept the scientific methods of inner realization from the East, and can pursue their worldly activities for the good of others, instead of for a selfish purpose. Nor need the East accept wholesale the industrial methods of the West. Modern industrial life is a jungle, too, in some respects. All that is necessary is an acceptance of the Western spirit of progress and development in reference to the material life. Thus each may benefit by the example and teachings of the other. The East must see the Supreme in the material things of life, and the Occidentals must not forget the spiritual Goal in their enthusiasm for worldly activity. A balance must be struck.

No matter whether you are a follower of Oriental religion or of Westernized Christianity, ask yourself, "Am I happy?", "Am I making others happy?", "Have I found the answer to the supreme question of life?", "What is my highest duty?", "How can I find peace and bliss?". Yogoda will solve these problems for you. It will teach you the technique of Practical God-Realization, of spiritualizing the body-cells thru a definite system of physical development, of keeping in touch with the Supreme Source of Cosmic supply that governs all our material and spiritual life. This is the practical message for which Occidentals have been hungering and waiting for nineteen centuries. This is the message that will again fill the empty churches. People today fill the movie-houses —but the churches are comparatively empty. Why? Because there is something to interest and delight the mind in the former. Evidently not, in the latter. But Yogoda will supply this interest. It will show each man that the most interesting thing in all the world —is the Bliss-God within, and will give him the key to enter into this realm of unparalleled joys. All the pursuits of life offer only partial joy, though crowned with utmost fulfillment. But in finding God we have found the reservoir of perennial, unending and unsatiating bliss. For He can give what the whole Universe cannot give. He is the Whole—the Universe is but a part of Him.

East and West Need Balance
....Knowing God Scientifically

Once let the Occidentals know of this great Bliss-God and their whole attitude toward religion and the church will change. No sermon will be dull then, no church empty. For they will hold the key to prove the truth of His existence. They will be listening to words about One whom they have experienced and know to be true, to be near, to be living. In other words, they will be devotees of God because they have met Him, and not because theoretically it seems that such a Person must or should exist. Nothing can ever satisfy the heart of man except living proof. Yogoda brings that proof to his door. Just as it is necessary for the astronomer to look thru the telescope in order to see the distant stars, just so —it is necessary for the questioner of God's existence to look for Him thru the instrument of Yogoda. If one denied the existence of a distant star, and yet would not look thru the telescope to see if he were wrong or not, his opinion would be worthless. He cannot confirm his stand unless he has confirmed it thru the instruments of knowledge that are available. So no one may rightfully deny, or affirm, the existence of God unless he has practiced the methods of approaching Him. Yogoda is the telescope to see God; without it, you must rest your belief in God on unproved faith alone. With it, you can challenge anyone to disprove that God can be known.

To control the mind by psycho-physiological methods, to direct it Godwards, to be its leader, not its slave—that is Yogoda, whether you give it that name or not. Unless you know how to shift your attention from failure to success, from worry to calmness, from mental wanderings to concentration, from restlessness to peace, from peace to Conscious Divine Bliss within—then all life's labors are spent in vain. If you have attained this control, then the purpose of life has been gloriously fulfilled.

> Whether in the prison house of loneliness,
> Or heaven of blissful solitude;
> Whether fettered by the chains of labor
> Or resting idly
> In the peace of long-deserved rest,
> I care not if Thou art with me.
> Whether in mosque, church or temple
> It matters little
> If I love ....not Thy house and its creed
> More than Thee.
> In the revolving wheels of factories
> I want to feel Thy pulsing, marching life.
> If thou art in the factory
> I prefer that
> To Heaven without Thee.

Paramhansa Yogananda

Whether in Himalayan caves
Or crowded subway,
Whether in jungles of modern life
Or of Hindustan,
Wherever we go
Teach us to discover Thee
In all Thy secret nooks,
East, West, North, South—Everywhere.

DOORS EVERYWHERE

When I was blind
I found not a door
Which led to Thee.
Thou has opened my eyes!
And now I find doors everywhere;
Thru the hearts of flowers.
Thru the voice of friendship.
Thru sweet remembrance
Of all lovely experiences.
Every gust of my prayer
Opens an unentered door
In the vast temple
Of Thy presence.

SYMPATHY FOR AIMEE SEMPLE McPHERSON

The Angelus Temple of Los Angeles and its leader, Mrs. Aimee Semple McPherson, have been an inspiration to many souls. At present they are undergoing very unpleasant tests of experience. Let all Yogoda students demonstrate the Christ-spirit by sending Mrs. McPherson good thoughts and prayers for her welfare, since she has uplifted many. It is easy to talk of universal sympathy and understanding, but we must demonstrate it in our lives too. The talk of the parlor and the pulpits must be put into practice in the rugged outdoor life of the every-day world.

It is only sympathy toward our brothers and sisters who are in distress —through the wicked plots of others, or through their own error, that will bring a better condition of society—not persecution in the name of the law to satisfy man's satanic instincts of revengefulness and gossip. We must remember Jesus' warning, "Judge not, lest ye be judged."

Many newspapers are like vultures, scattering their feathers in their struggle to get near the carrion flesh of others' misfortunes and troubles. Murders and sensational divorce cases claim their headlines, while good deeds and good thoughts hide on the back pages, if indeed they are present at all. The newspapers now are full of Mrs. McPherson's troubles, but when did these same newspapers ever recount the glowing story of the good deeds she has done? If Mrs. McPherson has done no wrong, then what untold injustice and persecution is being heaped upon her! And if she has committed any error —then that error should be balanced against the great works she has done by inspiring thousands of people. And then it will surely be found that her good actions far outweigh the other side of the scale.

We should bear in mind that it is the favorite game of misguided souls, steeped in spiritual ignorance, to strike at the slightest errors of great people, and magnify them, with the heartless hope of thus destroying the reputation and the work which the latter have built up thru the trials and tests of years.

THREE RECIPES August 1926

Health Recipe

With the presence of any chronic ailment in the body, it shows the best of judgment to stop eating everything except raw foods—vegetables in their raw state, also fruits and finely ground-up nuts. Don't complain of stomach troubles, colds, headaches. These are always the outcome of lack of physical exercises or a faulty diet. Perform some sort of exercise every day until a perspiration breaks out over your whole body. Your colds and other similar ills will soon disappear.

Fasting, or eating raw foods, and drinking less liquids, is good for reducing flesh. People don't get results because they are not regular. One day they fast, and the next day they feast. In order to get noticeable results, follow the raw food diet strictly and steadily for months.

Intellectual Recipe

Read, mark and inwardly digest selected passages from great books. Discuss important topics with intelligent people. Thinking logically over a given idea is the best way to develop originality in your ideas. When thinking, keep your eyes closed, and your mind wholly concentrated on the object of your study. Do nothing with only half-attention or half-heartedly.

Good books are your perpetual silent friends. When you are worried or grieved, take a book and bury yourself in it. Listen to the comforting and inspiring words of the great minds of all the ages.

Spiritual Recipe

Making others happy through kindness of speech and sincerity of right advice, is a sign of true greatness. To hurt another soul by sarcastic words, looks or suggestions is despicable. Sarcasm draws out the rebellious spirit and anger in the wrong-doer. Loving suggestions bring out repentance in him. Repentance consists in thoroughly understanding one's own error and in abandoning it.

Repent of your indifference to Him without whom you cannot live or speak, or have entertainment or bridge-parties! Try to cultivate His acquaintance, being introduced to Him by a right Preceptor. All earthly friends who seem so real, will be unreal some day, will pass away—and the One who seems intangible —will prove to be your only true lasting friend. It is worth-while to know God, for all your life's labor will then not be spent in vain, as is the case with those who labor day and night for everything except God.

Talk to Him with a crying silent-soul in the depths of night, steadfastly, deeply, determinedly. Be like the nasty babies who are not allowed in the apartment houses, who cry persistently. Cry for God and do not stop until He comes to you.

THOUGHTS ON THE FLORIDA DISASTER

Nature's calamities are occasioned by the sum total of the multitudinous wrong human thoughts. Every event in Nature is the outcome of the thoughts of creation. We are all indissolubly linked together and bound up in a common fate. Our thoughts help to bond or to liberate the world at large. We are hungry, and we find all the forces of Nature, the earth, the sun, wind and water —working together to yield our food. The more spiritually civilized we grow the more we will control Nature. The servant of Nature rebels when the Master of the house of civilization sleeps.

That is why such a disaster as has recently happened in Florida deserves our universal sympathy. As a World Race, we are all responsible for it. Let us show our practical sympathy by responding to the call of President Coolidge and contributing according to our capacity to the American Red Cross Fund for Florida relief. We ought to help our brothers and sisters in distress as we ourselves would welcome such help if placed in similar circumstances. Thomas a Kempis once said, pointing to a condemned criminal, "There, but for the grace of God, goes myself." That is true from a limited standpoint, but from the universal standpoint, we may well say of every man, "There goes myself." We are not the creatures, but the creators, of this universe. Our thoughts and deeds have contributed throughout the ages to the making of tidal waves, of forest fires, of volcanic upheavals, no less than they have flowered forth in spiritual giants, in innocent children and in the soft petals of the flowers.

MESSAGE TO MY LOS ANGELES STUDENTS

Never before, my dear ones of Los Angeles, did you make me feel so much at home as you did this time on my vacation to you. I have now known the loyal ones through the test of time. It is wonderful to know one has real friends. True sincere friendship is the light with which we can help one another to see and pass through the door of Heaven. When in mutual service we forget the little self, then only will we see the one big Self of the Spirit running through us.

The sunny California climate, and the Oriental cordiality that I found on every hand, made me almost think I was back in India again. Certainly you made me feel, with your harmony and spiritual blending, that One Spirit existed in us; and I could not find myself apart. It was only after breaking three railroad reservations to New York that I found just sufficient separateness and individuality to be able to unwillingly leave you.

May you grow in every way, and broadcast the message of Yogoda to East, West, North, South. Remember and act according to the suggestions I lovingly gave to you.

SPIRITUALIZING BUSINESS—HENRY FORD'S FIVE DAY WORKING WEEK

The word holiday sprang from holy day. The holy day should be a day for introspective thinking and for developing the sacred soul qualities of man. Jesus advised the world to keep Sunday for basking in the sunlight of wisdom. The Hindus also reserve several days in the year for sacred spiritual purposes. Easter, Thanksgiving and Christmas correspond to many of the sacred days of the Hindus. The Durga Puga festival is as universally observed in India among the Hindus as is Christmas in the West.

Man is a spiritual and a material being. He ought to develop himself spiritually by inner discipline but he must be materially efficient by developing his business faculties. Primitive man was busy using all his mental faculties for satisfying the needs of the material life. His time was spent in hunting, eating and sleeping. Modern man scientifically tries to meet the present material conditions of life. What primitive man did unmethodically, modern man does methodically, and this method in his efforts for material success has indirectly improved his inner faculties.

The master minds of India believe in directly developing the inner faculties (1) of will power to fight temptation, (2) of feeling for serving fellow beings.

But if money-making for securing the material comforts of man is necessary, then making happiness is supremely necessary. For possession of material riches without inner peace is just like dying of thirst while bathing in a lake.

People crave different things ...as money, fame or spirituality, as a result of early habits and specific environmental influences. That is why the people in the East and the West lead a one-sided life. The East is more spiritually inclined and the West is more materially inclined.

Men cannot live happily by only spiritual doctrines or material riches.

Balancing East-West

To bring a balance into the lives of the men of the East and the West, the method of developing an equilibrated life must be adopted.

People in general spend six days of the week in making money and even Sundays thinking about it, but they hardly give any time for self-development. One reason why there is so much crime, so many murders and robberies, in spite of the developed civilization of the West, is because people are too busy securing the commodities of material comfort, and have no time to think of the practical values of following moral and spiritual principles.

If material poverty is to be avoided, spiritual mental poverty is to be abhorred, for the latter is the cause of all human suffering. A practical spiritual man is the happy man, and only the happy man is the successful man. One hundred per cent material prosperity among the inhabitants of a city will not prevent murders and crime. Following the universal principle of mutual service, spontaneous cooperation, love for the spiritual life and disciplining the human sense-cravings are extremely necessary for the harmonious, happy, healthy, prosperous life of a city.

Official records annually show that almost one billion dollars are stolen by young men and woman ranging from the age of fifteen to thirty. We have the New York newspapers' report that 400,000 more meals this year were served in the jails than last year. Why is all this? Because man's attention is not yet fixed on the vital problem of "The Art of Living." Why not use the money used for erecting and keeping up jails to create How-to-live schools which will prevent children from becoming criminals? Criminal offenders grown worse in jails are let loose in healthy society for further spread of this bacteria of crime.

Most people will say, "Oh, I am too busy with my business to think about 'The Art of Living.' Oh, we all know about that. Some day we will come to it but all we want now is money."

But let us consider what purpose money would serve if one succeeds in making millions after a complete nervous break-down and utter loss of poise and happiness.

Since God has given us hunger and since we have a physical body to look after, we must have money and earn it honestly and scientifically by serving the right needs of our fellow beings. Business life need not be a material life. Business ambition can be spiritualized. Business is nothing but serving others materially in the best possible way.

People label those stores that start out with only the idea of making money, commercial and money-making dens. But those stores which first concentrate wholly on serving customers with the best articles at a minimum cost, are the ones that will always succeed and will also advance the moral development of the world.

I never forget the remark of a fine salesman in a large shop, where I was selecting an overcoat for myself. "Sir, I am not trying to sell you something, I am trying to find out exactly what you need." He knew I could buy a two hundred dollar overcoat, but he sold me a sixty dollar one which exactly suited me in every way. Besides I was pleased to get what I needed at a reasonable price. He certainly secured in me a permanent customer for his company. If he had sold me the costly overcoat, I would never have gone back there again.

Hence people should spiritualize their business ambition by starting out with the idea of serving the proper needs of their fellow beings. Man should make money not only by serving and getting something in return, but also for the sake of using money for creating philanthropic institutions which serve public needs. When one makes a great deal of money by making others prosperous and again uses that wealth for helping others to help themselves, that is spiritualizing ambition. Wealthy parents, who leave too much money for their children, have choked the development of self-created, self-earned ...evolution, success and happiness.

That is why I agree with Mr. Henry Ford in helping people to help themselves and not in humiliating slave-breeding charity. Hence it is only by having ambition and crowning that with the idea of service ...that all materially ambitious people will find a spiritual reason for making money. Besides the brainy man must have ambition or he does injustice to himself by crippling his faculties. By injuring himself, he sets a bad example and thus hinders the progress of humanity.

The one reason why all Oriental peoples have been more spiritually inclined is because they took life more easily, refused to convert themselves into business automatons, and had more time for contemplation. Of course, many Orientals used their leisure for feeding lazy habits instead of spiritual realization, but as a rule, the Oriental people have an awakened spiritual perception.

Our Western brothers have used all their time in developing only the material and intellectual factors of life. They are too busy to enjoy the fruits even of their material labor, or to know much of peace, relaxation, and bliss. Many Western brothers are enslaved by their less important engagements and forget their highest engagement with the blissful Ideal-life of God-contact.

So the Western brothers must make time; though their struggle for a livelihood is greater, due to their more wintry climate, still, by their extensive use of machinery, they have an advantage over their Eastern brethren, and can thus save time by using it less in dancing and amusements, and more in the deeper studies of life. Business activities, money, these are for the comfort of man, but blind greed for them must not rob him of his happiness.

Six full days and nights of machine-like existence, and part of one day only for spiritual culture, are not balanced. The week should be allotted to work, amusement and spiritual culture—five days for money making, one day for rest and amusement, and one day for introspection and inner realization. In America, life is altogether too fast; in the Orient, it is altogether too slow. A balance has to be struck. Man must have some free time to find himself. One day a week—Sunday—is not enough, because it is his only holiday and he wants it for rest and is too tired to meditate.

Under a five day working week, as proposed by Henry Ford, people could use Friday night, Saturday and Sunday for getting away from the noisy city environment and thus increase their longevity. The Chicago Chief of Police says that man's longevity could be increased by eleven years if the city noises were cut out and man's nervous system calmed down thereby. Almost every family in America nowadays can afford an automobile of some kind, and with it, they can get out of the cities on week-ends and refresh themselves in the peaceful retreats of nature, living the double life of a hermit in the woods, and a warrior in the field of worldly activity.

Since ultimate wisdom, i.e., knowing everything that can be known by the maximum use of the human reason, is the human goal, then why not learn the art of living rightly?

We must begin with the children as well as with the adults. The plastic mind of the child can be moulded into any shape with the cooperation of self-disciplined, reformed adults. Desired habits can easily be created in children because the will to perform is mostly free except for a few innate tendencies. Adults have to battle and expel old habits in order to lodge good ones. But all habits, whether in children or adults, must be cultivated through the medium of spontaneous willingness. In training children in a balanced life or in habits of paying equal attention to the earning of money and to the acquisition of spiritual happiness, the time and method of training has to be considered.

People lose their balance and suffer from money madness and business madness only because they never had the opportunity of culturing habits of a balanced life. It is not our passing thoughts or brilliant ideas, but our everyday plain habits which control our lives. There are some very busy business men who make millions without being irregular or nervous, and there are other business men who become so engrossed in making money that they cannot think of anything else and do not wake up until something terrible happens to them as sickness or loss of all happiness.

Many psychologists say that the later periods of life are but the repetitions of the training which one receives between the ages of two to ten or fifteen.

Spiritual sermons inspire the minds of children to better action but that is all. Actual practical discipline for roasting the seeds of pre-natal habits lodged in the sub-conscious and super-conscious minds is necessary. This can only be done by scrubbing the brain cells of seed habits with the electricity of concentration thrown within. Children ought to be brought up with a spiritual ambition to make money only for the sake of service. Modern children are mostly brought up in a wrong atmosphere where money-making is the goal, so they try to get rich quick, often by the hold-up method. If making money anyway is the goal, then why shouldn't hold-up methods prevail?

But it lies in the hands of the modern adults to uplift the future children and bring them into a balanced life. As long as the adults will remain intoxicated with a one-sided material life, so long will the children's hopes remain unfulfilled.

Thus in order to save the future world by saving the children, the modern adult must wake up, and cultivate balanced habits of material and spiritual life.

Most heads of concerns work five days a week from nine in the morning to three in the afternoon and generally take Saturdays and Sundays off. They have some poise, more home life, but they spend most of their time in playing golf and too much dancing, instead of giving some time to spiritual culture.

In order to lead a balanced life, adults must educate themselves and realize that business ambitions are only for making themselves and others happy. Without this realization, strenuous business activity only produces nervousness, greed for money, lack of social qualities, miserliness and disrespect for all good principles; only with this realization of service for others can life be really happy.

Thus I think Mr. Henry Ford has inaugurated a new era in spiritualizing business life by proposing a five day week. Jesus asked people to have Sundays for the Son or Wisdom's Day for culturing Knowledge, but people are so busy all week that they want Sundays for relaxation and amusement instead of giving it to God or introspection. The clergymen and priests, who are opposed to having movies and diversions on Sundays, ought to sympathize and cooperate with Henry Ford's plan of working for only five days a week, because the hard-working man could utilize all Saturday for relaxation, gardening and amusement, and use Sunday wholly and solely for church or temple or mosque work or self-discipline through the technique of concentration and meditation.

I know many prominent, intelligent business men ...who in their heart of hearts are discontented with everything and are craving for God and Wisdom, but they are helplessly carried away by their habits and too many engagements. They sacrifice their highest engagement with God, Truth, higher studies and more home life, for money making or some useless engagement.

So it is extremely necessary that the five work day a week plan of Henry Ford be carried out by all business concerns. Truth-loving real world patriots should cooperate for giving working people Saturday, a day for amusement and relaxation, and Sunday, an exclusive day for culturing habits of meditation and contacting good men, good principles and the highest good, the God-Bliss within.

As the art of war needs certain training, so does our battle with active life need certain training. Untrained warriors are soon killed on the battlefield; so also men untrained in the art of preserving their poise and peace are quickly riddled by the bullets of worry and restlessness in active life.

The five day working week plan is extremely desirable and necessary in order to give people more time to enjoy nature, simplify their lives and their imaginary necessities, enjoy the true needs of their existence, get to know their children and friends better, and best of all, get to know THEMSELVES.

WHAT I MEAN BY THE WORD "HINDU"

The term "Hindu" is used often in a misleading sense. Its proper meaning would include only the religious adherents of Hinduism. But it is commonly used in a racial and national sense, and I myself was guilty of so using it in my article on "Ethnologists vs. the 'Common Man'"* in the July-August 1926 issue of East-West. The right word to use in a national sense, when designating the different people of India, would be "Indians" or "East Indians." Thus, all Mohammedans, Hindus, Parsis, and other peoples that live in India are Indians, while only those professing Hinduism are Hindus.

The name Hindu was first given by the Greeks to those who lived on the banks of the river, Indus. The word Hindu is a corruption of the word Indus. According to the Vedas and all our sacred books, and the investigations of eminent western ethnologists, the people of India belong to the Aryan race. Most of the Europeans, the Persians,+ the Hindus and the Semitic Mohammedans all come from the same Aryan race. The type of their skulls, noses, features, and the origin of certain languages being traced to Sanskrit, has led to the accepted conclusion that the above-mentioned races were all Aryans.

In my article on "Ethnologists vs. the 'Common Man'", I meant to include within the scope of the word "Hindu" which I used, all Mohammedans, Christians, Hindus, Persians and various other East Indians that live in India, and it is for them as much as for the Hindus (using the latter word in its proper religious sense) that I wrote my article explaining the fallacy and injustice of Justice Sutherland's ruling that East Indians are not "white persons." These East Indians who, having lost the white color of their skins by living in the hotter regions of India, therefore cannot be American citizens according to Justice Sutherland's interpretation of the word "white," as he ignores the theological and accepts the "common man's" viewpoint. In other words, if the Oriental, dark-skinned, Jesus Christ came to build a church in California he could not own it. Yet strange it is that Jesus Christ is worshipped in every Christian church.

The East Indians have ample space to live their simple, spiritual lives, in India. All I ask is that America should save herself from the spiritual error of disowning her own brothers and sisters living in the far East.

The Latin, pater, Sanskrit, pita, colloquial, pa, English, father, colloquial, papa, all these words come from the Sanskrit root pa, which means protector. The Aryan father was called pita, in the agricultural stage of civilization, because he protected the cows. The Latin, mater, Sanskrit, mata, colloquial, ma, English, mother, all these words come from the Sanskrit root ma, which means the measurer. The Aryan mother received the name mata because she measured the milk and distributed it to her children. The Anglo-Saxon, dohter, Sanskrit, duhita, English, daughter, all these words mean the same thing and they are derived from the Sanskrit root, duh, which means to milk the cow. In this manner, by the analysis of

thousands of words, philology has proved that the Hindus, the English, the forefathers of the Americans, the Persians, the Semitic Mohammedans, all belonged to the Aryan race which originally spoke the same Sanskrit language.

The inhabitants of the northern Himalayas in India, especially in Kashmere, which is spoken of as the epitome of the world, are for the most part white-skinned, and some have blue eyes and blonde hair. As one travels to the hotter southern regions of India, one finds the skin of the people getting darker and more tanned. Many white-skinned Americans and Europeans, living for a long time near the sea or in the hotter parts of India, will grow tanned beyond recognition.

The immigration law and the citizenship status in America should be based on the quality of an individual and not on his color. For color is God-made and sun-made and not of man's own choosing, whereas qualities are developed by individual effort. The present erroneous standard of color discrimination in America may invite the white human dregs and degenerates of Europe and may shut out dark-skinned, world-inspiring savants like Mahatma Gandhi.

Justice-loving and truth-loving America, you should not put a loose brick of an unjust law in the foundation of your civilization. Wake up, dear Americans, and fight this great error in the history of your civilization. Keep the mental firmament of America pure and broad as the heavens.

*The article referred to appeared in the July-August issue

+In this connection, it is interesting to read an inscription left by King Darius at Persepolis, about 559 B.C. It reads:

"A great god is Ahuramazda, who hath created this earth, who hath created that heaven, who hath created man, who created the gladness of man, who made Darius king, sole king of many, sole law-giver of many.

"I am Darius, the great King, the King of Kings, King of lands peopled by all races, for long king of this great earth, the son of Vishtasp, the Achaemenian, a Persian, son of a Persian, an Aryan of Aryan descent." (BROWNE.)

Christmas Message
To My Beloved Yogoda Students
Of America

DOORS of joy, which may have been long closed within us all, should be thrown wide open at the coming Christmastide, in memory of One whose divine example has lit the way down twenty centuries.

This is my prayer for you all on this occasion of spiritual Christmas, that you keep those little doors of joy open so that the ocean of Christ-Consciousness may continuously, uninterruptedly, flow into you.

Instead of bestowing material presents on those that you love, give them spiritual books and spiritual gifts, which will remind them always of the necessity of attaining Christ or Universal Consciousness thru meditation and universal love and service.

Material favors, dinners, exchange of gifts during Christmas, are purposeless without the attendant spiritual consciousness for which the Christmas holidays were originated.

Make up your mind that this Christmas you are going to supremely try to revive in you the principles for which Christ lived and by which he deserved to ascend to Heaven or God-consciousness.

Be determined to endeavor so that your consciousness will ascend to heavenly heights.

May this newly awakened Christ-love enable you to see the underlying unity which pervades the East and West, the North and South, all races and nationalities, all children of the One Father.

"Peace on earth, good-will toward men."

Amen! (Christian Om); Om! (Hindu Om); Amin! (Moslem Om).

Three Recipes December 1926

SPIRITUAL RECIPE

Prayers have been offered, scriptures have been read, chants and hymns have been sung aloud to God, yet He seems to be as silent and as mysteriously unknown as ever.

Today a man is Hindu, tomorrow he changes to a Buddhist, day after tomorrow to a Christian Scientist, and the next day to a Catholic or a Baptist or something else. Why is this?

It is because man has believed in different faiths or opinions of men about truth and scriptural sayings but seldom analyzed them by the light of personal investigation for verifying truth by the methods used in modern science. God is not moved by prayers or praise nor by atheistical outbursts and denials of Him. He answers through law. Hit a stone with your knuckles or eat sulfuric acid and the laws of God answer. Break His law of life, and punishment and suffering comes. Think rightly, behave rightly and God answers through peace.

Hence the only way to know God is to persistently use your deepest concentration mixed with your utmost devotion in the silent hours of the night, at the break of dawn, or in the hidden glow of twilight, in demanding an answer to your prayers. Pray and use your dogged will steadily day after day, week after week, year after year until the cosmic silence of ages is broken and you find your answer. You will not have to wait for ages, for you will find in deep prayers that His Spirit of Bliss will hover around you and will talk to you through the voice of peace.

Remember the only way to know God is by persistency, regularity, and depth of loving effort.

HEALTH RECIPE

The origin of almost all of the diseases which I have mentally healed thru the power of God, I find in over-eating, improper eating, misuse of sex life, lack of exercise, and above all in bad environment.

Disease warns one that nature's physical laws are being broken. Nature speaks to man through her laws.

The careful man, following health laws, suffers rarely compared with the careless man who does not discriminate about his diet. Eat less, eat finely ground nuts, raw vegetables and lots of fruit; and exercise. Walk daily. Bathe your body in the bacteria-killing sunshine every day. Now that winter and its healthful outdoor sports are here, take time to go skating, skiing and walking. Breathe the fresh, crisp, invigorating air of winter. By these means, methods of physical and mental healing will be unnecessary, for disease will be dispelled.

Even then, the doctors and mental healers will be kept quite busy and successful if they concentrate on keeping people well. Let the doctors receive good fees for keeping their patients well. The Chinese pay their doctors for keeping them well, and when they get sick, payment stops.

Obey God's physical laws of hygiene and proper eating, and keep yourself mentally disinfected by the strong faith that nothing can harm you, that you are ever protected.

HOW TO MAKE NUT CANDIES

Mix half a teaspoonful of brown sugar with one tablespoonful of finely ground pecans or almonds.

Pecan candies are very wholesome and easily digested.

Almond candies, according to the Hindus, are very helpful in building moral character. Give nut candies to your children. Give to your friends good candies which will strengthen them and not cause them to add slabs of flesh to their bodies. Every extra pound of flesh in the body overworks the heart and causes it to pump the blood through one mile of artery in order to irrigate the added undesirable territory.

Stuff California dates with very finely ground pecan nuts, one teaspoonful of ground nuts to each date. For variety you can use pistachio or almond nuts. These are the best candies you can eat —Nature's candies.

Fruit Salad Dressing

Butter the size of an egg, 1/2 cup of sugar, the juice of one large orange, juice of 1/2 lemon, 2 eggs, 1/2 pint of whipped cream.

Cook the butter, sugar, lemon and orange juice, and eggs well beaten, in double boiler until smooth, let cool, and then fold in the whipped cream.

Delicious with any fruit salad, especially salads containing sliced orange and pineapple, or sliced grape fruit and seedless raisins.

VIBRATORY HEALING

Human life can be likened unto a house fitted with three windows .... of the Body, Mind and Soul. Thru these openings come pouring forth the three kinds of divergent perfect light of God—known as Health Rays, Faculty Rays, Wisdom Rays. These triune Rays are responsible for the perfect health, mental equanimity and enlightenment of the soul of man. That is why man is spoken of as being created in the image of God. But then arises the question, if man is made after God's likeness why does he suffer in so many ways? The answer is, man —a Divine Child— shares the independence of the Divine Being. Man essentially was made as a God—but as such ...he has the privilege and free choice of God to eclipse that image with error, or to keep it unobscured and dazzling ....with rays of health, power and peace. Man has the peculiar independence and free power to live in the house of life with its health, strength and light-giving windows ...open or closed. Thus it is that when he closes the windows of life, the Ultra Violet Conscious Cosmic Rays are shut out and he lives in the darkness of physical disease, mental disquietude or abysmal soul-ignorance.

Most people have one or more of their windows of life ...shut and jammed for years. That is why they suffer from chronic maladies. Their rescue lies in the knowledge of the law by which they may open their windows themselves and bask once more in the all-healing Conscious Cosmic Rays.

Man wants instantaneous healing by God's power but he fails to understand that the work of healing lies within himself and that God never wanted him to be sick in the first place. God gave man the original privilege and free choice to receive Rays or shut them out. God cannot change His law arbitrarily just by the bribery of special ceremonies or blind prayer or partiality. He can be moved only by law and love. Love is law. When man closes the health-power-and-light-giving windows of life and keeps them closed indefinitely, he must himself make the effort to open those windows again to let the freely-willing-to-help, knocking-to-enter, Light in. Hence, all physical diseases, psychological inharmonies and soul maladies born of ignorance ...come from man's own fault of shutting out the Rays of God. And the logical, lawful conclusion is, whether knowingly or unknowingly he shut the breath-giving windows of life, he must open them again by self-effort. Ignorance of law cannot be an excuse for escaping the effects of a law which is broken.

There are many ways of opening the three jammed windows of life. Those ways can be generally named as Healing. And Healing in general can be classified as Physical Healing, Psychological Healing of worries, fears, nervousness, etc., and Spiritual Healing of soul-ignorance.

There are many kinds of healing, each of which can be used in healing physical, mental or spiritual diseases.

Of the different kinds of healing by medicine, injection, affirmation, massage, nerve or vertebral adjustment, by imagination or will or faith, Vibratory Healing is of great importance.

Vibratory Healing consists in creating and sending vibrations to diseased individuals, internally by energy charged by will-power or externally by super-consciously-impregnated chants, intonations of the human voice, enlivening words, phrases and affirmations.

The methods of internal vibrations of energy can only be done by a system of spiritual exercises such as Yogoda offers. Willingness and determination keep the blood vitalized with pep and life-energy. If even the layman can keep his mental initiative, willing-to-work attitude all the time, he will find his blood charged with life-current, making it immune against the invasion of bacteria. Keeping yourself smiling from within, pulsating with joy, and in ever-readiness to act, spiritually ambitious in helping others, all these not only are good exercises for the mind but keep the body constantly supplied with Fresh Cosmic Energy descending into the body thru the door of the Medulla Oblongata. Strong Will pulls energy from the Conscious Cosmic Rays surrounding the body through the door of the Medulla Oblongata. Man shall not live by bread (food chemicals) alone but by every word (vibratory life-energy) which flows (into the body of man) thru the mouth of God (i.e. the opening of the Medulla thru which the Conscious Cosmic Life Principle enters the body of man). Hence strengthen your Will and determination in everything. Your body shall be internally vibrating with life current. A man of strong Will, by his highly vibrating mind, can shake out disease, failure and ignorance. But the Will vibration must be stronger than the vibration of physical or inner disease. The more chronic the disease is, the stronger, steadier and more unflinching should be the determination, faith and effort of the Will to get well.

In connection with singing, chanting or intoning away physical disease or worry or spiritual ignorance, one must know the law of intonation, from high to low, low to whisper, whisper to mental, sub-conscious to super-conscious ...Chanting. This is the method of converting loud meaningful words into realized experiences--assimilating the truth of a word or words by chanting loudly and mentally until they become a part of the soul's realization.

Or one must induce the super-conscious, peaceful state first and from that stage chant mentally or whisperingly or loudly as he pleases.

But in all cases the intonations whether mental or physical (i.e. audible) must be injected with super-conscious mentality, faith and steadiness in the beginning or at the end, to be effective in accomplishing a specific healing.

Mental chanting is best for individuals, loud chanting ranging from low to high or vice versa is good in congregations.

Before chanting, the law of repetition should be understood or explained. Some western minds often fail to grasp the changing depths of conviction in Hindu chantings and see only a monotonous repetition of a word or words. Of course repetition of words without understanding their meaning with deep and deeper feelings and realization is useless. That is what the Bible meant by saying, "Take not the name of the Lord thy God in vain," that is, do not say, "O God, O God" without attention or while thinking of other things or while the mind is wandering. Long intellectual prayers full of word-jugglery may satisfy the intellectually hungry but they are only the empty noises of a victrola without the soul in them.

It is better to say just one phrase as "O Father, heal me," or "I am well for Thou art in me" extemporaneously (as it comes) repeating it vigorously from low to high or high to whisper and lastly from a whisper to mental affirmations until one feels what he is saying, i.e., repeating a phrase with varying depth of soul-feeling until one realizes the meaning of his utterance in every fiber of his being. This is At-onement with one's own affirmations through loud and mental chanting.

And the moment the phrase reaches the super-consciousness and the inner conviction ...a volley of energy will shoot down and vibrate and heal the diseased tissues of the body, mind and soul, electrocuting physical bacteria, paralyzing mental fears and conflagrating ignorance into ashes.

In our Hindu Tantra (Hymnal) Scriptures we find the advice that all mystic incantations, seed words, have to be revivified in the soul of the chanter, vitalized and specifically intoned or changed in order to produce the desired results. Mere repetition ...without deep feeling of mantras or incantations —does not produce results.

It is a fact that if a born and universally-known coward says loudly, "On, ye brave, march on with me to glory or the grave," it would have very little effect in rousing courage in people. Healing affirmations like "The Father is in Thee, be Thou well," in order to be efficient must be uttered only by him who has felt the Father in Himself.

The police commissioner of Chicago declared recently in a bulletin that if the sounds of vehicles, etc., could be cut down, city people would live ten years longer. In other words, inharmonious noise affects the nervous system of people, weakening this medium through which vital energy is supplied to all the principal organs of the body, the circulatory system, brain, etc. With the deterioration of the nervous system, the energy and thermal supply of the blood becomes low, making it a fit home for bacteria of disease.

On the contrary, harmonious sounds, chants impregnated with Super-Conscious Soul-force, Will-Power and Faith, awaken the drooping tissues of the nervous system by rousing Vital Energy in them. Hence the external method of vibrating the voice according to the aforesaid methods can heal all inharmonious conditions of the Body, Mind and Soul. A sincere kind word, an inspired song, a soul-solacing voice of wisdom have dispelled many sorrows and inflamed into many the light of lasting joy.

Paramhansa Yogananda

OCEAN OF INTUITION
(Swami Yogananda and Grace Thomson Seton)

Beneath the ocean vast of intuition,
Deeply cast yourself.
You touch the Cause Supreme,
Spread with pearly wisdom's beam;
And watch
Tumultuous difference and want ...retreat,
When your soul the Supreme Soul would meet.
Armoured by Will of Steel.
Untouched by lamentation, worry sharks;
Moving in deep wisdom's light,
Your darkness disappears.
Soul solace will appear.
With heart made pure and clear,
You will see Him everywhere,
One, one Living Sea, eternal, near.
The storm of breath
Has roused the waves in stealth,
Over thy mental sea.
Speak thy Command,
"My storm be calm,
All, all waves to melt in One-Soul-Sea."
I said,
"It was but in a dream
That I found myself

Balancing East-West

Soaring through clouds of life and death.
I am awake.
For me there is neither birth nor death,
The form of the dream-vase will go.
Its too-little-living-space within
Vanished into the Greater Space."

FOUR RECIPES May 1927

Food Recipe: Making a Hindu Curry

When curry powder (Major Gray's) is mixed with either egg, or vegetables, etc., it is called egg curry or vegetable curry. The curry powder is a mixture of turmeric and a few other spices.

Do not eat curry every day as it causes thirst and too much love of taste. But once in a while it is good to use, as it stimulates the generation of saliva and the flow of the digestive juices.

Take a teaspoonful of curry powder and mix it well in a tablespoonful of water. Then fry it in one tablespoonful of hot melted butter for a few minutes until it becomes a little brown and the water almost evaporates. Now mix this well by stirring it in a glass of hot water. Boil the curried water for ten minutes. Add two tablespoonfuls of raw whole wheat flour gravy and boil for four or five minutes. Half a tablespoonful of melted butter and a quarter teaspoonful of salt. Then pour this on the boiled sliced eggs or boiled or fried vegetables and then heat curry and eggs or vegetables on the fire for five minutes.

Eat more ground-up raw vegetables, finely ground-up nuts (pecans, almonds, pistachios) and lots of fruits. The best meat substitute is ground nuts.

Include sunshine and oxygen in your menu.

When you are tired, it is not only food or sleep or rest which can revive your energy. The internal way of dispelling fatigue is to vibrate your body by your Will Power. You will also be surprised to find that if you run for ten minutes, or bask for half an hour in the sunshine, your fatigue will be removed.

Intellectual Recipe

Read the "Imitation of Christ" by Thomas a Kempis. A few lines daily from the Bhagavad Gita by Sir Edwin Arnold called "Song Celestial." Read from Shakespeare one page daily. Read a history of philosophy. Read the Christian Bible, ten lines each day from St. John. Read the poems of Walt Whitman and of Emerson. Read Tagore's "Gitanjali" and Francis Thompson's "Hound of Heaven."

Intellectuality is improved by introspecting and mentally assimilating the subjects that you study. Always first understand what you read and then assimilate what you feel is right and reject what you feel to be incompatible with your reason. But do not pass hasty judgments. You must aim to know everything of some definite study and something of everything.

Prosperity Recipe

Most people fail and are not prosperous because they have hypnotized themselves with the consciousness of their failures and they do not make repeated steady efforts to succeed. Along with repeated efforts about anything, creative effort should be attached. That is, energy and effort should not be wasted on a wrong venture but on the right business suited to you, and found out or created by your thinking penetrating self. The world is full of imitators and there are few creative workers. The one who creates does not wait for opportunity, blaming the fates, circumstances and the gods. He seizes opportunities or creates them with the magic wand of his Will, Effort and Searching Discrimination.

Spiritual Recipe

In the study of spiritual books, be warned against the self-sufficiency of the intellect. Although you may hear or read the words, "Cosmic Consciousness" many times, that does not mean that you know about it. The best way to understand scriptures is to read and study, and not read ...only satisfying the intellect, and pass on. Intellectual study of the scriptures without corresponding realization produces vanity, and false conviction that one knows, and is detrimental to realization, but intellectual study of the scriptures with the sole desire to learn, know and feel, does lead to realization.

Before studying scriptures, calm and steady yourself, then take two or three lines and meditate several minutes on them. Then when the meaning becomes one with yourself, close the book and go about your business. Do not hurriedly go through any book of deep spiritual nature. For if you study such a book only intellectually, you will be falsely satisfied and will not want to realize the truth in it because you became apparently satisfied by intellectually knowing it. The way of studying scriptures by realization will awaken new inspiration in you. You have listened about spiritual recipes long enough. That will not satisfy you. You must try to digest them yourself. One hour of regular meditation is more than one month of theoretical study of scriptures. In meditation direct knowledge is received.

MEANING OF "YOGODA" AND "SAT-SANGA"

"Yogoda" means the system which teaches one to harmonize all the forces and faculties that operate for the perfection of body, mind and soul. "Sat-Sanga" means "fellowship with truth."

A VISIT TO MT. VERNON

In honor of the birthday anniversary of "The Father of his Country," Swami Yogananda visited Mount Vernon on February 22, 1927, to lay a wreath on Washington's tomb. He was accompanied by a score or more of his Washington students. The Swami delivered the following address to his students and the assembled visitors at Mount Vernon:

"As Washington performed his duty he never forgot the Giver of all gifts. That is what inspired me in his life. In India he always inspired me with this thought. His love for Truth was greater than love of party politics. I believe that though patriotism is necessary, it should not exclude Spiritual Truth because patriotism which excludes international well-being is built on loose stones. But patriotism which is firmly built on the everlasting source of Truth, that patriotism which loves Truth and Truth Alone, that nation is based on such patriotism as Washington possessed ...and the great good that he did to the world and to America, is ever awake with us. He is ever living in the minds of the world, and we must always be inspired by his example ...for he inspired not only thousands, hundreds of thousands, but millions.

"Most great men that serve live... hundreds of years before their time. He came, he conquered, he mastered himself and the situations in which he was placed and then withdrew and led the life of a hermit in seclusion here. There are politicians ....and politicians—those puny ones who cater to the mob sentiment and who put the national mansion on a loose foundation; but men like Lincoln and Washington have always tried to solidify the foundations of the national mansions with the eternal rock of Truth and Spirituality. The politicians who are going to live forever are the direct beneficiaries of his labors, his aspiration, his trials, and great strength. The whole world, after all, should remember that these national boundaries are all man-made. Time shall again erase these boundaries and as we love to love our nation we must always remember and regard the love and patriotism of all other nations. And if you love co-operation, harmony and patriotism, then you must love the patriotism and independence of all other nations. One's own patriotism must not exclude the patriotism of others. Our national ideals must not militate against other ideals ...but we must find harmony in nations. It was for ideals like this that great men like Lincoln and Washington lived and died.

"In studying Washington's life and his principles, I find he was a man of wide vision; he did not live by the stereotyped customs of his time. He lived for the ideal of freedom and independence inspired only by the Love of Truth and not by party politics. He is not only an inspiration to America's best ...but he is a source of inspiration to all nations. His love of Truth, his great strength, deep understanding, not only made him America's national hero, but all nations of the world are proud of him and glorify him.

"Let us all with united hearts bless the soul of George Washington that he may forever live in our memory ...not only in image, but a perpetual source of spiritual inspiration of liberty. With Thy grace, with Thy strength, in Thy name, O Spirit, our One Father, we are all gathered here to worship the national hero, the international hero, the inspirer of millions, and we wish him good-will, eternal good-will for the great services that he rendered to us. In the name of Jesus Christ and the Great Spirit and with our hearts filled with sincerity, love and gratitude, we offer this wreath in the name of India, America, and all nations."

Swami Yogananda At Congress Of Religious Liberals

A Promotional Poster

OVERCOMING NERVOUSNESS
(A lecture delivered at the Washington Auditorium in Washington, January, 1927.)

Calmness is the ideal medium through which we should receive everything. Nervousness is the opposite of calmness. Today nervousness seems to be the world's disease. He is your best friend who humbly suggests to you how you may be benefitted.

Many people think that by forgetting disease you get rid of disease. You may forget disease but disease does not always forget you. Two men were standing on the bank of the Ganges when they saw a wonderful black blanket floating by. One of them jumped on the wonderful black blanket but he could not get loose from it ...could not get away from it. The other man said: "Why don't you leave the black blanket?" He replied: "I want to leave the black blanket but the black blanket doesn't want to leave me." It was a black BEAR.

Nervousness is the deadliest disease. It looks very simple but has far-reaching consequences. It is better to destroy disease in its infancy. Many people blame poor nervousness ...but nervousness has no brain to be nervousness. It's the innate side to nerves. Nerves have no mind of their own, no power of their own to be nervousness.

What makes nervousness? Think of a house telephone. You send messages and receive messages through the same wire. If you talk angrily through the telephone, do the wires get nervous? No! The medium is the wire itself and the electricity passes through the wires. Similarly, in your body, you have a telephone system called the nervous system. When I pinch my arm ...the sensation of the pinch goes to the brain. It hurts me and I don't like it. Nerves send the response.

When you are excited it disturbs the nerve force. So you ought to be very careful not to get excited. What happens when you get excited? You send a flash of energy into the nerves. The nerves are just like a fine wire. If you send too much current—1,000 volts, it will suddenly burn the wires. Excitement creates energy and if you are excited, you send too much energy—unbalanced energy—more energy to some parts of the nervous system and less to others. When you are very angry, you burn the nerves of the brain up.

Then again, why shouldn't you be nervous? If your ordinary telephone gets out of order, you call the electrician and ask him to put it in order again. But when nerve wires, through excitement, become worthless and useless ...when the nerve tissues become destroyed ...where is the electrician who will fit you up with a new set of nerves? So you can't afford in any way to destroy your fine nervous system. These nerve wires of your body have been grown from within, and if they are destroyed ...you cannot replace them. Medical science has not found the way to replace them.

What is the function of the nervous system? It is your means of getting in touch with the world and of keeping your sense of touch alive. It has the same function as your ordinary telephone in the house. The nervous system is the telephone that sees, hears, feels, etc. The nerves supply the current to your heart, brain, etc. Everything is carried on by the nerves. They act as a telephone also to supply the eyes, ears, olfactory nerves, etc. Nervousness burns the nerves, cutting off the supply of current or energy. Nerves are your medium of contact with the world. Nerves are the medium of vitalizing all the different organs of your body, of the senses and every particle of your body. The disease of the nervous system is the cause of all diseases. Yogoda has a special technique by which you can revive tissues if you have burned them out; you can revive tissues by sending energy into nerves that have been destroyed. Each cell and tissue in the nervous system is a living thing. Each nerve tissue and cell is intelligent. Nerves take messages from the brain to the outer world. You must know how to treat nerve cells so that they will not be destroyed. Keep them cheerful always. Causes of nervousness are mental excitement, wrong diet, and wrong environment.

When an animal dies, its trainer knows if it wasn't fed scientifically. When a human being dies, we say: "Well, Heavenly Father took him"; whereas white bread killed him perhaps. Wrong thinking, eating and environment ...cause nervousness. There are two kinds of nervousness—psychological and mechanical. Superficial or organic. Psychological nervousness is due to mind excitement—when energy is created it excites the nerves and tissues and burns them out. If you indulge in the habit of psychological nervousness all the time, thereby flashing energy into certain nerves, the nerves get burned and you are the victim of physiological nervousness. It's generally due to lack of proper diet, lack of right company and lack of right attitude, right peace, that you become nervous.

The best way to get rid of nervousness is first to remember choice of company. Tell me what kind of company a person keeps and I will tell you what he is. We always love the company of those who flatter us. This weakens us, though. We should like the company of those who tell us the truth and help us to be better. If we always live in the company of flatterers, it is bad for us—for our spiritual growth. Once there was a Master who had a disciple who criticised everything the Master did. He died, and his disciples came running joyously to their Master and said: "Master, that man who is all the time troubling you, he is dead." Then the Master began to weep. The disciples said: "Why do you weep; you should be glad you are rid of this terrible man?" The Master replied: "No, I am sorry, my teacher is dead." His criticism acted like a warning. To criticise is bad, but if you can stand criticism it is wonderful. Brutal, harsh criticism is like hitting a man on the head with a hammer. There is nothing greater for helping people than the power of love. The gentle power of love which comes to others as suggestion, as the voice of suggestion, is better than criticism. Too much criticism is not good, but suggestion is better. Always remember this, if you want to criticise, do it to help and not to satisfy your spirit of revenge within. Criticise lovingly to help. Judge not. Judge not others, only yourself. Spend your efforts in judging yourself and you will spend it profitably.

Be careful in the choice of company. Keep company with people who are calm, strong and wise, with a deeper nature than you have. When a criminal is put into the company of a greater criminal, that does not help him. When it is time for him to leave, the warden says: "When are you coming back?" When nervous people are in the company of other nervous people they cannot get better. Always choose calm company. If nervous, mix with those who are not nervous. The best way is to analyze yourself and find out that anger, fear, worry and all such things ...do cause nervousness. As soon as you are angry, disturbed or afraid, you burn the nerves. Fear burns the nerves of supply to the heart. Feeling timid destroys the nerve endings. Too much sleep drugs the nerves and too little sleep is hurtful to nerves. Treat nerves as a whole—treat them by sending messages of calmness and peace. The messages you send from the brain to the world will then be sent calmly and likewise, all received, will be received calmly.

Now, about fear. Analyze a little. Why should you fear? <u>Wisdom</u> only can make you free. Understanding the law ...God's law. If I go into a dark room, take a stick and pound the darkness, break the table, will the darkness go? No. But if I bring the light in, it goes immediately. Don't be afraid. That won't do any good. Bring the light of reason. As long as you are not dead, you don't know whether you are going to die or not. When you're dead, it's all over. What's the use of fearing? By fearing, you not only create nervousness, but you move toward the very object of fear.

If you are perfectly calm you will AVOID EXCITEMENT. If you are too much elated about making money, you will often make wrong speculation or investment. If you are calm, no matter how many propositions people may bring to you, you are always able to separate sentiment from fact. If you fear too much, you bring the very things you wish to avoid. You are destroying vitality of nerves and drawing sickness. When you are full of power and strength and life, it destroys disease. In anger, you burn the nerves out. The reason why you should not be angry is that it poisons the blood. Angry vibrations affect circulation. An angry mother can poison her milk that feeds her child. Cultivate peace, calmness and cheerfulness. The more cheerful and calm you are, the better it is for you. The more you worry or are angry or afraid, the more you are losing poise. The more peace you have, the less nervousness.

How can you obtain poise? If it's difficult to earn money, it is much more difficult to obtain poise. Make a triangle and on one side write SWEETNESS, on the other side write CALMNESS and at the base write HAPPINESS; sweetness in speech, mind and body. People have two kinds of nature—the drawing room nature and the home nature. The home nature is when we feel that we are natural ...but we wish sometimes that we are not natural ...because in our naturalness we express ugliness. Many people go out all dressed up ...but inside, passions are boiling and raging within. Inside the house they say: "I am angry." Outside: "Oh, how are you?" Be calm in speech, in mind; be calm in your triune unity. What you think ...you must testify—what you think and speak, your body, soul and mind, everything ...must testify. We must have UNITY of MIND, SPEECH and BODY. Attain calmness; attain peace; attain happiness; attain poise.

Every night before going to bed, say this: "I am the Prince of Peace ...sitting on the throne of Poise." Poise is your center. Whether you act quick or slow, you will never lose your kingly attitude of peace. Jesus, Son of God, is the prototype. On Sundays people get religious. One day is better than none—better than nothing at all. But every day ought to be God's day with us. Christ has given us a great ideal ...that we may live the life of Christ. "To all those who receive Him ...He gave the power to be SONS OF GOD". Everywhere Jesus demonstrated peace. He passed through all situations but He had poise and peace. Jesus demonstrated peace in His speech, mind and body.

For ordinary nervousness take a cold shower bath. Splash your face with cold water. Partial fasting is good—to go without breakfast or lunch. Keep company with cool, calm people.

Always act calmly—be calm in everything; be calmly active and actively calm, have a good diet, but above all move in the company of calm people. Get away from the city once in awhile. Above all, remember that you should learn the method of controlling energy. You can contact Cosmic Energy and bring energy into your body, not through imagination. Your body is like a little bubble of energy in the Cosmic Energy, God is everywhere. He controls planets, stars, everything that you see and yet He is not disturbed. He is above this world, yet He is in this world. You must reflect the image and likeness of God.

THERE IS NO STRANGER NOW

Amid the jungle of human souls,
Amid strange, flowering faces
Which ne'er I saw before,
I oft cognize again
Those of yore
That I knew always.
Yet some remain, ever remain
Stranger, though we meet again and again.
There are some, since seeing first
Are ever my own to the last.
In trembling joy
My memory wakes
To meet again
Those forgotten faces.
But many a brother sleeps
And dreams of me, a stranger,
To whom there is no stranger now.

THREE RECIPES July 1927

Spiritual Recipe

Man is born with the material consciousness of animality predominant in him. The soul is clouded over with matter and material instincts. Like a caterpillar in a cocoon, man is surrounded by his silken, clinging, temporarily sweet prenatal and post-natal tendencies. He must cast them off and spread the gorgeous, delicate wings of his hidden soul ...before the silkman death gets him.

Be not afraid, though your sins be as deep as the ocean or as high as the Himalayas. The soul remains unpolluted, like age-long covered gold. All you have to do, is to wash off the dirt, and the spiritual rays will shine forth thru your joy.

Direct contact of God, thru silent persistent demands of prayer at night and on waking in the morning, can alone satisfy the doubting soul. Thru the technique of meditation, God must answer. You have Him in your hands.

The trouble is, people are afraid of God and want everything else but Him. They pretend they are shedding tears for Him when they really want an automobile or a million dollars. God, being the nearest to our thoughts, knows this and it is not possible to deceive Him. So He stays away for centuries from most of the churches and temples and human hearts. It is proper to pray for the fulfillment of your righteous desires, but once in a while, show that you want Him also. They are self-deceivers who are satisfied with gorging themselves with dogmas and beliefs without actual contact of God. God cannot be bribed by man's beliefs. He will only come when you are no longer satisfied to know Him thru the intellect merely.

We must be earnest and play the part of the persistent babies, not allowed in the apartment houses, who ceaselessly cry to arouse the attention of the Divine Mother. The spiritual babies who cry little in prayer and who fall quickly asleep—to them the Divine Mother does not come.

Pray, cry persistently, until you hear Her Voice in the hour of Silence.

Balancing East-West

Don't be satisfied until you are sure that you have heard Her Voice and can always hear It at will in response to your prayers.

Intellectual Recipe

This month read "Christ of the Indian Road" (Abington Press) by Rev. E. Stanley Jones, a Methodist missionary who went to India to convert the people and who himself returned as a convert "from Christianity to Christ."

Another fine book for this month's reading is "Laotzu's Tao and Wu Wei" by Goddard and Borel (Brentano's, New York). The spirit of the Gita and the Upanishads is in the teachings of this ancient Chinese philosopher.

Read the "Physical Culture Magazine" every month.

Read scientific books, too. Each new finding of science reveals the glory and wonder of God. Begin with physiology and hygiene, and then study botany, zoology, astronomy or whatever most attracts you. New discoveries are constantly being made and you should keep up with them.

Read and think and absorb the good ideas of any book by sifting them from confused vague sentiments. A book is usually a mixture of facts, and inferences of doubtful truth. Separate these sands of unproved theories from the sugar of facts as the good ant does.

Health Recipe

Do you run everyday? If, when you run or go upstairs, you feel a pain in the chest or are quickly out of breath, take care. You have a lazy heart, suffering from lack of proper exercise. Begin to take daily walks and increase your speed until you can run without panting. Then run every day.

Oranges and Bananas

A bowl of orange juice and pulp served with a banana sliced to paper-like thinness, is not only delicious but nourishing and can take the place of meat. Bananas contain more nutrition than fish, lobsters or crabs. They are grown by nature and free from all poisons.

Cheese Salad

Small squares of your favorite cheese served with chopped hearts of lettuce and topped with thousand island dressing, is appetizing and healthful. If desired, add a few nuts or raisins or pieces of sliced orange. Now that summer time is here, live as much as you can on fruits and raw foods.

THE FIRE

Penetrating dense dark forests of Ignorance
I created a Path of Light.
First I set fire to a few frailties
And bramble-bushes of prickly desires;
My fire grew,
It spread over tall vanities, thick arrogances.
The whole forest of World's Delusion is ablaze.
The wild beasts
Of passions and mortal fears
Are burnt.
Wading thru the ashes of past human errors
I shall create a path for all.

REFORMING RELIGION BY SCIENCE

Like the slaves of yore, Religion is imprisoned and enslaved in the house of Dark Dogma. A great war on ignorance must be launched in order to declare the freedom of the bond-slave religion from the hand of superstition. Primeval religion was born in the womb of the unscientific seeking of man for the origin of the mysteries of his being, future life, nature's violent phenomena, God, et cetera. A few prophets have risen during the ages, with their intuitive wisdom, exhorting people to believe in their doctrines. But did science ever uphold their doctrines by actual investigation?

Alas, there has seldom been, except sometimes in India, any real research on pragmatic, life-moulding universal religion, in a true scientific way. About the nature of water and electricity—all scientists are agreed, because they thoroughly investigated their constituents and properties, but few are sure whether Hinduism, or Buddhism, or Judaism, or Confucianism, or Mohammedanism, or Christianity, is the real means to ultimate salvation and the right solution to the problems of life. Why?

Because religion has never been taken seriously by real scientists (except in India anciently) as a matter of life-long research and scientific study in such a practical way as would show the origin, end and purpose of human life on earth.

Religion mostly has been handled by dogmatists, self-chosen reformers, self-elected members of God's mystic counsel. Religion has been patented, trade-marked and peddled by quack spiritual doctors with unscientific but profuse advertisements of its efficacy. "Mine is the only one, the best," is the declaration of most cults. But there should be a standard for judging what is best, just as the standard of quality of goods determines which store is the best in town, even though all claim to be the best.

What is the Standard?

So all the cult shops selling religion declare their goods are the best. What are you going to do? How are you going to find out the proper standard of judging the good, bad, better, best religions? Saying "my religion is best," believing in a mass of unproved statements, swelling the number of dogmatic followers, building big temples, or churches, or stupas, or mosques; hymning chants to emptiness, praying without receiving answers, will not make a religion true, good or lasting.

People sometimes say "O, join the - - - - Church and you will soon have your own automobile." Others are heard to say, "I just joined this, because the members give their business to their own people."

The Good religion has done thru the ages, by reminding people of an Ideal, either thru religion or reasoning, or thru fear and fanaticism, ... can never be denied. Yet, unscientific religion has been the cause of the tyranny of the caste system, et cetera, in the East, and of the class system, Spanish inquisition, burning of martyrs, in the West.

Unscientific Religion

Cruel wars in the name of Crusades have been fought by Mohammedans, Christians and other religious bodies in the name of their God. Unscientific religion today expresses itself in Hindus calling Christians "heathens" and in Christians returning the compliment to them by the same epithet. Why don't the orthodox Brahmins of India eat with the pariah (outcast) when his Scriptures say, "He is a man of realization who looks upon an elephant, a dog, a pariah, a Brahmin in the same way"? Why were Inquisitions and burning of people at the stake for their religious convictions, perpetrated in the name of the Bible, ...when Jesus taught such tolerance that he said his followers should offer the other side of the cheek when one side was hit? Why don't the Bishop of Canterbury and the Pope of Rome exchange pulpits—are they not followers of the same Christ?

Why do I hear in America, "O, we have a nice class of well-dressed, well-to-do people belonging to our church." Is not religion and God for the rich, poor, intelligent, weak, illiterate alike, as a panacea for their disease of ignorance?

Why does the minister's true soul freedom, his emancipating, independent thought, have to sleep on procrustean beds of dogma, there to be lopped off and amputated? Why has the minister to look for rich people, and cater to their whims, in order to support his church? Will expensive church-founding and bringing people, more or less unwillingly, and from a sense of "duty" merely, to attend them—will such methods solve the problems of life and salvation thru religion?

Why do most people more eagerly go to the "movies" and pack places of amusement, instead of the churches? Why? Many think that dancing, festivities, movies, Billy Sunday dramatics, or sensational sermons can draw crowds to the church, and urge their use there. But how can the churches, with their third-class performances, compete with first-class pleasure-haunts, dance-halls and movie palaces? It may not be entirely useless for a church to adopt such methods and some good may come of it. But the point is, why seek substitutes of true religion, deluding the unsatisfied Self? Religion should not try to compete with ordinary recreational activities—it should rather offer a distinct, individual and characteristic form of social service by giving peace, enlightenment and spiritual strength, and not merely offer temporary pleasure or outward stimulation, for these can be better afforded by the theaters and other pleasure agencies.

Churches and temples and all religious organizations must give more. They must be united in their efforts to find their goal instead of being torn by mutual jealousies and party feelings. "Ah, we are the best church because Rockefeller belongs to it!" some say. This is delusion. God makes the most powerful monarch as well as the "unknown soldier" to return to the same dust, bereft of all their material possessions, though still possessing their spiritual qualities.

Above all, church funds, instead of being completely tied up in heavy mortgages and ornamental edifices, could be better employed in inducing the greatest scientists of the East and West to make real investigations for a practical technique of making the body, mind and soul of man ...perfect, harmonious, ever-strong, quickly developing, better and happier.

Ideal of Yogoda

Such is the ideal of Yogoda, for it means, technique for balanced development of body, mind and soul. For the first time, this technique for, and emphasis on, the three-fold simultaneous development of body, mind and soul, is offered to the world.

Scientists should test, in the lives of growing children, the methods offered by all religions and should thus discover by practical application, the one which works the best and brings the greatest good to the greatest number. And then they should broadcast the knowledge they have earned, in the name of truth. The truth should be tested by the government of each people, standardized, and introduced into school, societies and universities, in order to bring the maximum results.*

Religions, or opinions and beliefs of men about religion, are many—but true religion or real spiritual experience by any human being, whether Hindu, Christian or member of any sect or school of thought, will be discovered, in the course of realizing God or truth, to be one and the same. There is only one Truth, there cannot be two or more truths.

In India, where much scientific truth has been discovered by Yogis and Swamis in religious experimentations, the word "Dharma" means "those immutable principles which protect man permanently from the three-fold suffering of disease, unhappiness and ignorance." Destruction of suffering, according to the Hindu Sankhya philosophy, involves the permanent destruction of all possibility of any return of suffering.

Life Still Uncertain

With all the modern inventions and comforts of present-day civilization, man's life is still uncertain, unsafe. He does not know what is going to happen to him at any time, or when he is going to be unhappy or die without his desire.

That day, when man is able to dematerialize or convert his human body into its constituent electrons and basic consciousness, and then materialize it again into organized living physical flesh, as Christ did, and as Hindu Yogis do, then he will be free, and will suffer no more thru the collisions of other forms of matter, which result in pain, disease, disintegration, accident or death.

Religious effort must be applied to the conversion of the human body into life energy. "Man shall not live by bread (solids, liquids) alone, but by every word (vibratory energy) which falleth from the mouth of God (medulla oblongata)." Energy in the human body which converts food into energy, is the direct real source of life, and not food.

As electricity or pure energy cannot have automobile accidents, rheumatism, appendicitis, cancer, tuberculosis, nor can it catch cold nor be stabbed, killed by a sword, shot to death by a gun, nor burnt by fire, so, when practical religion teaches us to be energy, we will then attain immortality and will reclaim the lost God's image in us—not until then.

Angels of Energy

God made us angels of energy, encased in solids—currents of life dazzling thru the material bulb of flesh. But we are now concentrated on the frailties and fragility of the bulb, and have forgotten to feel the immortal indestructible properties of the Eternal Life Energy within the changeable flesh.

Even protoplasm is immortal. So is thought. Everything is indestructible, even in the world of matter. Then why this illusion of mortality and death?

Listening to the muffled cries of millions of people stricken with a consciousness of disease, mental suffering, and Soul ignorance, let us cast aside party prejudices and formalities, let us unite our hearts to fight Ignorance—the Great Satan of all religions. Let science, instead of devising more articles of impermanent material comfort for human beings, be engaged in making man himself invulnerable to the destruction arising out of his inventions—death by airplanes, electricity and automobiles—and conscious of his own powers of superiority to disease, drowning, unconsciousness, pain and tragic or premature death. Let science discover and teach the method to consciously leave our bodies so that we may pass from this world to the next consciously and without struggle and pain.

Let us separate the dross of superstition from real religion by burning it in the furnace of Scientific Investigation and Realization, and by their practical application to life. Om! Amen!

Practical systems of God-realization.

It is true that India today cannot boast of material wealth and scientific progress, but she still has the fountain that can quench the soul-thirst of those who are weary of materialism and who would find the ...inner peace and eternal wisdom. And America can help India with her superior knowledge of organization, machinery, invention, sanitation and material progress. Is there not a beautiful harmony in this cosmic plan, the one nation shall furnish what the other lacks, so all may realize their interdependence and common brotherhood?

SAMADHI

Vanished are the veils of light and shade,
Lifted the vapours of sorrow,
Sailed away the dawn of fleeting joy,
Gone the mirage of the senses,
Love, hate, health, disease, life and death,
Away are these false shadows
On the screen of duality.
Waves of laughter, scyllas of sarcasm,
Whirlpools of melancholy,
Melting in the vast sea of Bliss.
Bestilled is the storm of Maya
By the magic wand of intuition deep.
The universe, a forgotten dream,
Lurks subconsciously
Ready to invade my newly-wakened
Memory Divine.
I exist without the Cosmic Shadow
But it could not live bereft of me,
As the sea exists without the waves
But they breathe not without the sea.
Dreams, waking, states of deep Turia, sleep,
Present, past, future no more for me,
But the ever-present, all-flowing I,
I, everywhere.
Consciously enjoyable

Paramhansa Yogananda

Beyond the imagination of all expectancy
Is this, my Samadhi state,
Planets, stars, stardust, earth,
Volcanic bursts of doomsday cataclysms,
Creation's moulding furnace,
Glaciers of silent x-rays,
Burning floods of electrons,
Thoughts of all men past, present, future,
Every blade of grass, myself, and all,
Each particle of creation's dust,
Anger, greed, good, bad, salvation, lust,
I swallowed up, transmuted them
Into one vast ocean of blood
Of my own one Being.
Smouldering joy,
Oft-puffed by unceasing meditation
Which blinded my tearful eyes,
Burst into eternal flames of Bliss
And consumed my tears,
My peace, my frame and everything.
Thou art I, I am Thou,
Knowing, Knower, Known as One
Tranquilled, unbroken thrill
Of eternal, living, Ever-new Peace.
Not an unconscious state
Or mental chloroform
Without wilful return.
Samadhi is but an extension
Of my realm of consciousness
Beyond the limits of my mortal frame

Balancing East-West

To the boundaries of Eternity,
From whence I, the Cosmic Sea,
Watch the little ego floating in Me.
Every sparrow, each grain of sand,
Falls not without My sight.
All space floats like an iceberg
In My mental sea.
I, the colossal container of all things made.
By deeper, longer, continuous, thirsty,
Guru-given meditation,
This celestial Samadhi is attained.
All the mobile murmur of atoms were heard,
The dark earth, the mounts and seas
Were molten liquid,
The flowing sea changed
Into vapours of nebulae,
OM blew o'er the vapours
And they opened their veils
Revealing a sea of shining electrons,
Till, at the last sound of the Cosmic Drum,
Grosser light vanished in eternal ray
Of all-pervading Cosmic Joy.
I, the ocean of mind, drank all creation's waves.
The four veils of solid, liquid, vapour, light,
Lifted aright.
Myself in everything
Entered the great Myself.
Gone forever
The fitful flickering Shadows
Of mortal memory.

Paramhansa Yogananda

Spotless is My mental sky,
Below, ahead and high above.
Eternity and I—one united ray.
I, a tiny bubble of laughter
Have become the sea of mirth itself.

*Super-consciousness, in which the One Reality in all substance and phenomena is perceived.

THE RAMAKRISHNA SWAMIS

Sometimes there is a kind of professional jealousy even in spiritual work and religious organizations of all types. Certain ministers and priests, as well as amateur "Swamis" and "Yogis", betray narrow-mindedness in this respect. Even an average good man belonging to one sect often will not speak well of another good religious man like himself, because the latter happens to belong to another sect. "O, well, find out for yourself how he is," says this kind of religious man, even though he knows in his heart that his brother of another sect is really good.

Such intolerance and jealousy is nowhere out of place so much as in spiritual work. In this country, where true religious teachers often have to undergo various forms of soul-crucifixion and trials of all kinds, it is with sympathy and understanding that I view the efforts of other teachers to bring the message of spiritual knowledge and freedom to America.

So I take pleasure in announcing to East-West readers and Americans in general, that the Ramakrishna Centers in America are bringing a beautiful spiritual message to this country.

One very fine Ramakrishna Swami, Paramananda of California I have known since 1920 in Boston. He invited me to his Asrama (hermitage) in Massachusetts and California several times. He is doing much good in America thru his devotional teachings.

THREE RECIPES October 1927

Health Recipe

Masticate your food well; drink no ice-water while eating, as it cools down the temperature 30 degrees and may cause indigestion. Do no mix starchy foods with liquids (i.e., eat no bread with milk, et cetera) as liquids dilute the saliva required to assist digestion.

Fast one day a week. If complete fasting is difficult for you, then fast on orange juice.

Reducing by fasting sometimes upsets the stomach. This condition can be prevented by frequent drinking of a small glass of buttermilk or orange juice mixed with a small amount of lemon juice.

A glass of orange juice with a beaten yolk of one egg makes an ideal breakfast.

Raisin Drink

Mash up two tablespoonfuls of raisins which have been soaked in hot water. Mix with one glass of water and a quarter of one lemon. Shake. This drink gives. "pep."

The Liquor-Habit

Many investigators claim that most young men and women are drinking more than in pre-war days. They say that everybody nowadays is expected to offer his friends liquor at dinner-parties. Some say that rich people have their cellars and vaults filled with this liquid of Satan. The poor say, why deny us when the rich have it? Some say the prohibition law was passed by a trick when the boys were away fighting. Others say family life has improved since prohibition. Some say the bootlegging of poisonous liquor is killing many good but thirsty people and that light wines and beers should be given.

Anyway, it is true that right education instead of clubs and machine-guns and prison, is the best method of eradicating a deep-rooted popular habit. Yet people should not break a law when it has been passed by their own representatives.

In India, certain licensed shops sell liquors. A few rich people and some laborers are addicted to drink. The vast middle class and lower classes never touch it. Ninety-nine per cent of India's young men are free form the liquor-habit. One Hindu girl in a hundred thousand will not be found drinking. Why? Not because of a law but because of their family training and moral consciousness.

American parents should look after the moral health of their children. Parents should chaperon their children at dances and on automobile rides, and should protect them from friends who have a bad influence on them and who urge them to form injurious habits like drinking.

Liquor benumbs the senses, deadens the reason, inflames the baser passions and animal instincts, and young people under its influence may turn into reckless drivers, hold-up criminals and moral degenerates. Liquor is the enemy of reason, the great paralyzer of good judgment, a destroyer of mankind and the seed of a million evils.

"Never Fed, Ever Satisfied"

Once the liquor habit is formed, it is hard to get rid of. In the feeble-minded or emotionally unbalanced, even one drink may form a formidable habit. As with most habits, the law is "Never fed, ever satisfied—ever fed, never satisfied." The best way for a man to kill a liquor habit is not to go near drinking places or drinking people, and to associate with stronger and better people than himself.

Liquor corrodes the stomach, benumbs the senses, and destroys intuition. It anaesthetizes the spiritual brain-cells, and eventually destroys permanently their "radio" quality of tuning into God-consciousness. No instrument can ever be devised fine enough to perceive God—only spiritual brain-cells of man can do that.

Awake! Young men and women! Fight the liquor habit! You can never really like it, only your habit compels you to indulge in it. Separate your death-bent, destructive inclinations from your true inclinations which always want to take you Godwards.

So remember always that it is for your own best interests to avoid liquor, regardless of what the law may be. Do that which will bring you lasting happiness. The Bhagavad Gita sings:

> "Good pleasure is the pleasure that endures
> Banishing pain for aye; bitter at first
> As poison to the soul, but afterward
> Sweet as the taste of Amrit. Drink of that!
> It springest in the Spirit's deep content.
> And painful Pleasure springeth from the bond
> Between the senses and the sense-world.
> Sweet as Amrit is its first taste,
> But its last
> Bitter as poison."

Intellectual Recipe

The following books should be read by those who want to know the real India and her people—their manners, customs, daily life, religion, home influences and India's real soul as expressed in the average life of the Hindus.

These books were written by Margaret E. Noble (Sister Nivedita), an English-woman, who conducted a Girls School in Calcutta and who travelled throughout India and lived there many years and was accepted by the people as one of themselves. In that way, she came to know India's inner life and home life and religious life in a way that is not open to the vast majority of writers on India, who find the real life of the people a mystery that they cannot penetrate, due to the lack of understanding and sympathy with which many writers on India approach their subject.

The following books by Miss Noble, published by Longmans Green & Company, London and New York, and procurable in most public libraries and thru any bookstore, are recommended to my students and their friends as giving a true and fascinating picture of Indian daily life and thought:

> "The Web of Indian Life."
> "Footfalls of Indian History."

Balancing East-West

"Studies from an Eastern Home."
"Cradle Tales of Hinduism."
"An Indian Story of Love and Death."
"Religion and Dharma."

Spiritual Recipe

Try to attain the state of realization described in the poem "Samadhi" which appears in this issue of EAST-WEST, by repeated, deeper, continuous meditation, with the help of a true Guru (preceptor), if you want to feel God in this life. Forsake self-delusion, self-deception, false satisfaction of thinking you can know God thru the outward formalities of any cult or "ism" merely. The eternal fountain is within yourself, and there it is you must seek it, patiently, persistently and unswervingly.

HAMID BEY, "MIRACLE MAN"

I met Hamid Bey, with his good friend, Dr. Hereward Carrington, in Buffalo recently. I was quite impressed with the beautiful spiritual gleam in Mr. Bey's eyes. I sang the song, "O God Beautiful!" for him. Ever since then he has been singing it.

Hamid Bey is an Egyptian from the Soudan, famous land of sheiks. He was reared under an austere mystical training, and the feats he performs are a part of the religious rites of his sect.

Mr. Bey showed me that by touching anyone's wrist he could divine his thoughts. Each thought has a certain vibration, and by contact with the pulse of the person thinking the thought, Mr. Bey receives the same vibration and consequently thinks the same thought. Later, he demonstrated to me his method of physical trance, in which he fell into my hands, breathless and almost lifeless. The stethoscope revealed that his heart-beat, at first fast, slowed down to an intermittent beat, and then got very slow.

Mr. Bey can remain underground, buried for twenty-four hours, sealed in a air-tight casket, and can hold a thousand pounds on his chest. He controls his pulse at will—its beats appeared and completely disappeared at his will. He also pierces his body with long needles without bloodshed. The marks almost instantaneously disappeared after the needles were withdrawn. He thrusts these needles into his throat, cheeks and tongue without pain. He can produce blood from one puncture and withhold blood from another. Most of these things he performed right in front of me. In the various cities where he visits he often gives demonstrations before gatherings of eminent physicians and surgeons. In New York City he submitted for burial for three hours. On this occasion his body was sealed in a casket and placed six feet underground. The doctors who were present admitted that they could not explain the feat other than by Hamid Bey's declaration that by self-imposed catalepsy, he renders his body almost lifeless.

Passing needles thru his cheeks and certain other of Mr. Bey's feats are performed, after long practice, by manipulating glands of the throat and by pressing certain nerves on the head. These are very interesting physiological phenomena showing that man can control the functions of the heart and all other organs of involuntary action. This is known to Hindu Yogis and Swamis who practice Yoga, as well as to mystics of other sects.

Of course, it must be remembered that without the love of God and without wisdom, such control and feats are just physiological jugglery and a detriment to spiritual realization. But Hamid Bey loves God, and he tells me he loves Him more and more since he heard the song, "O God Beautiful."

He has a good wife. "I often wake up in the night, sit upright, rebuke sleep away, and talk to Him," he told me. "At first my wife did not understand to whom I talked. But now she does, and we both love 'God Beautiful.'" "O, how I love to hear him say that! I told him to tell everyone wherever he goes, that prayer without love of God is meaningless and that people should talk to God every night when no one is watching or listening. That is a sure way to know God easily. Otherwise, a thousand shows of prayer will fail to accomplish any spiritual result.

I told Mr. Bey to produce trance by love of God, rather than merely by glandular pressure, as results produced by devotion are safer and greater. Generally, it takes another person to arouse Mr. Bey from his trance. But, in the conscious trance of devotion, or Yoga, one never loses consciousness but transcends the material consciousness and comes back to consciousness of matter at will again. That is the conscious communion with God the Yogoda aspires to teach.

Mr. Bey can put small animals and sometimes certain types of men into the cataleptic state. Medical science as well as metaphysical science should investigate the results and possibilities for usefulness of such phenomena.

"SAYINGS OF SWAMI YOGANANDA"
IN WASHINGTON "HERALD"

The following "Sayings of Swami Yogananda" were featured in the "Washington Herald" each day from February 15th to March 2nd, 1927:

Inner Riches

"Possession of material riches without inner peace is just like dying of thirst while bathing in a lake.

"If material poverty is to be avoided, spiritual poverty is to be abhorred, for the latter is the cause of all human suffering."

"Wealthy parents who leave too much money for their children, in most cases have choked the development of their self-earned evolution and happiness."

Service

"Life must be service. Without that ideal for all the world, for all human beings, the intelligence which God has given men is not reaching out toward its goal."

"Business is service. And only that article is fit to sell which is a good article and helps the world."

"Business is necessary, and it is a great impetus to man's ingenuity. But if it is devoted solely to money-making it is unworthy of its mission."

The Battle of Life

"As the art of war needs certain training, so does our battle with active life need certain training."

"Untrained warriors are soon killed on the battlefield; so also men untrained in the art of preserving their poise and peace, are quickly riddled by the bullets of worry and restlessness in active life."

Balancing East-West

"People need more time to enjoy nature, to know their children and friends better and, best of all, to get to know THEMSELVES."

Scientific Analysis

"Every tomorrow is determined by every today."

"We should analyze the life of man, as it were, in a laboratory, find out what it is, and then devise means to make it what it ought to be."

"Customs and mannerisms are non-essentials. The real development of man consists of the development of his mindpower."

The Fire of Concentration

"The sun's rays, concentrated by a lens to a fine point, produce heat of such intensity that it will ignite wood, cloth or paper. Similarly, the mind, concentrated by scientific methods, burns up the veil of doubt, the cause of all failures, and makes shine the light of discrimination."

"The all-accomplishing, all-mighty power of attention can only be felt when one knows the technique of concentration."

Training Needed by Children

"Modern children are mostly brought up in a wrong atmosphere where money-making is the goal, so they try to get rich quick, often by the hold-up method. If making money IS the Goal, then why shouldn't hold-up methods prevail?"

"As long as adults remain intoxicated with a one-sided material life, so long will the children's hopes remain unfulfilled."

"In order to save the world of the future by saving the children, the modern adult must wake up and cultivate habits of a balanced material and spiritual life."

Cause of Crime

"Crime is caused from lack of equal opportunities, unbalanced material and spiritual life, lack of knowledge of the art of living, bad company, want of ideals, and, above all, early bad habits."

"Its only remedy is right education and cultivation of good habits at a plastic period of the child's mind."

"The material scientist uses the forces of the body and of nature to make the environment of man better and more comfortable, and the spiritual scientist, who uses mind-power to enlighten the soul of man, can be of even greater service."

The Cost of Luxury

"How people forget that increase in cost of living too luxuriously means the corresponding increase in using too much nerve and brain energy, and the expenditure of longevity, to gain the conditions of a luxurious life!"

"Most people become so engrossed and engaged in making money that they cannot utilize the conditions of comfort after acquiring them."

"Break your self-satisfied immovable, old dogged bad habits of idolizing your less important engagements and utterly ignoring the most important engagements with wisdom."

A Balanced Life

"Engagements with Over-activity and Idleness both lead to misery. Let the secretary of your true judgment arrange your life's daily itinerary."

"The one-sided business man, forgetful of his other duties of life, is not the truly successful man."

"First come first served. That has been mostly your worst calamity. The unwelcome habits that came earliest in your life have kept you quite busy now and have crowded out many worthwhile things of life."

The Light of Friendship

"True, sincere friendship is the light with which we can help one another to see and pass through the door of heaven."

"When in mutual service we forget the little self, then only will we see the one big Self of the Spirit running through us."

"All the pursuits of life offer only partial joy, though crowned with utmost fulfillment. But in finding God we have found the reservoir of perennial, unending Bliss."

Your Own Responsibility

"It requires greatest skill to live life evenly, rightly and successfully."

"No one else will answer for your actions, though others often become instruments in keeping you enmeshed in useless frivolities and so-called important engagements."

"The world creates in you bad habits, but the world will not stand responsible for your actions springing from those habits."

Know God Thru His Law

"If we praise God all day long, He does not come. If we blame Him, He does not come. Praise and blame do not move God. We find God through His law."

"God shows no partiality at any time or place. He is everywhere. We cannot cage God."

"Heaven does not come to us by aeroplane or special delivery. We have to bring Heaven here ourselves."

The Power of Attention

"Every action, insignificant or important, should be performed with quick, alert attention."

"Absent-mindedness blunts the needle of attention."

"Attention is the needle that cuts the grooves in the record of the memory cells."

THE ROSE

There is the rose—its petals, perfumed gloriously with the perfume of the Soul behind the veil. Behind the veil of petals, we find Beauty; behind the veil of perfume, we find the suggestion of some attractive secret; behind the color, the resplendent color of some hidden beauty.

The rose came, born of the Great Beauty; the rose dies, melting into a Great Beyond; the rose is the language of the hidden Soul; the rose is soft, tender, alluring, everlastingly giver of joy, and as such the rose will not fail to give joy to all those millions of human beings that are going to come in the future; the rose has charmed and pleased millions of Souls who have gone beyond; the rose is still charming millions of Souls that are now here; the rose is the preacher of eternal Joy; the rose is a bringer of pleasure; the rose is a reflection of God; the rose is sweet, because the God in it is sweeter still.

Love the rose, but love the Maker of the rose more, much more, for without His beauty, the rose could not manifest in its resplendent beauty; the rose is visible ...visibly alluring, but the beauty behind the rose is invisible. With Vision behind the mortal veil, watch the INVISIBLE BEAUTY, the Beauty which is invisibly alluring, which is the home of all roses, all flowers, all beauty, all life.

REALIZATION versus BOOK LEARNING

Western philosophers have always assumed that Truth can be known by dialectics and reason. Immanuel Kant was the first one to question if man had the faculties required to know Truth adequately. The great Sage Patanjali, who lived long before Kant, gave conclusive proof that settled the dispute about the nature of the instruments of man's faculties required in knowing Truth.

A thirsty man once went to a lake and craved at the sight of it to swallow all its waters. He found, however, that he could not drink more than the capacity of his little stomach. So sits there by the vast lake of Truth many a thirsty philosopher and seeker who aspire to drink all of its waters and hold all its mysteries within themselves. But alas, they know not that this can not possibly be done. To swallow all the waters of the lake of Truth, one must have a stomach as big as the lake.

Ordinarily a phenomenon is known by the senses, perceived by the mind, and cognized by the inner ego. All human experiences depend for their data on the testimony of the senses. The power of inference comes after and draws conclusions from the material supplied by the senses. If smoke is seen to emerge from a distant hill, John concludes the hill is on fire. Why? Because he had seen fire and smoke together before. But in this case, it was not smoke but a cloud of dust on the hill. John was mistaken in inferring the hill was on fire. Whenever the data furnished by the senses are wrong the conclusion is wrong. Hence though the power of inferential reason has its uses, still it is incapable of proving the ultimate nature of Reality.

Limitations of the Senses

Our sense radios can only intercept certain rates of vibratory message of qualities, appearances—not the substance, the thing-in-itself. Our senses give report of phenomena, not of noumena. Look at an orange—you perceive the color, touch, smell, taste; one perception at a time. A combination of these perceptions is called an orange; none knows what the thing, the orange, is in itself. The orange is not the color, nor the taste, nor the softness—but is the force which combines these qualities harmoniously to produce the effect of an orange. A manufactured orange may be produced with a sponge, orange juice, orange scent, and orange skin, to look, taste, and feel like an orange. As our senses only perceive qualities separately, an artificial combination of the color, taste, smell and touch may easily lead the senses and the power of inference to believe a manufactured orange to be a real orange.

None knows what the real orange is. Perhaps it is the intelligent combination of differently vibrating atoms representing color, taste, solidity and smell, around one nucleus. Our senses do not tell us that, but our wisdom does. The vast universe is nothing but an ocean of energy lying about us; high overhead as rivers of the milky way, twinkling stars, solar systems; beneath our feet as solid earth. The physical body with its ethereal thoughts, the sparkling lakes, heaving oceans, sky, air and fire—all are but the vibrations of the same cosmic energy. Yet the senses differentiate and tell us the delusive story that the solid hurts us, the liquid drowns us, the fire burns us, the sky does not hold us, the gas chokes us. As ice appears from water, steam, hydrogen-oxygen gas—so appears the universe as the solid earth, oceans and vapors. All are the manifestations of one and the same substance. All the ninety elements of which the whole universe is comprised is made of one electronic energy which in turn is composed of conscious cosmic energy. Our senses tell us only of the most superficial aspect of matter, deceiving us into thinking that ice is cold, heavy and solid and that the steam is hot and fluid, and that the atoms in it are composed of burning luminous electricity.

Our senses do not tell us the truth—that the electrons laden in a small pencil could explode a skyscraper, and that the energy released from the electrons constituting a human body could explode a part of Mount Everest. If our senses spoke the truth we would see the earth not as solid, liquid and gaseous, but as rivers and glaciers of electrons. Each speck of dust would appear a rolling mass of light.

It might be reasoned that though our senses deceive us, our powers of reason can give us new truths. That is true. We must, however, remember that all the knowledge derived from experiments carried on by the help of the microscope, mathematics, and fine instruments, has to come through the senses. The senses, and the reason working on their testimony, have only told a millionth part of the truth about the nature of matter and all things. But yesterday atoms were considered ultimate—now they are further analyzed to contain the finer materials of electrons. Thus neither the senses nor the power of inference, which builds knowledge on sense testimony, can be trusted to tell us the truth about the earth, the universe, the human body, or the mind.

Authority is not Proof

Every religion claims its Bible to be of divine origin. Some hypocrites have even buried books, written on old papyrus, underground, grown grass on them, and then led mobs there under supposed inspiration to dig out and recover the "God-given book." How are you going to find out which book represents truths? The number of believers cannot be the proof. Galileo, one single man, believed the earth round and suffered prosecution on that account, while all the people of the world believed that it was flat. Hence the belief of the millions of followers of the Christian Bible or the Hindu Vedas cannot establish the immutable universal nature of the principles inculcated in them. Of course by reading and hearing sermons from the Bible and Vedas we can find certain moral advice and suggestions of right human conduct which can benefit all races for all times. But that does not prove the deeper Truths mentioned in them. The Vedas and the Bible both declare God as a living, kind, responding Ruler of the Universe. But reading those words does not prove it. Has anyone consciously seen Him? Our senses see the color in flowers and our mind perceives the beauty, but who can tell that One Intelligence pervades the Universe? Who can tell that the Vedas and the Bible are infallible? Isn't there some husk, some crust of superstition in both books? We have to separate the husk from the kernel. We must find the Truth as separated from the language and limitation of expression used by its propounder.

Therefore the sage Patanjali, the founder of the Yoga system in India, who flourished several centuries before Jesus Christ, says that the authority of the scriptures is not proof of its Truth, because the scriptures, no matter who propounds them, have to be received through the sight, hearing, limited imagination, and the reasoning powers of the reader. All seekers, all denominations, whether Unitarians, Universalists, Baptists, Methodists, Episcopalians, Congregationalists, Christian Scientists, Swedenborgians, Catholic or Hindu Christians, all interpret the Bible according to their own degree of development and power of reasoning. That is why there are so many cults formed out of the one universal teachings of Jesus Christ.

What Is the Proof?

The proof of applying the laws of Patanjali in finding out the Real Truth about the pure universal teachings and Scriptures, undiluted by the limitations of our opinions, is to live it in life. I asked a knave if he read the Christian Bible. He replied, "I have read it a hundred times, Sir; I know all about it." "Alas," I said, "You know nothing about it because you are still a knave." That is why in ancient India the Vedas and the Hindu Bible of Bhagavad Gita were not printed for centuries. They were handed down through the memories of devout disciples and only some knew all the truth. Others were told not more than they could realize at one time. Nowadays, any Yoga book or scripture or the Christian Bible can be bought for a few cents and intellectually swallowed. Swallowing one's own ideas about the scriptures without digestion ...only creates a greed for more books and more new ideas, but chronic indigestion and spiritual non-assimilation will result.

Everywhere we see Pundits, living, moving dictionaries crammed to the brim with intellectual knowledge. But have they the ability to put all that wisdom they have memorized into practical achievement and manifestation in their life and character? If not, then their knowledge is vain and is really ignorance.

This is happening in the West and in the East. Each phase of intellectual study of scriptures must be substantiated by corresponding realization and then a little more should be read and realized and so on. Every theory and belief must be practiced and its truth found out. Belief is no safety, for it produces the ignorance of false satisfaction born of dogma. It crumbles at the storm of reason. Skepticism is refusal to investigate further. It is self-inflicted punishment.

The Power of Realization

Sophistry and intellectual belief may produce temporary satisfaction but they are short lasting, vanishing like soap bubbles before the blast of deep scrutiny. Followers of the Hindu and Christian teachings should build their faith on the unshakable rock of realization. According to Patanjali, any real inner Christ teachings cannot be understood through the testimony of others, or listening to their interpretations, but can be grasped only by testing them directly by the power of intuition. I know I exist. I am not the body—it is my body. I think. I am not the thought. Therefore this consciousness of the I-ness in every man cannot be perceived through the senses. What cannot be perceived through the senses, cannot be inferred about through the reason. Then how do I know I exist? From direct perception of my intuition and not through the intermediary faculties of sensory perceptions and reason.

Through the ages the red pages of history tell of many religious Inquisitions, burning of martyrs and so-called witches, wars of the crusades, and so forth—brought on by not only the limited interpretation but misinterpretation of Christ's teachings. Jesus Christ was crucified once but his teachings suffer crucifixion every day at the hands of men and cults of limited vision. Jesus Christ's teachings cannot be understood by reading the Bible a thousand times or thru all life and several generations, but can be known only by living and trying out the book in every-day life. What you listen to, what you read in books—try to mediate on that long enough to be one with the thought underlying it. Then try to manifest that realization in practice. Realization comes from constant wide-awake meditation, with ever-busy, ever-searching mentality to convert theory into solid knowledge thru practice.

Scriptural Realization

All beliefs must be thoroughly scrutinized. Overstudy must be avoided. Indis-criminative study, especially of religious books written by novices or untried enthusiasts mostly results in indigestible hashes of imagination, emotional outbursts, and diluted realization. Patanjali Yoga Philosophy, the Christian Bible, the Hindu Bible—Bhagavad Gita, and a few other books written only by men of real realization, must be studied, a little at a time, and meditated upon for hours or for days together. The best time to read scriptures is after practicing meditation when the intuitive feeling is awake.

My Master, Swami Sri Yukteswar Giriji, once told me one of his experiences in the real studies of the scriptures, in a hermitage. His great Savant Guru (teacher of Gita) was sitting surrounded by his disciples. The sacred book was open before them all. They were looking steadfastly at one passage. A half hour passed, then they closed their eyes. A half hour passed again, the Master explained for a few moments the same passage upon which they were concentrating. They all meditated motionless for an hour—then the Master asked a question, "Have you understood?" One of them answered "Yes, sir." The Master replied, "No you didn't—let us meditate again." They meditated for another half-hour. Then the Master asked his disciples again, "Do you all now understand what you read?" No one spoke. Then the Master said, "Our study today is over." He then turned to my Master and asked, "Have you read the Bhagavad Gita?" My Master replied, "No sir, although my eyes and mind have run through its pages." His Guru smiled and with great joy said, "You are the only one of thousands I have met who said that. But indeed you have read it. When one is engrossed in knowing, he does not have the time to think whether he knows or to say he knows. He is too busy knowing—others are too busy saying they know, that's why they have no time to make the effort to know."

Sacred and inspiring books are helpful in stimulating the desire for realization, if a little at a time is assimilated. Otherwise overstudy of books produces vanity, false satisfaction, that one knows when he does not know at all. Ramakrishna said, "I pity the ignorant, I love the unread man of realization, but I consider a bit of straw the man of book learning without realization. I can blow him away by a puff of questioning about realization. I admire, love, and respect a man who has realization as well as the intellectual knowledge of different scriptures." Let not love of book reading or ceremonial diversions be the delusion to divert you from realization. God realization first, books and everything else is of secondary importance. Have Him and you have everything. Seek ye the kingdom of God first, and all things will be added unto it—all wisdom, prosperity and beauty. Get the tree of life, and you shall have each of its fruits too.

NICHOLAS ROERICH

The article on "Activity" by Nicholas Roerich, and his painting, that appear in this issue of EAST-WEST, will give joy to those of our readers who are discovering Roerich for the first time. This great Russian painter is international in his message—he understands the soul of India no less than the soul of America because he is one with all humanity.

To list the manifold activities and gifts of Professor Roerich is to reveal a man to whom all departments of knowledge are open. He is painter, architect, writer, poet, jurist, musician, publicist, explorer, professor or archaeology, educator, sage and prophet. His paintings have won the highest expressions of praise from the leading artists of every country, and the Roerich Museum in New York is perhaps the only Museum in the world which is dedicated to the works of a single living master.

At present, this indefatigable seeker after knowledge is heading the Roerich Art Expedition, now in the heart of Mongolia for archaeological excavations. He recently presented the Mongolian Government with his painting, "The Great Rider." Officials of that government have asked Professor Roerich to design a temple of jasper and porphyry which the painting, along with other objects held sacred by the Mongolians, can be suitably housed.

Paramhansa Yogananda

TO THE AURORA BOREALIS

(Over Forest Lake in Minneapolis)

From the heart of the northern horizon
A dim palpitating fountain of flame
Spread flickeringly
Thru the dark stray clouds and the milky way,
And across the space overhead;
Softly glowing liquid fleecy lights
Rose, quivered and flooded the southern land.
Aurora lit the sky,
Played with shadows within the deeps of the limpid lake
Fluttered scintillating transparent lights
Flowing o'er the stars
And the sky o'erhead,
And shining on rippleless lake beneath,
Then floated like dream waves of light
In my mental sea.
Still thoughts like stars would flutter
Thru the dim mental clouds;
My wisdom's aurora light
Would rise from medulla's horizon
And spread, tremblingly lighting
The dark vapors of mind.
Thou lone matchless imitator of all these—
O Aurora! spreader of light and joy
O'er cloudy hearts—

Balancing East-West

Thou reminder of bursting glowing light in my forehead!
Some invisible lamps on the left or extreme right
Would throw sudden iridescent red
Or blue sky-kissing search-lights
Then the ends of those lights
Would send out etherial mystic flames
Which joyfully bounded and vanished in the eternal ray.
Ever burning radium, thou aurora
—My fountain of strange colors—
Flooded my mental sky
Illumining the opaque darkness
Behind which the Light of all lights hides.
It was a vision of ever-changing rolling molten light—
Trying to coax the stars, trees, water, earth and all matter
To melt their grossness
And become the cosmic light;
Aurora, there is hope,
For I shall liquify in my Samadhi's fire
All grossness of my mortal being and all creation's dust.
Matter shall change to light,
The darkness will burst into atoms of leaping fire,
The little soul will breathe with the eternal breath—
And with each birth of my breath
New solar systems will be born
And with the escape of each eternity's breath of mine
Many a universe shall cease to breathe;
The feeling of the body will fly
To feel the universe;
No more shall I clasp but a little clot
But in my bosom I shall bear the burden

Paramhansa Yogananda

Of the twinkling atomic vapours of nebulae,
All shining stars, planets and all living things.
For I am the life
And my big body is the universe;
I am smaller than all little things made,
I can hide behind a speck of electron;
And I am bigger than the biggest thing that breathes;
I am the life which shattered its littleness
Into the bigness of all big things;
I am most subtle, the subtlest of forces
Is thick enough to hide me;
Yet everything speaks of me.
I wake with the dawn.
I exercise my vital muscular rays in the sun,
I sleep in the night—
Oft peeping thru the twinkling lights,
I smile in the moon,
I heave in the ocean,
I paint, and wipe away,
The pictures on the canvas of the sky,
I make the dew-drop and conjure the flowers
With my invisible wand,
I whistle in the canaries and sing in the nightingales,
I melt and sigh in human breasts,
I whisper thru conscience and roar in the thunder,
I work in the noisy wheels of factories,
And I play hide and seek
With the sky, stars, clouds and water
As the light of the Aurora.

THREE RECIPES December 1927

Food Recipe

Rice

After washing rice always cook it in a double boiler. To one cup of rice, add two cups of hot water. Then put the double boiler on a medium gas flame for half an hour. It is not good to eat rice all mushy or with the water drained from it after boiling. The best rice in this country is Florida wild rice. Each grain is an inch and sometimes an inch and a half long. Put one cup of cooked Florida wild rice with six mushrooms chopped up with a teaspoonful of curry powder and four tablespoons of butter.

Natural, brown, unpolished rice gives physical stamina and mental strength and concentration. White polished rice is practically worthless, most of its precious nutritive elements having been removed.

Rice has been called the Father of all Cereals. It was the original cereal food of the American Indians. To this day it is the chief cereal food of most Oriental countries. It was interesting to read recent press dispatches stating that Premier Mussolini has been discussing with visiting tradesmen his project of introducing rice as the daily food for Italians, in an effort to do away with the necessity of importing wheat. One of the first and most important changes that the Duce made on his rise to power was to banish the worthless white bread that the Italians, in common with most other peoples of the world, had been using, and to restore the dark whole grain wheat bread to favor. It can therefore be assumed that if Mussolini decrees that rice instead of wheat will henceforth be the daily food of the nation, that he will introduce the brown unpolished rice and not its pale emaciated shadow, polished white rice.

Avocado

Half an alligator pear chopped up in small squares mixed well with two or three tablespoonsful of Thousand Island dressing is delicious and a meal in itself. Alligator pears contain more nutrition that a steak and do not contain the impurities of the latter. A pear costs about fifty cents. After all, it is cheaper than meat. It is the best meat substitute. All abstainers from meat should always eat natural meat substitutes and thus avoid growing weak and going back to meat eating.

There is a Syrian proverb: "the enemy of man is his stomach." Remember that this bodily machinery has been given to you to enable you to accomplish certain works on this material plane, and that you should guard it and take care of it as your most precious possession. The chief abuse of the body lies in overloading it with unnecessary food. Eat sparingly and notice the great change in your health for the better. The proper combinations and quality of food should also not be overlooked. A supply of raw fruits, vegetables and nuts should be included in the regular diet.

Prosperity Recipe

It is the greatest shame for a person not to be able to support himself or his family. People without backbone acknowledge defeat and beg. The torture of poverty is a better incentive than the drug of satisfaction born of receiving things through begging which slowly poisons the health of the incessant fighting spirit within us.

Fight to the finish. Never turn back. Never say, "I could not find the way so I give up." Ask the way if you have made mistakes but never give up. Many give up when the difficult turns in the path come. Failures should consult and associate with the successful persons and not with failures. Make up your mind you will succeed.

Spiritual Recipe

To all those who receive Him, to them He gave the power to be the Sons of God.

It is best to take on single passage of Scripture, each day, and meditate on that one thought and meaning alone. Great illumination can come that way. Scriptures that are too hurriedly read do not reveal their inner regenerative significance and power.

Paramhansa Yogananda

MIRACLES OF RAJA YOGA
Its Western Misconceptions

Hypocrisy and Hats?

It was while applying for a passport to go to Vancouver, B. C., that an immigration official became sarcastically fascinated with my yellow turban, the national headdress of the Hindus. The officer looked at me with pity and said, "Do you gaze at crystals, tell fortunes, swallow swords? Are you a snake charmer?" I said nothing but presented him with one of my books, and when he had read a few lines and had a look of apology in his eye for his rash inference, I looked at him smilingly and said, "Dear officer, did you know that the Hindus never had any factory where they knew the art of making crystals? Crystals are of western origin. Hence it is news to me that the Hindus gaze at crystals.

"As regards fortune telling, you have quite a number right here in America as well as in India. But whenever you meet an American gentleman do you ask him, "Are you a fortune teller?" Every Hindu is not a fortune teller. They don't believe in flattering an unmarried woman by telling her fortune, saying that she is going to have a good wealthy husband, and then relieve her of three or four dollars. Wise Hindus can teach you how to solve the problem of life. Your present poverty or opulence, disease or health, is brought about by your own past actions. Your present life will determine your future life. They diagnose scientifically how the law of cause and effect apply to human actions and lives. They do not believe in fate, i.e., anything happening without cause. Hence the Hindus do not like fooling people by telling them what is going to happen through the trickery of imagination, equivocable words, or by fraud. The real Hindu astrologers make a scientific study of the law of causation governing human actions and they are not satisfied with telling you the past or predicting your future only. They teach you the art of averting an unwelcome event or stimulating the fruition of a desirable event coming to you as a result of your past evil or good actions. Good astrologers tell their students only what will benefit them, and do not like to satisfy idle curiosity. They say there is no use in telling you what is coming to you anyway unless one can also show you the way to control or regulate your self-created destiny. Otherwise ignorance is bliss."

I said to the immigration officer again, "Sir, I haven't had the singular, dangerous experience of swallowing swords or taming cobras, which our wonderful street magicians often do in open daylight before the gaze of people." These snake charmers and sword swallowers are our street magicians. They are skilled in slight-of-hand tricks at the same time. They do perform magic by producing optical illusions. Herein the eastern magician is superior to the western magician."

Then smilingly I asked the officer again, "I have seen some hypocritical western people wearing hats and dress suits, but I never connected hypocrisy with the wearing of hats. How did you happen to connect snake-charming with my turban?"

By this time the officer was smoothed out and in a very friendly tone he said, "I am sorry. Many good turbaned Hindus have to suffer the persecution of public opinion because some turbaned Hindu fakers have produced a wrong impression on our people."

I replied, "Well, but you cannot expect all Hindus to forsake turbans because some Hindus have not done right, just as I cannot expect all western brothers to forsake their hats because some practiced hypocrisy while wearing hats. Western tourists go to India and watch our poorly dressed coolie laborers, and see the performances of the street magicians or fakers, and they think the Hindus need to wear swallow-tail coats and neckties to be civilized. Well, you can dress a cow with a swallow-tail coat and necktie, but that would not make it civilized. Neither would a turbaned cow dressed in a robe become a spiritual Hindu."

Customs and mannerisms are non-essentials resulting from certain climatic influences. The real development of man consists of the development of his mind-power.

So the American tourist visiting India must take care not to misconceive the real Yogis of India. The real Yogis are distinctly different from the magicians, sword-swallowers, instantaneous mango tree growers. The latter are our magicians and street entertainers. The former are Great Men, very difficult to recognize due to Their child-like simplicity, yet possessing miraculous powers like those of Christ.

Physical and Mental Miracles

There is no difference between physical laws and super-laws or miracles worked by the knowledge of the mechanism of the human mind. The Americans work miracles through use of physical laws; the Hindus work mental miracles. The operation of radio and tele-photo cameras are still miracles to many Hindus, and the workable miracles of the mind ...so often displayed by the Yogis of India are unknown to the Americans. In these days of marvels of constant inventions it would be wise for the Americans to at least investigate thoroughly the discovery of spiritual miracles by their Hindu brothers. Miracles are nothing but the operation of super-mental and cosmic laws. Jesus and the master-minds of India know how to operate them. To ordinary people such work appears as miracles, but they are really the result of the natural operation of certain higher, hidden laws.

Need for Raja Yoga

Yoga means uniting Mind-Power with Cosmic Power. Raja Yoga consists of those principles of concentration which were easily practiced even by the Rajas or royalists of India who were engrossed with the multifarious duties of their states.

These methods of concentration, or Raja Yoga, which bring power over one's own destiny and which can turn failure—material, moral, social or spiritual—into success ...can fit in with the busy and worried life of the American Rajas and Maharajahs, the American millionaires and billionaires. Human nature is everywhere the same. The American needs poise and spiritual strength just as much as the Hindu does. The American, because he makes the machine work hard for him, has more time than the Hindu, who has to work with his hands for his living. The American business man has more time than the proverbially spiritual Hindu to devote to developing mental miracles.

The superiority of acquiring miraculous mental powers over the acquirement of business skill is this, that the former has no limitations, whereas the latter has. The ordinary intelligent business man may be broken down by hard competition. When his business intelligence is exhausted he utterly fails. But the Hindu savant says that when your intelligence gives out you don't need to give up. One can use his unlimited super-powers for the materialization of a desire. As God is all-powerful, so also, by Raja-Yoga, or uniting with Him consciously, man becomes likewise powerful.

Miracles Historically Recorded

I will give below a few authentic, historically true, miraculous achievements of the Yogis of India ...showing that they lived far ahead of the modern times and performed miracles still far remote from even the comprehension of modern material science.

About seventy years ago, the holy city of Benares was agog with the miracles of Tailanga Swami. He was two hundred fifty years old, and it is said He used to remain below or floating on the surface of the Ganges two or three days at a time; He read peoples' minds like books; He drank poisonous liquids by bowlfuls without dying, and seemingly had done all the miracles of Jesus Christ. The story goes that once, for disregarding the laws of the city, He was put in jail. He was seen the next minute walking on the roof. He had many wonderful powers. Can science tell us of anyone else who has lived for two hundred and fifty years?

The Miracle of Sadhu Haridas

Another miracle of Raja Yoga was demonstrated when Sadhu Haridas permitted Himself to be buried alive under-ground for five months. In the sixteenth century, in the court of Prince Ranjit Singh—emperor of the Punjab—and under the seal of French and other European doctors, the miraculous performance of Sadhu Haridas was historically recorded. The emperor buried this Saint Haridas (after waxing the body all over and then sewing it in a sack which was then sealed in a stone chest) several hundred feet below the earth in his own courtyard for five months. Millions of people waited for the news about the Saint when He was disinterred after five months had passed. The stone chest was opened, the clothing and wax were removed, and the body was examined by French and English doctors and pronounced dead. Yet in a few minutes the Saint Sadhu Haridas blinked His eyes and came back to life. Boom! went the cannon from the ramparts of the emperor's fort at Lahore (Punjab, India), heralding and declaring that the Saint Haridas had come back to life. Millions witnessed this event, and in any comprehensive historical book on India this occurrence will be found recorded.

There are such Saints who once in a while publicly demonstrate these powers even to this day. My teacher's teacher gave a demonstration similar to that mentioned above, to my mother. But it is considered a spiritual degradation and blasphemy against God's laws for great Yogis to give such above demonstrations merely to satisfy the idle cravings of curiosity-seekers.

It took me a long time to understand my Master and His miraculous power, though I had close contact with Him. I have seen miracles, and of all the wonderful things witnessed, I shall declare to the world that I secured my A.B. degree through this miraculous power. I used to always visit and stay with Him, and neglected my college work so much that I hardly knew where my college books were. Two days before the university examination, I told my Master I wasn't going to appear at the examination. His demeanor changed suddenly and He said, "Then all My relations with you cease this instant." He insisted and said, "All I ask of you is to appear at the examination." He declared I would pass even though I had not studied. I agreed reluctantly, thinking I would write about His teachings in the answer paper to questions on the writing of Shakespeare. I just agreed literally to carry out His behest.

Next He asked me, at first gently, then vehemently, to go to a certain friend of mine and ask certain questions of him every morning of all those days that my A.B. examination lasted. This Calcutta University A.B. degree, in some respects, is more difficult to obtain than a Harvard A.B. degree. There is so much injustice and difficulty set in the path of those being examined. I did as my Master told me; and strange to say, whatever questions this friend of mine unconsciously told me to prepare for, I found those very questions in my examinations. After the first day I declared to the world that I was going to pass, and when I received the A.B. degree, my parents and friends, who had given up all hopes about the success of my college life, told me I had performed a miracle. That is why I am fond of putting the A.B. after my name in all my books and articles. The A.B. title reminds me of this singular experience. When I questioned my Master, Sri Yukteswar Giriji, He just replied that faith, works and knowledge of super-mental law can work miracles, where physical efforts of man fail.

I remember that a friend of mine, seeing me a devout follower of my

Master and negligent of my studies, had once ridiculed me and said, "I am sorry to tell you that your Master and God won't make you pass your examinations." And half in faith and half for the sake of argument, I replied, "Why not?" Little did I dream I would see the fulfillment of my saying later on.

My Master is still living in flesh and blood in India and I dare not tell all the wonderful things I have seen. This much I can say: throughout the whole western world I have not found a single one like Him. I would accept all the poverty, famine, and inconveniences of life in India .... in preference to the comfortable American life, just to sit at the feet of one like my Master. Americans who are good listeners and love real progress now ought to go deeper than mere listening to the philosophical message of India's spiritual science. They should learn the technique by which the super-miracles of the mind can be understood and the higher laws applied ...to make life not only financially successful, but blissful in every way.

YOUR MOST IMPORTANT ENGAGEMENT

First come first served. That has been mostly your worst calamity. The unwelcome habits that came earliest in you life have kept you quite busy now and have crowded out many worth-while things of life. The social world moves on the wheels of certain habits. Few realize whither the social machinery is headed—to the chasm of ignorance or towards the mire of petty engagements, which choke the steady progressive activities of life.

How many times card and dancing parties, over-gorged amusement hunger, time-killing, progress-murdering mental idleness, initiativelessness, ambitionlessness ...have stood in your way and persuaded you to ignore and break your engagement with worth-while objects of life, even though you are fastidiously punctual in keeping daily engagements with useless doings.

When an overdose of drugging sleep makes you lazy and a late riser on Sunday mornings you forget your real engagement. On late waking you find the delaying-to-dress habit stands in your way, beckoning you not to go out of your home, and you easily break your engagement with the spiritually-stimulating atmosphere of the temple or church.

Your business engagements are important, and for them you sacrifice your equally important engagements of daily physical exercise, or of bathing the nerves and mind with showers of peace by meditation.

Evenness of Development

Just because your business engagements have been considered most important, they have always come first in your consideration. And they yet remain most important and they will remain so until you are called away in the Mystery beyond. But I preach evenness of development and of demonstrating prosperity—I do not believe in the spiritual sense being drugged and chloroformed by business madness or any kind of madness. Many think that unless one is "at it" day and night he is going to be left behind. That is not true. The one-sided business-bent man, forgetful of his other duties of life, is not the truly successful man. It requires greater and greatest skill to live life evenly, rightly and successfully. He who only keeps engagement with money is left behind by God. Yet God talks to us very loudly through the pangs of hunger which He has given us so that we should get busy and make money to support our physical bodies. Yet it seems that just maintaining our physical bodies by using up all our mental powers is not the goal of life. There is little difference between eating food from a gold plate or an iron plate. The food in both cases is equally satisfying to hunger. Then why concentrate on unnecessary "necessities" or go on constantly multiplying self-created, useless desires for more? To create such meaningless demands for luxuries is to be engaged night and day, giving one's life blood in the pursuit of getting things which one does not need.

The West is suffering from over-production due to concentration on unnecessary objects of luxury—and the East is suffering from lack of adequate production and the supply of many real necessities. The height of contrast is reached when we find some Western ladies wearing shoes with fifty dollars' worth of jewel-studded heels—and most of the Eastern women going wholly without shoes amidst clay and rain and maybe catching cold.

Overactivity vs. Idleness

In the West many factories close due to competition and over-production, and the East suffers from want of factories. In the West the people are too busy finding the will-o'-the-wisp of comfort; in the East some people try to preserve comfort by not being very active and by dreading material activity, which produces laziness. Comfort can only be acquired by a balanced attitude, a self-mastery which makes it possible for one to be comfortably active and actively comfortable. Engagements with Overactivity and Mr. Idleness both lead to misery. It is high time for the modern man to shake his drowsiness of centuries and systematize his life. The primitive man led a wild life in everything. The modern man has learned to apply science, psychology and system to his business, which are nothing but devices for his material comfort. The real man ought to apply the system and science to make his health, prosperity, social and international-world life and wisdom ...better and of scientific certainty. In order to do that he must not give all his time to business, which only ensures the hope of physical comfort. How people forget that increase in cost of living too luxuriously ...means the corresponding increase in using too much nerve and brain energy, expenditure of longevity ...to gain the conditions of a luxurious life! Besides, most people become so engrossed and engaged in making money that they cannot utilize the conditions of comfort after acquiring them.

Systematize and schedule your engagements—let none, especially your bad habits, sway or influence your judgment. Let the secretary of your true judgment arrange your life's daily itinerary.

Culture Habit of Meditation

Your engagement with business is important, but your appointment of serving others is more important, and your engagement with Meditation, Home, God and Truth is most important. Don't say you are too busy with worries and cares of keeping the wolf from the door to get time for the culture of Heavenly qualities.

Break your self-satisfied, immovable old dogged bad habits ...of idolizing your less important engagements and utterly ignoring the most important engagement with Wisdom. No one else will answer for your actions, though others often become instruments in keeping you enmeshed in useless frivolities and so-called important engagements.

O sleeping Image of God, wake up—make the determination and the effort to know the right law which will enable you to keep your most important engagement with yourself—to know thyself (Soul).

Do not say, "I will meditate on the Cosmic Being tomorrow." That tomorrow will never come. Begin your meditation today. Today's practice will stimulate the desire to meditate tomorrow deeper, whereas this day's negligence will weaken your craving. Do not be lured by bad habits and paltry useless-vanity-engagements into crowding out God-contact.

The world creates in you bad habits, but the world will not stand responsible for your actions springing from those habits. Then why give all the time to the world? Reserve even an hour a day for actual soul to soul God-realization. Doesn't the Giver of the world itself, of your family, money and everything, deserve one twenty-fourth part of your time?

Your greatest and most important engagement is with God and seeking His Truth through the eyes of wisdom and daily discipline!

WASHING SORROWS WITH MOONBEAMS

I will steal the milk of honeysuckles
Like Krishna of yore,
I will suckle the perfume
From the breast of the rose,
Roll over the velvet green
Or run after golden wings of gossamer.
I want no companions
But quietly wish to roam
With my nursing breeze.
Where the sheoli flowers
Dressed with pearly dew and showers
Rest on the throne of green gold lawns
For a while I will stand
My homage to pay to their scented majesties.
With the wings of the birds
My spirit joyfully flies
Over unknown fancies ...everywhere.
Thru the voice of birds
I will sing in silence.
I will spread with the vast blue;
With threads of sunbeams
I will sew my tattered joy.
With the moonbeams I will wash my sorrows,
With the night
I will obliterate my dark experiences,

Paramhansa Yogananda

With the dawn
I will create my new world of eternal joy.

RECIPES February 1927

Intellectual Recipe

Before starting to read always select logically written books which deal with vital subjects that will benefit your life. Read a little poetry every day. That will keep your feelings exercised. Read a little from modern physical science, study a little medical science and hygiene and add to these a little study of some book that will make you laugh. This will serve as a mental appetizer and will quicken the flow of your intellectual saliva.

Intellect can be developed by the habit of daily mental exercise in reading and thinking over certain logical philosophical statements. Finding out your own views, after you have read a good book, is of inestimable value in assimilating true ideas.

If you mix sand and sugar together it is difficult for a man to separate them while eating, but in a mixture of sugar and sand the ant always gets the sugar and leaves the sand alone.

The blind reader, who swallows good and bad ideas indiscriminately, suffers from intellectual indigestion, chaos, and mental irritation, whereas the introspective reader, like the ant, separates the erroneous harmful or too sentimental views from beneficial and right expressions in the books he reads.

So select quality in the books you read, and above all discriminate and examine the salient statements in them as you read. Remember you are not a mental machine of recording others' ideas. Assimilate only the worthy ideas in books.

Success Recipe

Always seek to be worthy of the position just ahead of you. Use your will power and creative brain specially to create new success. Most of us follow the beaten track. It is the new energetic explorer on the pathway of success who succeeds.

Spiritual Recipe

If you read fifteen minutes, write twenty minutes, introspect thirty minutes and meditate thirty-five, you will be spending your time according to the grades of importance of your work.

Health Recipe

Eating three meals a day is an extremely dangerous habit. Many are being led to their graves quickly because they eat at the sound of the dinner bell. Ignore its ominous call if you are not hungry. It is good to eat at a regular time, for a psychological expectancy is created in the body cells which helps the secretion of the digestive juices. The intelligent cells like hungry animals at the Zoo wait for the dinner hour. But never eat unless you are hungry. Eat moderately, if you are hungry. Eat less if you are a little hungry. Eat nothing if you are not hungry at all. Omit the meals which you may try to eat with little hunger and this will sharpen your hunger for the next meal. Use your will power to resist the temptation of eating three meals every day, by which the whole system, including the cells, the heart, the nerves, the stomach, has to work continuously. Give your intelligent machine occasional rest by cutting off breakfast, lunch or dinner every day. If you are very hungry and are working hard, you may safely eat three light meals daily, but if you don't do much manual labor, then two meals a day are plenty.

Raw Vegetable Cutlet

One head of very finely chopped lettuce, two tablespoonfuls of finely ground pecans, three tablespoonfuls of cottage cheese, a pinch of salt, half a teaspoonful of sugar, juice of a quarter of an onion. Mix these ingredients and knead them as you would a lump of dough, then make them in the form of a cutlet and serve on a dish.

YELLOW JOURNALISM VERSUS TRUTH

ARE EASTERN TEACHINGS "DANGEROUS"?

Some years ago in Boston, while being interviewed by a newspaper reporter, I gave my views on the subject of education for boys, based on my experience as founder and principal of the Ranchi Residential School for Boys in India.

The next morning, the interview appeared in the newspaper with the headlines reading, "The Swami's Opinions on Flappers." Much mystified, I consulted four dictionaries without discovering any other meaning for "flapper" except "One who, or that which, flaps." This left me as much in the dark as ever, and I consulted some of my Boston friends. Imagine my surprise to learn that "flappers" meant "scantily dressed young girls." The small boys I had been talking about to the reporter had undergone a newspaper metamorphosis, emerging as full-fledged girl flappers!

Certainly the methods of exaggeration and distortion, and the free play of imagination and fictional skill that are employed by some newspapermen in lieu of sober consideration of facts and actual events, can make a harmless rope look like a vicious snake.

Press Necromancy

Some of the clever street magicians of India can, apparently, produce articles out of thin air. This magical ability to materialize something out of nothing has been developed to a high art by the press-necromancy of certain American newspapers. A constant stream of unwholesome wonders emerge from such newspapers' trick hat of imagination. The deluded public gazes in astonishment at what appears to be a whole forest of venomous cobra snakes but which is in reality nothing more than a coil of inoffensive rope.

It lies with the public to destroy the menacing influence of untruthful journalism in America by refusing to buy its tainted pages. One knows not where its poisoned shafts will strike next. The history of yellow journalism is a continuous record of broken hearts, broken homes, ruined reputations and blighted lives, unjustly brought about. The fruits of a lifetime of disinterested service to mankind can be reduced to ashes thru the soulless efforts of yellow journalism. Gold is its only god, and to that god, there is nothing too sacred for it to sacrifice. Truth is its plaything, useful to it only insofar as it allows opportunity for distortion, misinterpretation and exaggeration.

Catering as it does, to a depraved public taste that lacks sufficient moral and intellectual background to enable it to detect truth from falsehood, the only aim of yellow journalism is sensationalism and "thrills," without regard for any fundamental right, truth or principle. Thru lust for gold, it will crucify any man or any movement at a moment's notice, employing conscienceless writers, skilled in the crafty art of misrepresenting truth while clearly avoiding the technical charges of libel.

Propaganda against India

These words are called forth thru the recent wholesale and seemingly organized propaganda in certain unprincipled newspapers, and in several books and magazines, aimed against India, Eastern teachings, and Oriental teachers.

The regenerating, life-giving, soul-revealing philosophy of the glorious ancient Indian sages has been more and more coming into the limelight in America, due to the reverent interest and earnest study of thousands of truth-seeking, thoughtful, unprejudiced Americans, who are lending their moral and financial support for the spread and defense of India's eternal light of truth.

The shallow reasoning, race-prejudice and love of sensationalism at the expense of truth that characterizes yellow journalism and writers with the Nordic-superiority-complex, have recently been widely employed in an effort to block the waters of truth that have been flowing from India into America. As well try to stop the stars in their courses! So long as spiritual hunger persists in American, so long will the deathless message of India's saints continue to nourish the Western brothers.

In the cosmic plan and purpose, certain duties and responsibilities have been allotted the different races of mankind. At the present time, the

Western world leads in material development and scientific progress, and the Orient is humbly grateful to receive instruction from the West along those lines, sending its promising young sons by the thousands to Western universities and Western lands to study the superior knowledge of material conquest of nature in the West.

Because of India's great antiquity as compared with the extreme youth of European and American countries, and because of the centuries of concentration on spiritual problems by the greatest minds of India, it is seen that the individual contribution of Indian national genius to the well-being of the world is a spiritual one. India has sent very few of her great teachers to America, but those who did come, like Swami Vivekananda, Baba Bharati, Swamirama and a few others, were received with open arms and accomplished the spiritual awakening of thousands of American souls.

Would America Welcome Oriental Christ?

For thousands of years past, the Orient has produced the towering spiritual figures of history. The whole Western world professes to follow the Oriental teacher, Jesus Christ, altho if He returned to earth today, He would meet with the same race prejudice, immigration restriction and journalistic misrepresentation that other Oriental teachers of today have to deal with.

Christ, Mohammed, Buddha, Confucius, Laotze, Zoroaster and Krishna were all Orientals. Some of the greatest spiritual figures of modern times came from India—Ramakrishna, Swami Vivekananda, Mahatma Gandhi and Lahiri Mahashaya are well known to the Western world. India has produced in every generation scores of saints of such God-realization and spiritual grandeur that their lives have left an imperishable mark on Indian history and their names are enshrined in every Indian heart.

These differing manifestations of racial genius do not mean that Western nations cannot produce great saints, nor that Orientals are incapable of great material activity. In fact, there have been many glorious saints of the Christian church who have known God and have manifested His power. Similarly, even today the Orient numbers among her sons some of the greatest scientists, inventors and mathematicians of the world. But the emphasis on values differs in East and West. In India, spiritual advancement is considered the highest goal of life. Any man who devotes himself to that calling is held in the highest respect and reverence by the people. Many of the great Indian characters naturally gravitate to that path of life. There has never been wholesale religious persecution or religious intolerance in India.

But in the West, we find a different standard. Here the religious life is held in no such respect as it obtains in India, and in fact it calls forth some contempt as the "calling of a weakling" from large sections of the American public. Hence, the great American minds naturally gravitate toward material, scientific expression and development. Recognition and public acclaim are mostly reserved in America for those who can show the greatest amount of material accomplishment. In India, a man like Mahatma Gandhi is held in adoration by the masses, not for the results of his labor, but for the grandeur of his moral nature and the strength of his character.

Genius is Mind-Concentration

In both cases, it is concentration of mind that produces great spiritual or scientific geniuses. Western souls can certainly achieve union with God as readily as the Oriental, should they make the same effort. Similarly, any great spiritual character of India could become a world figure in science, should he devote himself to that line, instead of to spiritual duty. It is mostly the hereditary, environmental and racial influences that determine in what direction the innate force of character shall manifest. The sum total of man's nature remains the same, regardless of what activities he may engage in. The great cosmic forces that are bringing the same soul to earth again and again, in order to enable it to overcome its human nature and to uncover its divine nature, send that soul sometimes in a Western body, sometimes in an Eastern body, in order that the various environments may bring out the infinite possibilities within him.

India has been able to withstand the political upheavals and social vicissitudes of centuries, without losing her national individuality as ancient Rome, Greece and Egypt did. Why? Because of her great spiritual vitality, because of the thousands of great saints that have trod her soil and sanctified it.

The ancient rishis (sages) of India went deeper into the laws of life, nature and God than any other people in history. Many of the great modern scientific discoveries merely confirm what the Aryan seekers discovered centuries ago in a general way, about the atomic constitution of matter, the basic laws of the physical world, and the principles of man's mind and nature. For this reason, whenever a great scientific or spiritual figure arises, whether in East or West, his message does not differ in any essential respect from the ancient philosophy of India. "Truth is One, men call it by various names." There can be no two truths. Destroy all books, all traditional learning, and still the basic truths of life would be discovered all over again, exactly the same, by the inquiring spiritual mind with its penetrating insight.

Repetition of Ancient Truths

Hence it follows that every modern spiritual message of any power or vitality, is a repetition in a new form of the truths pronounced ages ago by the Aryan sages, who for centuries devoted themselves exclusively to investigating the spiritual laws, the potentialities of their own nature, and in outlining the various paths of discipline for various natures to follow in order to come into contact with their own divine nature and hence with the cosmic forces of the universe.

All the world's great religions are based on the same universal truths, and do not conflict with but reinforce one another. Practically all the various forms of religion, and the basic systems of philosophy everywhere, have drawn their inspiration from the Hindu Scriptures, as the oldest and most comprehensive in the world.

The Hindu Scriptures consist of the four Vedas (each as large as an unabridged edition of Webster's dictionary), the two epics Ramayana and Mahabharata, the one hundred and eight Upanishads, and the six systems of Hindu philosophy, Sankhya, Patanjali, Vedanta, Nyaya, Vaisesika and the Purva Mimamsa; and lastly, Bhagavad Gita. The Upanishads were compiled to summarise the teachings of the Vedas; the six systems of Hindu philosophy are abridged forms of the Upanishads, and the Bhagavad Gita is the substance of all.

Western Misunderstanding

There have occasionally arisen various forms of misunderstanding in the

West regarding Indian philosophy and teachings. One of the most prolific sources of misunderstanding has sprung thru the ignorance of Western translators of the true meaning of the Sanskrit terms. The Sanskrit language is the study of a lifetime, the most scientifically constructed and most comprehensive language mankind has ever produced, and the root language of all Aryan tongues. "Who knows my grammar, knows God," said Panini, the great ancient Sanskrit grammarian, and indeed anyone who has fully mastered Sanskrit possesses also the knowledge of all arts, sciences and philosophy, so intertwined are they with the construction of Sanskrit.

This barrier of language, then, confronts those enthusiastic Western brothers who would draw inspiration from the deep bottomless wells of Hindu Scriptures to give them to their Western peoples. So they have to depend on the often-mistaken English translations of Hindu scriptures. Without a thorough knowledge of the Sanskrit language and root meanings of the words, it is sheer madness on the part of anyone, Oriental or Occidental, to attempt to translate from the Sanskrit depositories of knowledge.

Mistaken Translations

It is appalling to contemplate the translations that some western brothers have made of Patanjali's famous "Yoga Aphorisms" and of the "Bhagavad Gita." They have made blunders, minor and major, to such an extent as to often give the exact contrary meaning to passages in the scriptures. To what confusion and chaos such mistaken translations have led, can be traced by the idea, prevalent among large classes of Westerners, that Eastern teachings are "dangerous" and "intended only for Eastern followers."

Thus I find, that although our Theosophical brothers have done a great deal of good in the world thru awakening an interest in the West in the literature and philosophy of India, yet some of them, thru their utter ignorance or very partial knowledge of Sanskrit, have created much panic and wrong ideas in the minds of Westerners by giving the impression, thru their entirely wrong translations of certain Sanskrit passages, that danger results from such practices as rousing of the Kundalini, meditation and other forms of inner development.

Theosophical Misconceptions

Such erroneous ideas have spread like wildfire, especially among Theosophical groups. It is a spiritual crime to frighten people away from spiritual practices and spiritual teachers, for therein lies the path out of the maze of life into eternal salvation, which no amount of mere intellectual understanding nor reading of the scriptures will do. Without meditation and spiritual discipline and definite following of certain technique laid down by the great ancient teachers of India, it is impossible to achieve union with the divine. To frighten people away, therefore, from such practices as given them by a qualified spiritual guide, is to mislead them and hamper their evolutionary progress.

Of course, casual travelers to India, and the general run of newspaper writers, cannot be expected to understand anything about these things, any more than they understand such things as Einstein's theory of Relativity or the theory of music. However, while they do not presume to foist their ideas on the public about Einstein and the theory of music, yet many of them do not let their lack of knowledge about spiritual subjects deter them from exhibiting their abysmal ignorance in that direction to the public.

True and False Students

The result of Hindu teachings should be judged by its influence on faithful disciples who have incorporated those teachings into their daily lives and who therefore stand as a witness to the power of such teaching to transform the whole of life. The results of Hindu teachings cannot be judged haphazardly form any stray individual who has happened to read a book on the subject or to take a class for a week from some Hindu teacher. Every organization, every spiritual group, lodge, church or temple has had experience with some abnormal neurotic, unbalanced individual, suffering from hallucinations, who joins it movement and then attempts to represent that teaching to the outside world, creating misunderstanding and commotion. Though such an individual professes himself a staunch follower of the particular teaching he has elected to join, yet as a matter of fact he knows nothing about it and pursues his own hallucinations, sometimes to the point of craziness.

No Causal Relation

The fallacy of post hoc ergo propter hoc (because after this, therefore on account of this) can be illustrated in the following way:

The clock was about to strike twelve. Someone said, "When I clap my hands, the clock will strike twelve." A man suffering with cancer of the stomach, went on a whole wheat bread diet. He died soon after, and a great hue and cry was raised against the eating of whole wheat bread. In these two instances, there was no causal relation between the clap of the hand, and the clock striking twelve, or in the eating of the whole wheat bread and the death of the man. However, to a superficial and thoughtless observer, it might appear that there was causal relation between them. Similarly, there is no causal relation between Eastern teachings and the crazy outbursts of fanatics and neurotics who profess to follow those teachings. The craziness exists in the mind of the individual and is caused by his own wrong actions in the past. No uplifting spiritual study can possibly produce craziness, but on the contrary, can and does restore unbalanced persons to sanity. The practice of Yogoda has cured many people of unbalanced and neurotic conditions. The worse form of craziness is to maintain that spiritual study and practice are injurious. Since all forms of consciousness are unbalanced, i.e., not the ideal state of perfect equilibrium, it follows then that it is far more beneficial to himself and to mankind for a person to be crazy bout God than about money, fame and pleasure as most people are.

Without intelligence, it is impossible to understand anything properly in this life. People should judge everything on its own merits and not on baseless assertions nor second-hand opinions. If one does not make an effort to know truth, to discover her beneath the veils that cover her, then one will never know his own real nature and will be the sport of outside forces and the slave of circumstance always. Contempt for anything, without investigation, is the sign of a deluded man who will come to grief.

Practice is Essential

One phase of Eastern teachings that should be stressed is that they can never be wholly comprehended unless one practices them regularly in his daily life after receiving them from a real teacher of actual God-realization. Otherwise, it is a case of the blind leading the blind. The great light that leads from the dark world of matter into the celestial powers of divinity, are not lightly bestowed nor lightly won, and no effort is too great to find the way and to follow it.

Those Western authors who write on the danger of awakening the Kundalini (coiled life-force at the base of the spine) and other Hindu teachings, are the last ones to know what they are talking about, having never practiced the proper exercises nor been instructed by a qualified Hindu teacher. They sound their erroneous warnings against Eastern teachings in order to offer, instead, their own Western-diluted Eastern teachings.

Many western brothers there are, who are enthusiastic to become teachers and interpreters of Eastern philosophies. To them I would say, that they will find more spiritual upliftment and insight into the truth of life, and more direct answers from the divine source within themselves, by one hour daily of meditation and Kundalini practice as taught them by a qualified Hindu guru, than they would get from twelve hours of daily reading of the scriptures.

Most would-be teachers of Eastern philosophy simply read the translations of Hindu scriptures, attempting to understand their meaning according to the measure of their own limited intelligence, and then, after entirely omitting the practical art of scriptural realization thru meditation (the only means of true comprehension of eternal principles) thru mental laziness, they try to teach others about Eastern truths.

Since meditation and concentration have been a highly developed art in India for some ages, ambitious Western brothers ought to sit at the feet of a qualified Hindu guru for a time before they consider themselves ready to offer their opinion to the world on the subject of Eastern teachings and the worth of Eastern spiritual practices.

Truth Not Eastern Nor Western

Truth is neither Eastern nor Western—it is the inalienable property of every soul that draws the breath of life. That is the true meaning of the equality of man—not the social nor political nor economic equality that many people often wrongly imagine will someday arrive, but the equality of every soul before God, the equality to seek Him and know Him.

Truth, however, must have a form and an individualized expression on this plane. It must express itself thru something, some material medium. They are mistaken who are prejudiced against any spiritual truth because it has an Eastern label. Label it must have, just as the infinite ocean must take the shape of the bowl it is put into, but neither label nor bowl can change the inherent quality of truth. Put it into what form one may, it shines thru as the same One Eternal Truth. "Lofty its declaration, sublime its aspirations, pure and tender its piety," Sir Edwin Arnold says of the Bhagavad Gita. What matter whether its message is called Bhagavad Gita or the doctrines of the apostle Paul? Would not its aspirations still be sublime, its piety pure? In eagerness to criticize the form or source of truth, many seekers fail to grasp the meaning of the message which alone is of any worth.

Modern Forms of Ancient Wisdom

The progress of Christian Science in the West is due to the fact that it is based on the great spiritual truth of the superiority of mind over matter. This glorious regenerative spiritual law, introduced in a new Christian form, is the same ancient principle known to the Hindu sages and all great teachers throughout the ages. Mrs. Mary Baker Eddy was acquainted with Hindu Vedanta philosophy and used quotations from the Bhagavad Gita in the earlier editions of her book "Science and Health." The Rosacrucian and Theosophist and many other spiritual movements in the West draw heavily from Hindu sources for inspiration. The greatest poet-philosophers of America, Emerson and Walt Whitman, were devout students of the Bhagavad Gita. Many of the most profound students of philosophy in Europe and America have not hesitated to humbly admit, like Schopenhauer, that "the Upanishads uphold me in life and death."

The East and the West must realize and be thankful for their mutual interdependence and need for each other. Thru the modern methods of quick transportation and communication, the nations of the world are now only a stone's throw from one another. It largely depends on their attitude now, whether they are going to concentrate on one another's differences and faults, and shatter one another with explosions of misunderstanding and hatred, or whether they will utilize their closeness as an opportunity for constructive exchange of their best national qualities.

Cause of War

Hate, unjust criticism, provincialism, religious bigotry, selfish commercial "patriotism," superiority-complex of being a ruling nation, race consciousness, color and class prejudices, unwise immigration laws and conscienceless journalism are the real ammunitions of war and self-destruction. God never has to employ miracles to kill the evil-doers—they fight and kill themselves by civil and racial wars and rejoice in doing so.

No nation is perfect. Even the most civilized land contains enough evil in its slums and criminal classes to appall the world. Any "literary" Westerner who feels the impulse to "expose" the faults or wrong conditions in some other land, such as India, should first reflect that he can find enough material in the slums of any large Western city to put Dante's Inferno to shame. Throwing mud gets one nowhere, and can be prolonged indefinitely on both sides. All the dark spots of the earth can be cleared up by mutual cooperation and loving help among the peoples of the world, and nothing else will suffice.

Truth is Invincible

False news travels with the wind, but truth has the power to travel against the wind.

I have my good-will always toward those error-stricken, misguided ones who seek to blacken India's name and India's philosophy in the eyes of the world. Jesus was crucified for doing good, and all spiritual teachers must be prepared to bear the trials that will come to them. Judas was the cause of bringing Jesus' message to the attention of the whole world. The enemies of India's immortal light of truth cannot dim its lustre nor withdraw its regenerative influence from the lives of those who seek it. The narrow-spirited critics of India and the concerted efforts of yellow journalists can never destroy the indestructible heritage of the sages of ancient India. Such critics will themselves see the true light someday and repent, like Paul, of their former persecution of a message that does ill to no man and good to all.

Mankind has only one real enemy—Ignorance. Let us all work together for its destruction, helping and cheering one another along the way.

Paramhansa Yogananda

THE RIGHTEOUS BATTLE

I never understood
Why for doing good
Christ was crucified.
For giving love, he met great hate,
For giving life, ah death he met.
I ne'er dreamt for doing good
He could be crucified!
He had no foes—
But could not help
If some did think
They had to be his foes.
Some die for fame,
Some die for lust,
Some die for golden dust,
But all must die.
The why not die as Jesus did—
Die, O, never to die again!
To cure dark hate with golden love
He died to live again.
To hate those who hate us,
To love those who love us,
Is the common mortal way
But to love those who love us not
Is by immortals sought.
Those who hated and fought
Unworthily died.

Balancing East-West

Jesus died for love,
He lives in human-hearted shrines forever.
Elder brothers who culture love
From Divine Mother above
Deal lovingly
With revengeful younger brothers
steeped in error
Who seek fault where no fault is.
Deal lovingly
But fight the righteous battle
With love in heart
To shatter their error apart.
But one must master love
Before he can battle righteously.
Battle for Truth,
Battle with love—
Not for victory,
Not for shaming others,
But to show
That Truth must reign
In spite of all.

SHADOWS

Beds of flowers,
Or vales of tears,
Dewdrops on the buds of roses,
Myriads misers of desert sand,
The little running joys of childhood,
The stampede of wild passions,
The ebbing eddies of laughter,
The drooping petals of hopes,
The haunting melancholy of disease,
The will-o-the-wisp of our desire,
Leading on from mire to mire,
The octopus grip of self-complacency
And time-beaten habits,
The first-born joyous cry of a babe,
And the last groan of death,
Are but shadows seen
On the Cosmic mental screen.
These are but shadows,
Yet they have, O, many shades!
There are dark shadows
And there are light shadows.
So even shadows may entertain.

SPIRITUALIZING THE NEWSPAPERS

"Blessed are those who do not indulge in sensational news."

Millions start the day with the gruesome sight of murder headlines in the morning newspapers. The sleep-refreshed young mentality starts the day's race for success with the dark cloud of wrong thoughts hanging over his mind. The law of "All's well that starts well" is trampled upon.

Newspapers have more or less become the tin gods worshipped by the mass mind. They can make or unmake a man, at least in the public eye. Human opinion, however, and God's opinion are different. One forsaken by all humanity may not be forsaken by the God of Truth. One worshipped by all the world may not be true to himself. He may not be acceptable in the eyes of Truth. It is the duty of truth-loving people to reform the newspapers since they almost completely control unthinking, child-like mentalities.

Modern journalism originated in the desire of man to know all about his fellow man and about his environment. The busy man looks at a paper and at a glance knows in what relation his business and social affairs stand with the community. Newspapers are the gods of information. They are the soul of modern business. They are the epitome of the city news. The modern world cannot get along without them. They can act as the breath of life to noble human activities or they can react like chlorine gas to asphyxiate people's independent thinking. Through the sluice-gates of newspapers the reservoir of human mentalities is constantly fed. That is why a truth-loving country should keep a strict eye on the operation of these gates through which the river of information flows into the public mind. Muddy and defiled water must not be allowed in when clean and sparkling streams are available.

Freedom of the press must respect the law by which true freedom can alone exist. Intoxicated with the wine of freedom, some newspapers often abuse their powers. They often do not know how to operate the gates of information. They have not learned how to exercise self-control and thus prevent the wild river of muddled information from overrunning and clogging the tank of human mentalities. Moreover, newspapers ought not to introduce poisonous news into the tank of human minds, for the thirsty, undiscriminative masses drink poisonous, unwholesome news wherever they find it and hence suffer with nervousness, worry, fear, and subconscious criminal suggestions.

Criminal Suggestions

In a few minutes a newspaper prints the headline: "Four hold-up men cleaned up a million. No trace of the robbers found." The weak and poverty-stricken, or criminally-bent mentality reads it and induces a few friends to join him to try to get rich quick by this unholy method. Unwholesome news whets the appetite for crime. Hold-ups at the point of the gun with the aid of automobiles were unknown in many parts of the world until the idea was unwittingly introduced into the minds of weak mentalities through the channels of western newspapers and movies. That is why sensational movies and newspapers should be gradually crowded out by educating the tastes of children and adults to a higher standard.

Some newspapers and some film producers, in order to be the best sellers of the day, vie with one another in breaking all gates of propriety, morality, purity, and truth in order to overflood and devastate human mentalities with their sensationalism. In order to reform sensational movies and newspapers we must first reform ourselves and our children. "Catering-ism" is the watchword in everything in America. Business, religion, lectures, all must be made to suit what is called "public demand." That is wrong, unless the demand is wholesome. If people want to eat cocaine, opium, cobra poison, or to indulge in a flattering religion which is afraid to even constructively criticize, or to hear only those lectures which gloss over and explain away their faults, should the business men, religious leaders and lecturers reason, let us give the people what they want, let us sell them poison, flattery and untruth, let us thus kill their souls and choke their mentalities of progress, it doesn't matter since we are getting rich? No right-thinking man would want society to be run along such lines. The law of honesty should be the policy of newspapers, movie concerns, business men, religious leaders and reformers. They should only cater to the wholesome taste of people. That will bring out the latent good taste even in apparently lost souls who have artificially developed a bad taste for good things.

Who is responsible if the described-in-detail crime news, murder headlines and indirect divorce suggestions begin to influence and mould the clay mentalities of children, burning and hardening them into fixed habit-thoughts of evil? Is not sensationalism responsible for taking a large part in suggesting crime to children and to weak mentalities? Let us save the masses from the drug of sensationalism. Let us have more newspapers with aims and platforms like the Christian Science Monitor and a few other American papers who are trying to be fair and constructive. The New York World has a "Department of Accuracy and Fair Play" which investigates and gives publicity to cases of false and unjust publicity. This is a step in the right direction.

Murdering Reputations

Some newspapers have grown bold and despotic in order to be the best sellers. They don't stop at anything. They libel a man, writing half-truths or evading the true facts about him, just for the sake of sensationalism. They give head-lines to scandalize him, and syndicate their news, for most papers take it and swallow it wholesale. They murder a man's life-long-earned reputation in a few minutes and go scot free, laughing. If the person is exonerated and the time for retraction comes, no more headlines. Most of the papers hide behind indifference, do not print the retraction, saying it has no news interest. If they do print it, they give it an insignificant place. If the man sues in court for libel, the process is endless and expensive, and some newspapers even encourage this as a publicity stunt. They employ the best attorneys to fight the libel case. If they lost some money they make up their losses by printing more sensational head-lines like the following: "Reverend John Denies He Was a Bandit and Criminal." The unthoughtful people are led to buy the papers out of curiosity and thus unknowingly patronize injustice. Some religionists will then raise a hue and cry and say, "Oh, don't sue the papers; that's against Christ's principles." That's a fine view, but why not root out the evil instead of allowing it to grow to be later endured by Christ principles?

Many people will remember the case in London a few years ago of "Mr. A.," Hari Singh of Kashmir, who was blackmailed by a woman and her accomplices. Under threat of blackmail and of newspaper headlines of scandal, the woman and her accomplices extracted seven hundred thousand dollars form the Prince. Later on we hear that the Prince told of this unfortunate experience to one of the English judges. The judge felt a righteous indignation and began to move heaven and earth to break the net of blackmailers who prey upon wealthy or noted people, public men and great ministers by falsely scandalizing them and extracting money from them on threat of newspaper head-lines. Thus we hear a law was passed in England by which all cases of blackmail involving noted persons are heard behind closed doors without the presence of newspaper men. When a case of this kind is settled, only a short correct report is given to the newspapers. No mention is ever made of the nature of the charge if the blackmailed man is found guiltless. Should not America enact such laws and safeguard the lives of public men and women which consist in their reputation? Besides, the English newspapers are very conservative and make thorough investigation before passing any remarks about a public man. The English libel laws are very strict and rigidly enforced, which is far from being the case in America.

No Public Man Is Safe

From a thorough study of the situation of public life in America, I am of the opinion that the reputation of no public man is safe from being wrongly newspaper-handled. Many newspapers try to create prejudice against individuals and nations to suit their nefarious ends of narrow, bigoted, short-sighted political views. Bad-motived newspapers, lecturers, books, movies and magazines can let loose all the messengers of evil—racial hatred, seeds of war, prejudice, too strict immigration laws based on pure injustice or political inequality or racial and color prejudice, gossip, scandal, love of criminal news, and thrills by the suffering of others. Such newspapers, instead of teaching Christ-love which promises forgiveness and spiritual help even to Mary Magdalenes, just try to foster intolerance and revengefulness, self-deception, and persecution of others for a fault which the persecutors themselves do not try to get rid of or sometimes for no fault at all.

Some syndicating news agencies at times make wholesale productions of lies and baseless scandals. I have studied and examined so many cases of untruthful exaggerations, whipped and bluffed untruths, that I wonder how the Sunday sheets of some papers containing sensational news can continue to exist.

However, one hardly ever sees any contradictions made by the persons persecuted. Why is this? I hear there is an unwritten law among some newspapers that when they are sued for libel they keep silent about it and that news is not syndicated. Since they control public opinion they don't want to turn the wrathful spot-lights of public opinion on themselves, whereas they rejoice when they turn those furious burning lights on some innocent person. Most papers gloat at the prospect of scandalizing someone. They are too ready and willing to use the materials cunningly supplied by blackmailers, but often quite unwilling to print retractions and save the reputation of innocent people from being murdered at the hands of evil publicity. Do Christian newspapermen consider this is right?

The Remedy

Seeing this condition of evil present amongst some conscienceless sensation-loving newspapers, I have a suggestion to make. Let the leading business men, ministers, and worthy public men of each city come together to form a board for educating the newspapers. Any public man or society scandalized by any unscrupulous newspaper or syndicate of newspapers should be invited to state its case and give positive proofs of newspaper untruth or false insinuations, to the above-mentioned board. Let the board members investigate and, when the person or society is found to have been attacked without adequate grounds, let them write or visit the mischief-making newspaper publishers and editors and exercise their powerful influence to make the newspapers give the same amount of space, kinds of type, position and page to the retraction as they gave to the attack. The city fathers should also write to the syndicating news agencies requesting them to print retractions for maligned persons. The syndicates and local newspapers should be made to consult the members of the above-mentioned board before printing any scandal about a prominent man or society. Last of all the newspapers must be taught by the board to respect others' freedom as they love their own.

Freedom of the press to print anything it chooses about anybody by writing in a clever insinuating way and distorting the truth should be accompanied by the freedom of giving the persons criticized a chance to reply in the same way. It is cowardly to attack a defenseless, forcibly-made-voiceless person. The same page, position, kind of types and forcible language used to criticize a person should be used in printing the reply of the person criticized if he so desires. There should be no putting off of the retraction or explanation by saying the news is old and uninteresting.

I once heard an account of a conversation between a reporter and an editor about a Peace Conference. The editor listened with disgust and obvious lack of interest in his eyes as the reporter related how smoothly the Peace Conference went along. At last the editor said, "Go put that news in ten lines of small type on the last inside page of the paper." The reporter realizing that he had not brought news of interest suddenly remembered a little incident which took place in the Peace Conference and exclaimed, "Sir, the President of the Peace Conference lost his temper in suppressing a crazy man who was saying irrelevant things and trying to disturb the Conference." The editor quickly turned to the reporter, his face beaming with the joy of evil smiles, and said, "Get busy, put headlines on the front page, 'The President of the Peace Conference Loses Peace'."

If some newspapers want to make half truths or exaggerated truths sensational they should make the real truth prominent and interesting too.

A Friend's Suggestion

A sincere friend of mine, Mr. Telford Groesbeck, a prominent citizen of Cincinnati, once said to me, "Please tell the newspapers in your lectures that we do not want the murder and scandal headlines at all. If they still think that some of the public need it or are interested in it, let them print about murders, arsons, divorces and gossip on a loose page and let them make the letters on that page as big and blood-red in color as they want, calling it 'Red Scandal Page.' When these newspapers are sent into good homes like ours let them be sent without that 'Red Scandal Page,' thus saving our children and homes from being infected with such destructive thoughts."

Half truths and distorted truths are worst than the blackest of lies. They are very hard to fight. Yet I believe that though evil travels with the wind, nevertheless truth has the power to travel against the wind. Catering to evil tastes will precipitate more evil, disorder, inharmony and suffering into society, and since newspapers are universally read by people, they should act like wholesome, reforming parents and not like murderers who secretly stab those who seek their protection. Of all social crimes, the crime of press distortion and giving prominence to scandals is of the most unfathomable harm to the rising world generation. Let us all by moral persuasion, love, determination and practical measures reform the newspapers and rid them of their epidemic of sensationalism.

Jesus and all world-teachers taught us to sympathize with and help people in error, whereas sensationalism creates the desire to rejoice in others' shortcomings. Christian newspapers that have sinned and indulged in sensationalism should repent and cease from further blunders. Let us spiritualize the newspapers. Let the morning and evening papers carry headlines on the front page containing the brave sayings of Jesus or the great prophets. Let men, women and children wake up beholding words of truth. Let them sleep, dreaming thoughts of restful, peace-giving truth and lasting joy celestial that dwells within them.

Paramhansa Yogananda

MOTHER'S EYES

I sought those two black eyes everywhere.
When my teacher or my brother rebuked me
Or were unkind,
I sought help every day
In the sweetness of those two black eyes.
In the harbor of those two black eyes,
I sought refuge.
She died. I cried, and I sought in the stars,
In the darkness of the night
For those two black eyes,
But I found them not.
Many other black eyes shone upon my childhood
But they were not those two black eyes
Which I had loved.
In the stillness of the forest
And the darkness of the night
I used to watch under the stars,
Watching in the darkness,
Looking for those two angelic,
Unapproachable black eyes,
But I found them not.
Now that my mind is awakened, I see
Those two black eyes everywhere.
In the eyes of the Divine Mother
I have found my own mother.
In the love of the Divine Mother
I have found my mother's love.

THE SCREEN OF LIFE

When roses bloom
And the dawn breaks the spell of darkness.
When fortune laughs
And praise weaves garlands
And glory makes the crown,
When little pleasures all dance around thee
When fickle festivity sings
The birth of a new born babe
In future sure to die,
When everyone shouts thy praises
And thousands follow,
You see His hands of showering blessings.
Yet there is a silent budding joy in every twig,
In the leafless limbs of the rosebush
O'er the snow;
There is a joy in waiting
For the streak of dawn in the darkness.
Through vapours of sorrow dim
Joy is seen with welcome.
Persecution sweetens long-tasted praise;
A bare head expectant of the crown
Has joy denied the head long-crowned.
The dance of darkness
Around each little flame of joy
Makes it burn brighter.
In monotony's mine lies buried

Paramhansa Yogananda

The caged air of bursting festivity;
Old age thrills with the thought of youth;
Behind the veil of death
Hides the promise of new life.
Behind the shifting scenes of life
The real life hides;
Behind the screen
Of unreal changing pictures of things seen
Lies the real drama of stable, unseen, cosmic life.
Shadows are lined with light
Sorrows bulge with joy
Failures are filled with determination of success;
All cruelties urge us to be kind.
Passing mirth, fame, wealth,
Proud possessions given
Only to be taken away again,
And the straw fire of passions, joys
And intoxicating friendship
Oft do hide Thee.
But when all are gone we look for Thee—
In solitude by friends and foes avoided
There's One unseen Who ne'er forsakes;
He may fly
When everyone shakes hand with thee—
When there's none
He may come to take thy hand.

THE PRESENCE by E. Charles
Reviewed by Swami Yogananda

I wish to recommend to all my students and to the public in general this book by E. Charles. It is extremely interesting, bringing out the most profound truths in a simple, readable and entertaining manner. It uniquely weaves deep mysticism with an absorbing love-story. I enjoyed it immensely, for it held my attention and interest on every page. It is a beautiful story of Ideal Love and Truth. Everyone should read it. The deep underlying meaning of many mysterious passages in the Bible is explained in a fascinating way.

The author says in the Foreword: "The human brain operates on much the same principle as the radio. If the electrical energies (the life forces) of the individual are largely lifted into the brain for regeneration, the potential range, or area, of the brain easily embraces the Fourth Dimension—the Super-planes, Powers and Bliss of the Higher Consciousness. (Those who know the highest type of Marriage have little grossness to overcome.) If the electrical energies of the individual are largely dissipated in selfish, worldly pursuits, speaking in radio parlance, the brain only picks up 'local happenings'."

This remarkable and engrossing story will be a wonderful inspiration to those seeking spiritual enlightenment as well as to those wishing to while away a happy hour in reading an interesting novel.

PRAYER FOR TABLE BLESSING

Heavenly Spirit, receive this food—
Make it holy.
Let not the impurities of my thought
In any way defile it.
It is for Thy temple.
Spirit to Spirit goes.

TWO RECIPES April 1928

Spiritual Recipe

Judge no one save thyself. Clean thy own mental house. Seeing thee, many others will be inspired to clean their own houses.

Look not for thy spiritual flower every day. Sow thy seed, water it with prayer and right endeavor, and when the sprout will come, busy thyself with the health of thy plant, picking out the weeds of doubt, indecision and laziness. Some morning you will suddenly behold thy long-looked-for spiritual flower of realization!

The Satan of the spiritual path has claws of bad habits, in which he tightly holds his victims to the rut of sense pleasures, away from the joys of eternal life. Do not be tempted by this Satan to forget God and your daily meditation. On the altar of prayer and meditation, lay your offering daily to God, and soon the Satan of bad habits will have no power over you. Before your strength, his hold will weakly relax. There is hidden strength within you to overcome all obstacles and temptations. Bring forth that indomitable power and energy!

Food recipe

Coconut

Grate a fresh coconut fine. Mix it with one cup of cream whipped with the yolk of an egg. This is an excellent substitute for meat in strength-giving qualities.

Egg-Plant

Sliced egg-plants slowly baked in the oven, covered with a little tomato sauce, make a delicious and healthful dish.

Whole Wheat Grains

Whole wheat grains, mixed with a little honey, and topped with whipped cream, is a meal in itself.

Eat less, chew well. Think not of your taste alone, but of your health. Summer is coming; eat fruits plentifully. Walk or run daily. Bathe daily. Avoid starches. Life can be much simplified by a simple diet. The time saved can be used on better things than catering to the body.

Paramhansa Yogananda

WATCHING THE COSMIC MOTION PICTURE OF LIFE

In this hall of life, we are all moving picture actors as well as movie fans. We entertain, inspire, and instruct others with the show of our experiences, and we ourselves watch the ever-changing interesting pictures of other lives.

The pictures of various events are filmed in the east, west, north and south. The various nations with their strange and colorful actings of diverse customs, traditions and occupations amid varying scenic and climatic environments, offer infinitely rich and inexhaustible material for producing life-films of ever-new interest.

Educational, sensational, comical, saddening and inspiring pictures are taken by the mind-camera of the average man, every day, anytime, anywhere. There are many comic films in life. Inspiring scenes help us when we behold the unrolled film of lives of great men and great adventurers like Lincoln, Gandhi, Lindbergh, Byrd, Emerson and thousands of other unique personalities, as well as the heroic figures of the religious teachers of the world, like Jesus, Buddha, Zoroaster, Confucius, Mohammed, Krishna and others.

We watch, moved and entertained, the mental movie pictures as filmed in Shakespearean tragedies and other great dramatic writings, in the house of our imagination. The pictures of world events, daily facts, evoked by our newspapers, hold our passing interest. the pictures of others' sufferings bring a tear, a determination to help them. Thru their sorrow, we find our own joy in helping them. The gods sympathize with and entertain themselves with the joy of helping mortals. If they cried, and became identified with the tears of others, they could not render help. For sorrow increases sorrow, which can only be diminished and healed thru contact with the potent salve of unshakable happy minds. Hence in watching tragic mistakes or misfortunes of other lives or of our own, we should feel only tears of joy because of our ability and absolute power to help. There cannot be room for the dark disturbing emotion of grief in children made in the likeness of God.

Balancing East-West

Individuals who are highly nervous, or who are suffering with the malady of melancholia, or anemic pessimism, or who are stricken with spells of despair at the approach of the least difficulties of life—these do not profit by watching the pictures of tragedy in other lives. They will have fainting spells; they cannot thus learn the lesson of the result of wrong behavior and thus desist from error, nor can they render help to those who are suffering, since they themselves are not free from suffering.

Thus, one must be thoroughly prepared mentally to profitably watch the motion picture of the tragedy of trying experiences in others' lives, in order to be able to render help in making others look upon life as only a picture for our entertainment and instruction.

The great wars of Europe and Asia, the natural cataclysms of earthquakes and floods, the famines, prosperous eras, influence of world-saints, statesmen and villains, the work of the colossal geniuses of the ages—the poets, business men, writers, courageous reformers, great lovers and heroes—these events and these natures all played their parts in the studio of the centuries.

Everything took time, everything seemed to last long to the consciousness of man. Each life seemed almost unending, each great event was all-absorbing, but when the Director of life called "Cut!" the film was over. The greatest lives, the complex knotted existences, the whole history of nations, your life and mine, past, present and future (if we could but see), which seem to drag on minutely, surely, slowly, could nevertheless be filmed and each life shown in a couple of hours. One's life, lived thru a hundred years, seems so long-drawn-out when taken thru the slow mental camera, but with the fast camera of true retrospection, one sees the whole panorama at a glance.

Is this life a movie show? The millions of geologic years, the constellations of heaven, the floating vapors, atomic combinations, earth materials, oceans, continents, nations and their histories, millions of births and the almost complete change by death every hundred years of all the earth's inhabitants, the various great intellectual, spiritual and material civilizations, their rise and fall—with this background, we can see all life as a vast ever-changing, ever-new, ever-entertaining mighty film in the hall of introspection. This life is a Paramount picture, shown in serials and by installments, infinitely interesting, ever-fresh, ever-stirring, ever-complex. The master minds and world-changing men like Jesus, Buddha, Socrates, Asoka, Mohammed, Caesar, William the conqueror, Darwin, Copernicus, Galileo, Newton and many other outstanding pioneers and leaders, are the great stars of the motion picture productions, who command universal attention from their audiences.

The picture of life must be always different to be interesting. One does not want to see the same comedies of lives or the same Pathe news of prosaic facts or the same tragedies of harrowing or gruesome experiences, all the time. One wants variety and can hardly bear to see the same picture twice. That is why the Great Director of the motion picture of life keeps everything changing. You cannot drink twice from the same running water, you cannot watch the same event twice. The water passes by; the events change; you are not now the same man as you were a second ago—your thoughts have changed, your sum total is in a different proportion.

Why not then take life simply as a motion picture show? To do that, you must steel your mind against sorrow. You must be prepared for variety. You must be a motion picture player, an entertainer, as well as one of the audience, in watching your own and others' pictures. While playing the part of combating disease, or fighting failures, or undergoing accidents, or enduring the trials of life, you must know you are just playing a part.

Just as an actor in the moving pictures is untouched by the sorrow he has to depict in his characters, so must you remain untouched by the changing pictures of inevitable misfortune, sickness, sudden failure and unforeseen obstacles in life. Sickness, failure and grief are so simply by the relative standards of human consciousness. A disciplined consciousness, united to cosmic consciousness, never inwardly experiences sickness or suffering or failure. As God's children, we are always perfect and we must recover that consciousness by wisdom and true understanding of the meaning of life and its problems.

Care not if you are not the principal player in the movies of life. No movie picture is made up of only one player or one event. Your part in playing, if short or obscure, is yet very important, for without you the picture of life is incomplete. In the Universal Director's eyes, he who plays his life's part well, whatever that may be, is made a star to shine in His immortal galaxy.

Our troubles mostly spring from not knowing what our parts are. This results from not developing our innate intuitive soul-faculties. Rouse the all-feeling, all-seeing Wisdom by regular meditation, and find your part. Then you must play or watch your own playing or the playing of others, be it the Pathe news of plain facts or a comedy of errors, or the tragedy of trying experiences, with an inwardly entertained mind. This is no room for pain, grievance or boredom in watching the movie of our own life. The retrospective consciousness of man can play all the noble parts of life joyously, untouched by suffering. These cosmic movies are all for our entertainment.

The great Director of the Motion Picture Company of life is made of Joy. We, as His children, are made in His image of joy. From joy we came, in joy we live, in joy we melt. He brought out this cosmic motion picture to keep Himself entertained. We, having come out of His being, are endowed with the same quality of superconsciousness by which we can watch the pictures of life, of birth, death and world events with the same divinely enjoying spirit. You watch a tragedy in a motion picture house, and when it is over, you say, "O, it was a fine picture!" So must you be able to look upon the pictures of trials of your own life and say, "O, my life is interesting with troubles and difficulties to be overcome. These are all my stimulants to show me my errors and help me to assume the right mental attitude by which I can watch with joy the fascinating spectacle of life."

The consciousness of man is made of God and is pain-proof. All physical and mental sufferings come by identification, imagination, and wrong human habits of thinking. We have to travel along the labyrinthine path of life, visiting many motion picture houses of varied experience, entering them with the consciousness of being entertained and instructed. Then life and death will be watched with an unchangeable, joyous consciousness. Our consciousness we will find to be one with cosmic consciousness. And with our cosmic consciousness, unchanged by the human waking of birth or the sleep of death, we will watch the Cosmic Motion Picture with perennial, ever-new Joy.

Review of The Creative East (by J. W. T. Mason)

A close study of the three great Eastern nations—India, China and Japan—has revealed to the author of this book not only their similarities but their striking differences. In what way each of these countries is competent to instruct the West, in exchange for the fruit of knowledge from the creative genius of Western peoples, is the thoughtful and stimulating theme of this scholarly little book.

Man cannot satisfy the cravings of his many-sided nature, Mr. Mason points out, without development of three modes of expression—utilitarianism, aestheticism and spirituality. To seek one fulfillment at the expense of the other two is to court disaster and eventual stagnation. The beauty of utilitarianism, as put forward by the West, is that it "permits man to subdue matter to his will," and to "create machine power to replace the drudgery of man power." Without incorporating this knowledge and practice into their national lives, Eastern peoples, according to the true reasoning of Mr. Mason, will not realize the full achievement and purpose of life.

The West, in its turn, tiring of a too marked interest in materialism, or the objects of creation, can discipline its soul and satisfy its spiritual hunger by developing its aesthetic power and spiritual perception, its intuitive sense of oneness with its Infinite Source. In the latter domain of wisdom, India stands supreme, the teacher of the ages. China's special genius is aestheticism, the cult of creativeness, the interest in the process of creation rather than in the created object. Her love of beauty, art, and propriety or social adjustments, is China's distinct contribution to the true wealth of nations.

Mr. Mason, pointing out where the almost exclusive interest that India gave to mystical science, and China to aestheticism, to the detriment of utilitarian progress, constituted their weakness, as unalloyed materialism may prove the nemesis of the West, speaks of Japan as the one country in all modern history who has been able, with some degree of success, to combine the three factors of harmonious life—utilitarian, aesthetic and spiritual development. Signs are not wanting, however, that China and India are rising to new life under the spur of Western and Japanese example and high material achievement. The West, also, is coming more and more to drink from the founts of inner spiritual wisdom that have sustained India thru so many centuries.

This little book contains many striking thoughts of true value. The soul of India, China and Japan is better revealed in these few pages than in many a weighty tome.

TWO RECIPES June 1928

Spiritual Recipe—(Interpretation of Gita)

The following is a spiritual interpretation of Chapter 6, verse I, of the Bhagavad Gita (Song of the Spirit).

Anastritah (not desiring) karma-phalam (fruit of action) karyam-karma (dutiful actions) karoti (performs) jah (who) sa (he) sannyasee (man of renunciation) cha (as well as) yogee (one who is united to God) cha, naw (not) niragnih (he who is without fire) nachakriyah (nor he who is inactive).

Sir Edwin Arnold has translated the above in his "Song Celestial" as follows:

> "Therefore, who doeth work rightful to do,
> Not seeking gain from work, that man, O Prince!
> Is Sanyasi and Yogi—both in one.
> And he is neither who lights not the flame
> Of sacrifice, nor setteth hand to task."

The above stanza outlines the middle path between the two extremes to which humanity gravitates in its march on the spiritual path. Complete renunciation of worldly activities is unpractical, for if every man forsakes the world to live in a jungle in search of God, cities would have to be built there or people would die because of lack of sanitation and proper food supplies. The schools of Christian, Hindu, and Buddhist monasticism have served certain good purposes, yet they are not ideal as they have grave weaknesses. They often foster idleness and unpracticality, and lack the trials of worldly struggle. The monasteries have to depend on the men of business for certain necessities and support, so their ideal could not be universal. Besides, outward renunciation of sense-enjoyments, without a corresponding inward renunciation, develops hypocrisy and a greater, though suppressed, attachment to material life. Outward renunciation is only helpful when the inward desire for sense-pleasures is satisfied by finding greater pleasure in God. Renunciation is not an end itself. It is not a method of self-torture. We should forsake objects of smaller consequence when they stand in the way of acquiring more tangible and more lasting spiritual happiness. Jesus renounced his life to acquire life everlasting.

Thus in this stanza, Gita emphasizes renunciation, not of a life in the world but of a selfish worldly life. The emphasis is laid on the renunciation of the fruits of dutiful actions, not on renunciation of actions themselves, as has been generally but erroneously supposed. Without action, life stagnates. Even the Lord is constantly engaged in action. Krishna tells Arjuna in the Gita:

> "Look on me
> Thou son of Pritha! in the three wide worlds
> I am not bound to any toil, no height
> Awaits to scale, no gift remains to gain,
> Yet I act here! and, if I acted not—
> Earnest and watchful—those that look to me
> For guidance, sinking back to sloth again
> Because I slumbered, would decline from good,
> And I should break earth's order and commit
> Her offspring unto ruin!"

Man should share the fruits of his activities and results of ambitions with his family, country, and world. The business man can be a man of renunciation if he earns money with the thought of the happiness of his family and fellow beings, and not just for his own comfort. The man who supports his family just for his own pride and comfort is not a man of renunciation, altho he is a better man than the selfish unmarried man. The man who unites his interests with the interests of humanity and works for humanity as he would for his own family, need not marry, but the man who avoids marriage to avoid responsibilities, is a selfish man and will not find the necessary spurs to achieve his own highest development.

The business man who spiritualizes his ambition by toiling and using his money, not only for his own family but in order to help others, is a man of renunciation. The Gita says that renunciation does not involve loss nor the flying away from worldly activities, but lies in spiritualizing worldly life, by acting for all and God.

Enjoy life with everybody. Include everyone in the circle of your family. Make money for helping others and making them happy, and not only for your own relatives. Gita thus advises one to receive the benefits of a life of renunciation and avoid the evils of selfishness. The consciousness of one who acts for himself becomes body-bound. The consciousness of one who lives for all, becomes one with the Cosmic Consciousness, which is identified with all. Hence, Gita says renunciation means the forsaking of the desire to enjoy one's own fruits of action for self only.

Then again, the other extreme to be avoided is acting all the time, and becoming a business automaton, keeping one's consciousness entangled constantly in the senses and their requirements. Over-activity and indiscriminate activity without reference to the spiritual life, is detrimental to spiritual progress. To perform all actions with the consciousness of fulfillment of a spiritual ideal is spiritual.

Outward renunciation leads to idleness, unpracticality, inactive stagnation. Over-activity makes an automaton of man and makes him forgetful of his highest duty to God. Without God's help, no fulfillment of duty to parents, family or country is possible. Over-activity makes one one-sided. It defeats the very purpose for which one acts, the purpose of self-development. Activity which robs one of joy leads to spiritual inactivity or soul stagnation.

Jesus told his listeners to seek the kingdom of God first and then all the universe of things belonging to Him will come also. This is good counsel for the extraordinary person who can think of nothing but God, and for those nations which are over-gorged with materialism.

But the Gita's saying is especially applicable for life as it is lived today by the average modern man, the business man, the professional man, the housewife, the laborer. The Gita says all actions are not wholesome; they cannot all lead to God. It says, first choose between dutiful and wrong actions. Every man should find the action which he should do, those actions which will harmoniously develop his material life, body, mind, and above all, his heart and soul. The average business and work which most of us find to do in this world is capable of leading to such self-development, provided the man seeks to discover its possibilities and to express them. All honest work is good work. All business that supplies the needs and requirements of mankind can be a work of love. Thru such work, we learn the lessons of service and cooperation, and justify our own existence in this world. The Gita says:

> "He that abstains
> To help the rolling wheels of this great world,
> Glutting his idle sense, lives a lost life,
> Shameful and vain. Existing for himself,
> Self-concentrated, serving self alone,
> No part hath he in aught; nothing achieved,
> Nought wrought or unwrought toucheth him;
> No hope of help for all the living things of earth
> Depends from him.
> Therefore, thy task prescribed
> With spirit unattached gladly perform,
> Since in performance of plain duty man
> Mounts to his highest bliss. By works alone
> Janak and ancient saints reached blessedness!"

Developing in an all-round manner makes right, dutiful actions inevitable. The Gita says, perform those right actions for developing yourself, not for your benefit only but for everyone's welfare. To eat right and live right is to build the temple of soul beautiful. To keep yourself healthy, young and good is to help humanity with the example of health, youth and goodness. To be rich and help others to be rich is to help the failure-stricken with brave thoughts of prosperity and the infinite treasures of earth that await development. Hence, the Gita says, work and be spiritual, not for selfish gains but for the purpose of inspiring others with the example of your life. To keep yourself sick, a failure in mind and soul and material life is to show a bad example to the world, to sow discouragement. The Gita says that such persons who perform actions for all-round development act as heavenly gates opened to invite lost souls back to God's mansion of joy. Gita says such persons are Yogis, are united to God, for they act, not to please themselves, since without Him they are nothing, but to fulfill the demands of truth, progress and God. They are men of renunciation, even though they lie in a palace and have millions, for they forsake the desire to perform actions for their own selfish welfare, and act to help all and to please God. It is not necessary and in most cases not desirable to live the life of a hermit or religious mendicant, to be a man of renunciation.

Gita distinctly says he is not a Yogi or man of renunciation who lives without sacrifice or who is inactive. Acting calmly, ambitiously for all, intelligently, interestingly, vigorously, undiscouragedly, doing right actions for harmonious development of self and of others, is Yoga and renunciation. Inactivity and wrong activity both should be avoided. They prevent the soul from expressing its inner qualities, and stultify it.

He loves God best who acts rightly. It matters not whether he works in the jungle of Hindustan or in the jungle of modern civilization. Both jungles have tests and difficulties. The former has ferocious tigers and the latter even more ferocious worries, temptations and struggles for living for false pleasures. One has to overcome both to gain freedom, to walk in joy, shorn of fear. Find the kingdom of celestial, perpetual happiness within, and heaven will reign in the territory of silence or in the noisy activity of the cities, wherever you may happen to be. God's voice must be heard in the cave of meditation as well as in the mart of modern business.

FOOD RECIPE

Curd Curry

Curd Curry is a good meat substitute. Boil one quart of milk in a double boiler or plain boiler. When the milk bubbles, add the strained juice of one orange and one lemon. Boil the milk until it curdles.

Strain the curd in a cheesecloth. Then bind the cloth tightly with a string. Put a weight on it that the water may run out. Then, after half an hour, cut the solidified curd in small one inch squares one-fourth inch thick. Fry them in butter till they are light brown.

They can be eaten that way, or made into a curry as follows: Take a teaspoonful of curry powder. Mix it with two tablespoonfuls of water. Fry the mixture in a pan with a tablespoonful of butter, until the water evaporates. Then pour one pint of hot water on it. Mix the curry well.

Put one-half pound of French fried potatoes and the fried curd into the curry water. Boil to neutralize the frying. The water will evaporate, leaving a thick gravy. Add a little melted butter and serve.

Paramhansa Yogananda

AFTER THIS

After the prison petals of life fade,
And the soul scent slips
In the mighty wind of life,
No more would I love a flower cage life—
Unless to mingle
The dew-drop tears of other prison souls
With mine
And show them the way ...I freedom won.
I would not mind to dwell in roses,
Daffodils, for a time,
If that is of my own free will.
But forever to stay behind the bars of beauty
Of violet, sun-gold rays, I care not.
I will be no more compelled to live
Even in a golden heavenly cage.
From flower to flower I will fly,
I will wear the blackness of the night,
Shimmering with the busy stars,
I will be the twinkle of their lights,
I will be the waking of the dawn,
And burst forth
With the warming rays of friendship.
I will be the shepherd of stray souls,
Or the humblest lamb in all His fold.
I will be the most famous man,
Or the least unknown of a cycle;
I will be the tiniest spark of light,

Balancing East-West

Or roll as the massive vapours of Life;
I will dash my mighty soul
To wash against the rocks of worldly life.
I will be the clouds, donning rainbow garlands;
I will puff bubbles of planets with my breath,
And float them on waves of space.
I will be the babble of the brook,
And the voice of the nightingale.
As emotion-waves,
I will surge in the sea of souls.
Holding the log of laughter,
I will float to the shores of Bliss.
I will sing through the voices of all,
I will preach through all temples and prayers,
I will love with the love of God,
I will think with the thoughts of all.
The hearts of all will be my heart,
The soul of all will be my soul—
The smile of all—my smile.

OVERCOMING PAIN AND SORROW

Matrashparshastu (the touches of matter and senses, verily) Kaunteya (O Son of Kunti) shitoshnasukha dukhada (produce the thoughts of coldness or warmth, happiness or pain). Agama paenonityah (they come and fade away and are short-lasting). Tan titikshasya Bharata (endure them, thou, O Bharata).—Bhagavad Gita, 2-14.

"Ideas of cold and warmth, pleasure and pain, O son of Kunti, arise from the contact of the senses and matter. They come, fade away and are short-lasting. Endure them thou, O Bharata."

By identifying the Ego with the senses the mind becomes disturbed, for it then cognizes only impermanent experiences; whereas, due to the soul's inner contact, the Ego hides within itself a dormant expectation for permanent equilibrated states of consciousness. The sense-identified Ego becomes deceived when it fixes its expectations on the fickle senses instead of the permanent-joy-giving Soul. So the Gita warns the spiritual aspirant not to get his Soul mixed up with the closely-associated senses, which will make him miserable and forgetful of his innate blessed state. The sensations of heat, cold, pleasure and pain are suggested by the senses and cannot be felt by the Ego if it keeps a strong undisturbed matter-disengaged mind. The word titiksha, or endurance, does not imply one should rashly expose the body to intense cold and heat and thus destroy it. If the body is sense-enslaved and unspiritualized, it should be protected from extremes, while mentally disciplining it to rise above its slavery. It is only when the mind by deep spiritual development realizes its aboveness, that the suggestions of suffering born of the senses do not register in the consciousness. Ultimately, when one sees the body as condensed spirit, through realization and not through imagination (as many try to do), then one finds that the spirit is above suffering.

(Kaunteya and Bharata are different names of Arjuna. Krishna calls Arjuna Kaunteya, or the son of a woman named Kunti, when he feels the weakness of Arjuna, and by way of encouragement, calls him

Balancing East-West

Bharata.)

Here the Gita gives unique advice as to what one should do when invaded by sensations of heat or cold, pain or pleasure. To protect the body from extreme heat or cold is not wrong. Artificially cooled or steam-heated apartments can temporarily comfort the body and remove the physical suffering arising from over-heat or extreme cold. These are the methods generally adopted by modern man. But constant ministrations to and changes adapted to the demands of the body often enslave it to the impositions of environment. Herein lies the fundamental difference between the East and West in their methods of combating suffering. The Bahgavad-Gita says in this stanza that an environment-enslaved body is a constant trouble to the mind. An enslaved body is apt to enslave the all-powerful mind.

A deep metaphysical problem is involved in understanding the psychology of pain. Stimuli of cold and heat touch the nerve-endings of the body and are transmitted through the nerve electricity and nerve wires as sensations. No one knows exactly what sensations are. We experience sensations as the immediate feelings produced by the contact of the senses and matter. Sensations of cold and heat are entirely different from the objects which produce coldness or warmth. The contact of a piece of cold ice or of hot water is only experienced as an idea. A sensation or first-flowing feeling produced in the mind through the contact of material objects is elaborated in perception. It is expanded into conception, and lastly, conception changes into feeling.

Feeling is that faculty which passes judgment on the experience of the senses. It expresses itself in terms of pain or pleasure of the body, sorrow or happiness of the mind. Sensitive feelings get so used to passing quick judgments on the nature of specific sensations which they experience that the all-powerful mind succumbs to their disturbances. Sensitive feelings magnify sensations and instead of academically and impartially experiencing the variety of sensations of cold and heat emanating through the body, they create pleasure or pain out of their attitudes of likes and dislikes which they whimsically form in their hasty judgment about the nature of specific sensations. Feeling classifies all experiences as being pleasurable or painful according to its likes and dislikes. If feeling could be neutralized, i.e., made impervious to short-lasting excitations or ephemeral pleasures and pains, then all experiences would be merely intellectually cognized.

That is why most wild animals (not those who become sensitive through domestication) and savages and children or those living close to nature, suffer much less from cold or heat or pain, due to their lack of unmagnifying mental sensitiveness.

Consciousness of pain, physical or mental, is purely mental and created by the Ego and feeling. One may reason, "If anybody hits the shinbone of my leg with a hammer I cry out with pain. I did not imagine pain," or "Imagination of pain, as in the hurt in a dream, and pain itself, must be different." But the only difference between imaginary and physical pain is that the former may be roused by imagination and the latter roused by feeling born of a sensation. Both of them are mind-born. Dream-born pains hurt as much in the dream-consciousness as actual physical pain.

Detached Mind Feels No Pain

Some hold that sensation is the feeling of consciousness of a certain state in the nerves and flesh. Even if this be so, sensations cannot be felt without the action of the mind. A knife may be thrust into the flesh of a person under chloroform, but, though the stimulus is present there, there is no sensation—nor is there any feeling to create pain. Hence this absolutely proves that when the mind is detached by deadening of the nerve centres, it cannot feel the nature of a stimulus as an inharmonious sensation nor can it create the feeling of pain. Sensation is nothing but a mental attitude born out of the state which a stimulus creates in the nerves or flesh. Of course the birth of a mental attitude as sensation must exactly correspond to the nature of a stimulus applied to the body. Sensations of cold, heat and such distinctions between various stimuli visiting the body give rise to the different consciousness, mental states or sensations.

At this point careful attention should be given to the idea of the genesis of pain or pleasure. All stimuli applied to the body at first just report themselves as distinct sensations cognized by the discriminative faculty of man. Gradually, immediately after that, the mind begins to recognize the sensations in terms of utility. A sensation, after its appearance in the body, begins to reveal whether it is harmonious or inharmonious to the conditions of the body. Thereupon the feeling becomes roused and begins to develop likes or dislikes from certain sensations. This innate feeling (in animals as instinct) instead of intellectually cognizing body-sensations as harmonious or inharmonious, begins to feel pleasure or pain. Strong liking of the human feeling toward a set of sensations produces the satisfied mental state called pleasure. Strong dislike of man's feeling to a train of sensations develops pain. That is why feeling-predominant people suffer heat or cold more than the better-balanced mentalities. Physical pleasure and pain are derived through long-continued mental habit. That is why harmful, distasteful drugs might give imaginary joy to some, and why the first taste of a wholesome, delicious fruit is sometimes repugnant to people.

Two children of the same age and health but varying in the degree of sensitiveness, made to walk twenty miles under the hot sun, or to undergo a minor, painful operation without the use of chloroform or local anaesthetics, will behave differently. The sensitive child may collapse during the walk, or cry or become hysterical during the operation, whereas the child of strong mentality may smilingly walk the twenty miles and not be afraid to do the same all over again. He may calmly watch the operation on himself as something wonderfully interesting. A doctor was known to perform the most complicated major operation for hernia on himself, cheerfully.

Hence my contention is that pain or physical pleasure, though they accompany body-sensations, are not created by the stimuli or sensations but by feeling, imagination and mental habit, born of wrong environmental and hereditary influences. Just as bad habits are so transmitted, so also the consciousness of pain has been bequeathed to mankind from its erring predecessors. As formerly the world bequeathed the strong erroneous notion of considering the earth to be flat, so modern man has been bequeathed the notion of pain from his ancestors who were not sufficiently versed in psychology to check the growth of the mental disease of pain or sensitive mentality.

In India, where there is a general notion that eating ice-cream in the winter-time predisposes one to catch cold, a Hindu friend of mine used to catch cold whenever he ate ice-cream in winter. When he came to America, he was surprised to find Americans eating ice-cream even in the dead of winter without any ill effects. He followed their example and suffered no more from those colds which had previously been brought on by his own expectations. Innumerable instances of such self-imposed troubles can be brought to mind by anyone.

Pain is Man-Made Delusion

Hence pain is a man-made delusion. We, being made in God's image of joy, never were meant to suffer pain. It appeared in man first in the nature of a mild desire to warn himself of the advent of an inharmonious sensation detrimental to the interests of the body. Later, instead of proving itself as a friend or a warner of the body, it turned out to be a veritable tyrant-torturer to cause the tears of mankind to flow. A baby, when operated upon, cries more through a sense of inharmony in the body than through pain. The famous doctor of an orthopedic hospital told me the children in his hospital vie with one another to be the first in being operated upon and regret it if they do not get the first chance. "But adults are entirely different—the mention of an operation chills their souls, due to imaginative and sensitive feelings," he said.

This hereditary error of pain has brought forth fears and cries from self-hypnotized souls, as the imaginary sight of an imaginary ghost makes a child tremble and shout with terror and pain. As an absent mind of a chloroformed person cannot create pain, so my contention is that a strong mind may recognize the presence of an inharmonious sensation in his body without being sensitive of a created pain. That is why the Spartan, Boy-scout method of training, and the Yogi systems of bodily discipline and endurance, are not meant for methods of self-torture but for lessening the suggestions of pain thru developing the resisting power of the mind.

Sensitiveness is the root cause, the primeval mother of all pain and mental sorrow. Pain is the dread of death, whereas it really is generally a cessation of pain.

Inharmonious physical sensations—for instance, of a thorn in the foot—give rise to the imagination of pain, as the inharmonious thought of the loss of a loved possession of friend may cause sorrow. Some imagination-born sorrows cause more suffering than excruciating pain-giving body sensations. I know of a man who died because of the corroding agony due to the loss of his beloved. He ate, walked, talked, but pined away to his death. He decayed faster than if galloping consumption had attached him. In fact he had tuberculosis from which he had successfully recovered, but even after being cured he faded into death—killed without any physical disease.

Thus it is wrong to acknowledge pain or sympathize with misery-making sensitiveness in people, for it strengthens the delusion of pain and sorrow. All wrong ideas such as breaking of bones, crash from an airplane, pricking of pins, the burning power of heat, or the freezing qualities of zero degree temperature, must be gradually overcome by the mind first and then by the body. The Bhagavad-Gita says that, instead of catering all the time to the whims of cold or warmth, learn to endure them by mental control. The Gita does not advise rashness by asking a man to put his hand in the fire or to lie without any clothing on the icefield. But in the final analysis it is found that the body, though trade-marked by limitations of the God-untuned human mind, still is nothing else but materialized consciousness. Since fire and ice are also materialized cosmic consciousness, they should not be the cause of engendering suffering to the body. Unless each human soul breaks away from the self-imposed imaginary limitations of the body, he is never going to learn that everything is spirit and condensed consciousness.

In India I have seen men who after great mental preparation by fasting, concentration and deep prayer can walk on blazing red-hot fire without harm. Besides, William James proved that by the suggestions of hypnosis, blisters could be produced on the body. Such is the power of the mind.

A matter-sensitive man should avoid rashness. He must not follow a method which may be powerful but which may kill him when he sees it. The cure must not be worse than the disease. He must train himself gradually. He must first realize that sitting in a draft does not produce cold. He must practice using less steam heat. He must never be afraid of out-doors. He must feel that the snow and the burning sun are but materialized God-consciousness just as his body is. Thus he must reason that these similar forces could not hurt his body or cause pain. He must realize that naught else but life exists and that pain comes only by permitting one state of consciousness to affect another state of consciousness.

Pain comes by identification, just as the mother suffers at the sight of her son's suffering through an accident. So also the mothering mind suffers if any inharmony is present in the body. It transfers its suffering to the body and vice versa. But perhaps another man watching the above-mentioned son's accident may feel hardly any of the pain that the mother feels. Sympathy or identification causes pain. One must be impartial and not excited. This does not mean that one should neglect an accident to the body, but that he may attend to its cure as detrimental to the interests of the body, but he must not feel pain.

A mentally sensitive man, a "touchy" individual, in his outward contacts and conversations with people, always feels hurt. He moans and says, "Oh, the weather is bad." "Oh, I read in between the lines of Mr. John's words, during my conversation with him, and, oh, he hurt me so terribly." Whereas a cheerful person, understanding the way of the world, in spite of severe tests of persecutions may wear a soul-warming smile and love his fellow-man as much as ever.

Thus it is that stimuli and sensations of heat and cold or of body wounds should be cognized by the mind only as ideas. The mentally sensitive persons are always troubled by even suggestions of a hot summer day or a very cold night or a slight operation. Man's body must be made pain-proof, until in it is found not the decaying, hurting, changing qualities of matter, but the invulnerable, unchanging qualities of spirit. Consciousness cannot hurt consciousness without acceptance. It is very difficult to hurt an ever-smiling wise man who considers all the injury done to him as due to ignorance. He refuses to allow his consciousness to acknowledge or accept others' inharmonious ideas. He knows that the Ego's process of cognition and any hurt-suggesting thought can only be linked by feeling. Thought can never be hurtful unless feeling overpowers it. That is, consciousness cannot be hurt by consciousness without conscious acceptance. Certain sensations in the body being inharmonious suggest pain, but that does not mean they should be given the opportunity by a weak mentality to be successful in producing pain.

Feeling, mental dislikes, haunting suggestions of ancestral habits, lack of mental training, ever-increasing sensitiveness, and nervousness, give birth to pain. Continued sensitiveness nurtures pain and in turn produces mental sorrow. Whereas a steel mentality which cannot be dented by the blows of accidents and physical and mental trials can remain untarnished, ever-shining, ever-piercing the veil of dark ignorance, destroying the vitals of the apparition of pain.

As awakened immortals breathing the ever-living life and primeval happiness, let us by endurance and discipline of body and mind destroy this reign of terror, haunting superstition of the imagination-born Emperor of Pain. God made man and God made Joy. Man made pain and he will have to know Joy always to be God again.

Suggestions for Overcoming Pain

When pain arrives in the body through cold or heat, hurt or disease, remember the following:

1. Your mind manufactures pain—during absent-mindedness or deep mental preoccupation or under the influence of chloroform, you do not feel pain because the mind is otherwise occupied and unresponsive to sensory impressions.

2. Pain is a friend which warns you of body-troubles, and is not intended to be a torturer. While adopting the proper remedies against inharmonious conditions in the body, do not give way to the suggestions of pain by allowing the mind to become identified with the bodily condition. Pain is short-lasting and has its limitations.

3. Divert your mind during pain by directing it into engrossing work. Keep calm and do not make much of the sensations.

4. Association with stronger-minded or less pain-sensitive people is beneficial.

5. The best way to overcome sorrow is to know that it springs from identification. Sorrow is not overcome by sorrow but by joy. Some sorrows we want to indulge in, but let not sorrow stay with you too long, for it will robe you of the richest of your soul's possessions—perennial Bliss.

Paramhansa Yogananda

IN THE ENDLESS LAND

Each night as I roam
In the sphere of slumber
I become a mystic and renounce
My title, body-weight, possessions, creeds,
I break the self-erected
Prison walls of limitations.
No more an all-pervading son of God
Caged in a dingy clod of brittle flesh
Or bound by the cords of birth,
Position, man-born narrowness or material ties.
There in the eternal ether of sleepland
I have no home, no country,
I am not Hindu nor Christian
Oriental nor Occidental.
My religion there
Marauding far and near
Is plundering joy from everywhere.
There's no lording god o'er me
But Myself.
The slave-god become the God
The sleeping immortal
Now the awakened Immortality.
An unseen God in an invisible plane
Drinking, breathing gladness,
Gliding in the Endless Land.
Free from haunting fear of a possible crash

Balancing East-West

And shattered skull.
No solids there to hurt me
No liquids to drown me
No vile vapours to choke me
No fires to scale my unseen form.
I shake off the memory of a fragile bony body
Remembering I am all space.
Being everything, how could aught
Dare me hurt?
Unknown to any, but known to Myself
I wake, walk, dream,
Eat, drink and glide in joy.
I am the Joy which I sought—
Which everyone seeks.
I was so little when I dreamt
In my mortal wakefulness—
I am boundless large now when I am awake
In my wakefulness omniscient.

Paramhansa Yogananda

FOUR RECIPES August 1928

Spiritual Recipe
Why God does not usually Answer Prayer

Watch yourself when you pray. Silently but strictly keep a keen eye on the truant child of your attention. Let it not run away beyond the precincts of the temple of your devotion. It is better to hold your attention by your own prayers which blossom in the garden of your heart. The mind likes fresh-grown thoughts of God instead of artificial flowers of others' prayers. God loves heart-made prayers better than book-made ones. When He does not respond, it is because He is often offered these imitation flowers of others' dry prayers. The bestowal of these flowers with indifference, absent-mindedness, cold formality or lack-lustre devotion is not the way to claim His attention.

The word prayer often smells of beggary. As sons of God we must not beg; we must demand and believe that what the Father has, we have. Our demands must not be one-sided. We must demand everything which is good for us and above all we must demand Him. Then, again, there must be power and persistency in the demand. Demanding, with disbelief gnawing at the heart, is futile. Unbelief must be put out every time it secretly slips in your sacred temple. Demand must be continuously and forcefully carried on if you want to see Him act. No matter if everything tells you He is not listening to your demands—believe not—laugh at doubt—be persistent. If you do not meet with success in receiving some little doll of matter which you are infatuated with, be not resentful to Him. Sometimes it is good that you do not get the things you want. Sometimes the Divine Father protects your fingers from getting burnt at the fires of passions in which you wish to plunge, being lured by their luminosity.

Even through unfulfillment, if you still keep steadily, deepeningly believing that the Father is listening to you and will answer you, you will be rewarded with his presence. As the miser loves, dwells on, craves and works for money, so do thou love God. As the new lover loves the beloved, so do thou love God. As a drowning man pants for breath, so do thou pant for God. As the mother yearns for her child, so do thou yearn for God. As the drunken love wine, so do thou love God. As the diseased crave health. so do thou crave God. As the sleepy want sleep, so do thou dive into God.

Intellectual Recipe

Read every book critically and with open-mindedness. Reject the froth and get at the substantial ideas. Read books according to the principle of classification: something of real novels, something of physiology, botany, chemistry, physics, astronomy, astrology, psychology; and everything of Scriptures and true books on realization. Go over mentally, thoroughly, after reading twenty-five pages of each book, and find out how it affected you. Books are your best friends. You can quietly hear Shakespeare, Milton, Emerson, Kalidasa, Krishna, Confucius, Plato, Buddha, Christ, talk to you, solace you and give you infinite advice. If you have no friends or if they are a drain on your time uselessly, consort with these wisdom friends by entering through the portals of real study into the eternally charming and interesting thought-land. Read something of everything, and everything of the one thing of living books on God.

Prosperity Recipe

My heart breaks to hear that even in prosperous America, three business men out of four fail in their business ventures. I analyzed the situation and find that, though most people love money, few know how to get it rightly or invest it rightly after having made it. It is not sin to make money to nourish yourself and the bodies of your family because they were given into your charge. A failure neglects to discharge his duties toward health, happiness and success created by God. It is virtue to make money to help God's work and thereby be worthy of the name of being created in the image of God.

Money-making is the next greatest art after the art of realizing God. All the good and philanthropic works of the world, all noble successes, have to be accomplished through money. No saint lived who directly or indirectly did not use money. But the great paradox and riddle of life lies in judiciously acquiring money. To love money is to be lost. That is the snare. You must use it rightly. You must use the right voltage of prosperity to shine through the bulb of your life—if you send a mad desire for prosperity, the bulb of your life will burn and become dark with the lust for money. Money is the source of infinite evil to those who rely on it as the lasting means of happiness. To those, it promises much until they have it. When they have it, they find themselves spent out—too late realizing that they have served a false God of the will-o'-the-wisp.

Yet money gives power, and if judiciously held with unattachment, one can use it to bring happiness to many and can himself outgrow the desire for material happiness.

It is easy to be idle or filled with hopelessness and thus desist from making a financial success. It is easy to earn money dishonestly when such opportunity presents itself. It is wicked by dishonest, organized craft to draw money away from the more needy. It is common to make money just for yourself. It is common to hoard money to satisfy the gold-craving.

But to earn money, abundantly, unselfishly, honestly, quickly, just for God and God's work and making others happy is to develop many sterling qualities of character that will aid one on the spiritual as well as the material path. Responsibility, knowledge of organization, efficiency, order, leadership and practical usefulness are developed in business success and are necessary for the all-round growth of man.

Food Recipe

Vegetarians should eat abundantly of bananas, cream or milk, ground nuts, cheese, cocoanuts.

1. Grated green cocoanuts with Thousand Island dressing, served on lettuce leaves.

2. Half of the heart of a lettuce chopped and mixed with honey, two tablespoonfuls of whipped cream and ground nuts on top, makes an ideal desert. It is better than pies and cooked desserts.

3. Raw food is nature-and-sun-cooked food with even temperature. Use it abundantly. But if you eat cooked food, let it be steamed or baked food without loss of the natural juices, which boiling evaporates.

THE MYSTERY OF LIFE AND DEATH

The dictionary meaning of the word "life" as the vital force distinguishing organic from inorganic matter has undergone a gradual change. Life is no longer a monopoly or organic matter. Inorganic substances like chemicals, by their attractions and repulsions, also show the presence of life. According to the experiments of the great scientist, Prof. J. C. Bose of India, even a piece of tin is living and its vibrations can be recorded during its life and death struggles. It can be poisoned and killed.

The old theory of matter as essentially different from spirit is gone. All matter including solids, liquids and gaseous substances can be converted into electronic energy and made to disappear into spirit. The old theory of matter being like a hot furnace, constantly losing heat and life, is exploded by Prof. Millikan of California. This eminent physicist found that not only is matter being disintegrated into energy or radiation, but that energy or radiation is again being reintegrated into matter. The cosmic rays, or "birth-cries" of the atoms, are radiations inundating the earth incessantly from limitless space.

"Matter and energy, time and space, are in a melting pot," declared Prof. Lovett Evans before leading British scientists recently, "and out of it will come we know not what strange relations of one to another. The enormously rapid developments of physics in recent years strike the onlooker dumb with almost religious awe. On further study, lines of separation previously held to be rigid will fade away, and there will be found to be continuity between matter and energy, between the living and the non-living, between the conscious and unconscious."

There is no difference between inorganic and organic life except that they are different manifestations of Life. There is nothing dead—the atoms in the flesh of even a corpse are highly vibrating and constantly moving with life. Different forms of life are manifestations of the same life-force. Just as ice, water, steam, hydrogen, oxygen gases are different forms of the same thing, so also solids, liquids, gases, stones, crystals, plants, animals and human beings both living and dead are manifestations of life. The spirit contained in matter, and matter, are the same, just as hydrogen oxygen gas contained in a closed jar made out of a block of ice is of the same essential composition as the jar itself. The thing contained is made of the same material as the container. If it were otherwise, matter and spirit would have to be the result of two co-existing infinite forces, which is impossible. As the ocean becomes the waves, so does spirit become matter. Spirit and matter are the same as the ocean and the waves. The waves are distorted ocean—so is matter distorted, objectified spirit.

The ocean can exist without the waves, but the latter cannot exist without the ocean. Similarly, spirit can withdraw all creation into itself by converting matter into energy, and can exist without any material manifestation, but matter cannot exist without spirit.

The waves, in addition to form, contain all the essential qualities of the ocean; similarly, matter, organic or inorganic, manifestly or latently, contains all the qualities of the spirit. Thus we can say that Life sleeps in the crude earth; dreams beauty in the flowers; wakes with power in the animals; and in man has consciousness of its infinite possibilities.

What is Life? Life is a wave of electrons and atoms, a wave of protoplasm, a wave of power, a wave of consciousness. Life is intelligent, organized motion. It becomes a clod of earth or melts itself into vapour—becomes a human being or a corpse. Stones, living beings, dead creatures, are waves in the ocean of life. There is no death nor cessation of motion in anything. Everything is living.

A wave is born; it rises to its supreme height, then falls or dies to rise again somewhere. Like everything else, the human body is a combination of three kinds of waves, or three co-existing waves, of electrons, life-force, and intelligence, knit together by a soul, rolling up and down the ocean of life. The birth of the baby is the beginning, the youth the crest, and the death the fall of the wave in the infinite ocean of Life.

Before and after death the soul rolls on as the wave of life and intelligence—but not as the wave of condensed electrons of which the body is composed. The body is shaped after the waves of life and intelligence. It behaves in exact accordance with the quality and measure of their power.

If life is eternal motion—then why does death visit the human body? This is the great question. Death is not cessation nor annihilation—for even matter is indestructible. (At death the life and intelligence waves, with the soul, slip away from the body wave.) The burned-away candle changes—but its weight and constituent ingredients can be found if the carbonic acid gas is held in a jar. Matter is life. Life is matter. Life is intelligence. Matter is sleeping intelligence. Since matter is indestructible, all life is indestructible.

The Infinite Is Ever New

But that does not mean life is not changeable. In fact, Eternal Infinite Life manifests itself through finite forms of flowers and living creatures. The phenomena of death or the illusion of change is reflected in all finite substances—otherwise the infinite would be limited, measured by finite substances. The Infinite would lose its nature by becoming the finite, definite, circumscribed and molded.

That is why the beautiful rose and the glorious youth, after expressing certain qualities of the Infinite, disappear as silent waves into the infinite ocean of life. The body is the froth of Life, of the intelligence and soul waves. The froth is temporary compared to the individualized soul wave.

Life is relative—some waves of life last longer than others, but they all have to express the Infinite variously and fully. They all emerge from and merge into the Infinite Ocean. The speck of star dust, the sun, moon, clouds, rainbow, the gossamer, the nightingale, whippoorwill all have to express the silent Infinite. Natural death comes when each object, each human being, has done its full share in expressing the Infinite. Untimely death of a youth suggests that he changes his diseased body vehicle and lodges elsewhere for better opportunities.

What is human death, what is its utility, what are its drawbacks?

As children are afraid to go into the dark, and as that fear is aggravated by tales of ghosts and goblins, so is the fear of death instilled into men. One should be consoled, for its is the necessary end of all living bodies. The fear of death is most foolish, for as long as one is not dead he has nothing to worry about; when one is dead it is all over. One cannot die twice in the same body.

Death Is a Reward

Physical pain in long-continued disease and mental suffering are sometimes worse than death. The oft-dreaded natural death or change of the body is a deep sleep earned after a troubled existence or a life full of struggle and activity. Death is the pension earned after a long term of activity in the office of life. Death is cessation of pain. Suicide under any condition is a spiritual crime, because it involves the quitting of the duty or test of life. The person who commits suicide is denied the privilege of peace, which attends the rightly-won pension of death. He who deserts this earth as a coward cannot be granted the pension of rest.

Physical pain and suffering of mind are both mental. The cause of pain which is in the body or the cause of bereavement which is in the mind—both are mental. A man suffers to see his beloved wife being operated upon, more than he would feel if a stranger's wife were being lanced. He would suffer most when he sees his own body being operated upon. Sensations in one's own body or in the bodies of others have to be accepted by the mind in order to produce pain or suffering. If a man's mind is disengaged from the body by superior means, such as meditation, or by artificial means, such as chloroform, and he is operated upon, he does not feel pain. So it is absolutely true that if man's feelings were rightly trained, he would learn to watch operations on his body without feeling pain. Pain and suffering are more in sensitive people.

The Caged Bird of the Mind

The pain and fear of death are due to self-created causes. If we get acquainted with what death is, we would find there is nothing to fear. The soul with its waves of life and intelligence grows attached to the physical wave of the body and fears to leave it, just as a bird, long used to a cage, hesitates to leave it though the doors are opened. The bird thinks, "Where will I go? Let me go back to the cage." Its confinement in the cage makes it forgetful of its free flights in the open skies. So the caged soul used to the limitations, diseases and frailties of the body is sore afraid of the infinite, safe, celestial regions of God, even when it is invited by death to make a change from the limited to the less-limited state.

As the baby is dead when it changes to a youth, so when an aged man dies he changes for something else. If life is lived rightly, death is a reward and a change for a better state. Some quit life, being forced out by failures in health or as victims to their wrong ways of living. But even failure cannot be a permanent stigma on souls—they must have opportunities in other schools of life, if they had to leave this school of life, being expelled by the exacting school-master of death.

Why do we cry when our dear ones die? It is because we sorrow for our own loss—we seldom consider the welfare of those whom we lose. If it be for the good of our loved ones to leave us for better training in other schools of life, we should rejoice instead of being selfishly sad and thus keeping them earthbound, hampering them in their path of progress by the broadcasting of our own selfish wills.

Terrible thought! If there were no death, fifteen hundred million people would monopolize the Infinite. The planets and the universes would trademark God with the sale of finitude. The Infinite would be exhausted. Life and death would lose the taste of charming mystery. Everything would grow old and stale. The Infinite is ever-new—so by His Infinite Magic Wand of renewing death He keeps everything ever expressing, ever remodeling itself into a fitter vehicle for infinite expressions.

Hence this paradox—the dance of death—shattering worlds, pulverizing skulls, crumbling roses, destroying fifteen hundred million people every hundred years, killing billions of fishes, trillions of bacteria and powdering sextillion countless atoms. The life beautiful is evolving, training souls in the factory of mighty death. Death is the cosmic furnace in which the dross of all objects and living souls is purified. Death comes to a dutiful soul as its promotion to a higher state; it comes to a failure soul to give it another chance in a different environment.

The Actual Phenomena of Death

The actual phenomena of death is something to be carefully noted. Many Yogis in India can say with St. Paul—"Verily, I protest by the rejoicing which I have in Christ, I die daily." I shall try to describe it just as I have experienced it. It is a voluntary or involuntary switching off of the life current from the bulb of flesh. Those Yogis who know how to operate their switch of the heart or control their heart beats—they quit quickly or stay as long as they want. I like not to overstay here but will merge my life current in the Infinite Electricity when my work is done.

The weight and feeling in the body, the love of sensual pleasures, sunlight, voices of friends, ties of family, love of warmth or cold, dependability on oxygen for life, love of food, dress, automobiles, furniture, houses—these are the common attachments of life and the body-bound soul.

When death comes it is variously experienced by different people according to their earthly mode of living. Just as people have various durations and qualities of sleep, so different people experience death differently. The good, hard-working man in the workshop of life goes to a deep, unconscious but restful sleep for a short while to wake up again in some other region of life. The man who neglects the duties of life or causes confusion often experiences something like nightmares or terrible dreams during death.

The moral man often has delightful dreams at death. The wise man experiences through death an infinitely better, safer haven.

During death the ordinary man finds every part of the body going to sleep. When your leg goes to sleep you see it, but cannot feel it belongs to you. Similarly, the dead man sometimes remembers his body distinctly, but cannot create motion in it. In death the power of touch goes first, then vision, then taste, then smell and last of all, hearing.

Dying People Can Hear

A student of mine had a much-loved sister dying in a hospital. The doctor in the room was saying loudly, "No hope for her, it is a question of a few more minutes before she passes on." The brother got angry and told everyone to leave the room. He shut the door and cried aloud: "Sister, come back!" And she came back to life though practically dead—when even her heart had stopped beating. When she was better she told how she heard the undiplomatic doctor discouraging her. It was only her brother's courage that simulated her will to energize her fast-deadening and rebellious muscles and nerves. This story illustrates the fact that it is highly unwise to discuss the condition of a dying man within reach of his hearing. His body or speech may be paralyzed but not his hearing.

Only those who have practiced the control of heartbeat and learned to live without oxygen—by eating less carbonized food and preventing the decay of tissues in the body through definite training in meditation—can consciously experience death at will as a rest from constant muscular activity and specially life's involuntary activity of the heart, lungs, diaphragm, circulation, et cetera. In heaven there are no crackers or soup, no breakfast, lunch or dinner, no water or oxygen or sunshine. Mortals should learn to live more by inner energy, unattached to the body. Those who learn in this life to live by spirit and are unattached to the body quickly realize the freedom of the soul from the bondage of oxygen, food and water after death. Death is a fear to the ignorant human animal—it is a transition to a higher state to the wise. To him it is a promotion in school to higher grades of life.

Even if you do not know the art of living more by energy as the Yogis of India and developed Yogoda students know, you can begin by ceasing to be attached to the duties of the body. Perform them with joy but with unattachment. Attachment is the self-inflicted torture brought on by ignorance. The ignorant dying man suffers through imagination even though he receives freedom from pain and leaves a minor inferior state for a higher one.

That life is not dependent on food or oxygen is proved by verified cases of men living long in a state of suspended animation. Life can exist in a corpse in a different form. A chicken heart can lie 16 years in a chemical syrup—longer than the life of a chicken. A crocodile lives 600 years. Life is vagrant, life a river appearing and disappearing in the desert of life.

Our Blind Physical Eyes

Death gives new robes to the soul actors to play new dramas on the stage of life. Death above all else is a transition to a better land—a change of residence. The wise man who has opened his spiritual eye finds that the death of earthly life gives him a new beginning in another supernal life. On this earth seeing we see not—a fluoroscope can show the bones of the fingers which the eye cannot see. We do not see the cores of light—blue, violet, aquamarine, orange, yellow, white, which bind the atoms and the earth together. We hear the gross noise of the world and a few sweet melodies and nothing more.

The wise man beholds in this life and after death with his spiritual eye not a region of chaos and dark sleep which the soul in ignorance after death experiences. Death is very attractive to the former—instead of terror he finds infinite freedom. The soul-bird of paradise finds its freedom from the limitations of the cage of life. The soul appareled in searchlights of multi-hues soars in infinite directions searching, claiming its lost territory of eternity.

In the mellow light of the other world, the wise perceive the inner sides of stars, stones, living beings, corpses, dust, iron, gold, earth, planets, dazzling with Infinite brilliancy. Every object which we perceive has two sides—the gross ugly outer side present before the physical eyes, and the inner, most beautiful side revealed to the eye of wisdom. The crude brick revealed by the physical eyes appears to be like a garden of electrons, when viewed through the spiritual eye. Human beings with skeletons, ugly sinews and red blood appear as beautiful many-hued living beings made of visible mellow materialized love. The rose of the human garden looks like a paper rose before the inner rosy lustre of its whirling atoms. Nothing fades there so quickly. Everything talks there silently. The roses talk to the souls with the language of spirit. The garden of roses lives by the breath of the souls, and the souls breathe the aroma of roses. The gentlest earthly flower—the lily, violet, drunk with gross sunlight—is not allowed to tread the sanctity of that fair garden of the gods. The mortal, enslaved by oxygen and sunlight, gorged with material food, faints at the delicate airless atmosphere of that divine supernal region. Darkness and gross lights equally lose their relative dualities in the darkless dark, lightless but all revealing soul-light of that sphere. The Yogis practice control of life and breathless state to be able to live in airless regions of living light, unburdened by the body.

The Life Beyond this Life

Souls in that region do not encase themselves in bundles of bones with fleshly covers. They carry no frail, heavy frames to collide and break with other crude solids. There is not war there between the solids, oceans, lightning, disease and man's frail frame. There are no accidents there, for all things exist in mutual help and not antagonism—all forms of vibration are in harmony. All forces live in peace and conscious helpfulness. The souls, the rays on which they tread, the orange rays which they drink and eat—all are living. They live in mutual cognizance and cooperation, breathing not oxygen but the joy of the spirit. There they live as long as they want, playing like waves on the infinite ocean of light. And there they melt into one another by celestial love as the ocean of light.

Balancing East-West

No bacteria, no thirst, no selfish desires, no heartaches, no lust, no pain nor sorrow, nor boisterous fleeting joy, no accidents, shattering bones and skulls, and no excruciating pain of parting, can ever visit there.

In that better region where change is not for decay—but where it exists like a cosmic magician to entertain with variety for infinite expression. There the law of change is governed by the wills of souls and is not forced upon them.

Let us not bury the soul in the grave and call death annihilation, but see it as a door through which bravely marching souls of earthly life can enter to find the all-alluring, all-charming region of our ever-luminous, ever-peaceful Common Cosmic Home. Mortal fears, heartaches, dreams, illusions fade—darkness of death changes into another infinitely beautiful universe. Why pity the dead? In wisdom—they pity us. They can see their super-region and us also with their spiritual eye, but we cannot see them with our gross spiritually blind physical eyes.

Insult not me
With your cries of sympathy
When I soar
To the land of eternal light and love.
It is I who should feel for you.
For me disease, shattering of bones,
Sorrow, excruciating heartaches no more.
I dream joy, I glide in joy,
I breath in joy evermore.
You are left behind
Oh, yet Life's wheels to turn and wind.
I have worked with diligence
In the office of life
And now I have won
My pension of earned peace.
I left the flickering shadows of life's shores;

Paramhansa Yogananda

I am living by the shoreless shore
Of the Eternal Sea evermore.

CHRISTMAS MESSAGE -1928

Greetings to all Yogoda students everywhere, on the occasion of the coming spiritual Christmas season.

The truth of Yogoda is marching steadily on through the territories of dark ignorance. New regions have been conquered by the armies of divine love. Soldiers of superstition, narrowness, misunderstanding and dogmatism are on the run. Wake, soldiers of Yogoda! Train yourselves in the art of self-control. Drill yourselves by regular meditation. The message of Christ was not of weakness. His message is of power, which can rout the legions of ignorance. His method of battle is more powerful than all the machine guns and bombshells of the world armies. Before the power of love, the asphyxiating gases of international hatred and bigotry, and the colossal ammunition of war, are belittled and strengthless.

To answer war by war, hatred by hatred, wickedness by evil, caste and class prejudice by retaliation, does not solve, but increases, the problem.

Let us make this coming Christmas season an occasion not merely for exchange of gifts and feastings. Let us rise above the plane of candies and gaudy things. Let us learn to hear the command of the Christ-general within us. Let us discipline ourselves to develop our sleeping spiritual powers, that we may conquer the Satan of ignorance, with all his allurements and delusions. Let us establish the Prince of Peace within us that we may meet our crosses and tests of life with power, victory and tranquillity. Let us learn to love those who love us not. Let us give battle to evil only by good. Let us meet religious bigotry by our inner conviction won by realization. Let us influence the error-stricken with our healthy spiritual examples. Let us live Christ in wisdom, love and meditation, and thereby show others how to be true disciples of the Christ they worship.

Let us break all our mental boundaries of color, creed and nationality, and receive all—even our inanimate and animal brothers—in the endless, all-embracing arms of our Christ-consciousness. This will be true celebration of the coming of Christ on earth.

Paramhansa Yogananda

ODE TO MY MASTER
Swami Sri Yukteswar Giriji

When thirsty for God
I left the portals of parental love
And became a wanderer
(Called by thy magnetic will)
In the sacred city of Benares
Where Ganges laps the feet of saints,
I met thee
—Thou polestar of my shipwrecked thoughts—
And was shown the Limpid Lake
Wherein I and all may quench our thirst.
Thou great bond of Sat-Sanga1
Fellowship's invisible cord
'Tween East and West,
'Tween two poles of boisterous activity
And calm spirituality.
In thy teachings science of matter and of spirit
Forsake their age-old feud
And meet in Yogoda's balanced realm
Never to part again.
The message of Babaji
And Mahasaya Lahiri
Has come through thee
To link truth and theology,
To bridge religions and realization,

Balancing East-West

To reach God by meditation,
To crush the walls of darkness
By the flood of wisdom's light.
Rise, sleeping world, awake!
Sons of God have come to take
The burden of your cries away.
O, awakener of the Christ in me,
With loving reverence I bow to thee.

1 Sat-Sanga is fellowship of religions and of the good in all.

2 Yogoda is the scientific technique for developing body, mind and soul harmoniously.

3 Babaji is the Supreme Master of the Yogoda Sat-Sanga movement in America and India. His disciples claim that he is several hundred years old.

4 Thou—Thou art Being and Breath,
And what Thou art can never be destroy'd.

QUICKENING HUMAN EVOLUTION

Do you realize how you spend your life? Very few of us know how much we can put in our life if we use it properly, rightly, wisely, economically. Economize your time—lifetimes ebb away before we wake up, and that is why we do not realize the value of the immortal time which God has given us. Time is spent in rushing, in racing, in getting nowhere. Very few of us stop, think and find out what life can give unto us. Do you know how may years actually you live? Most people sleep from six to ten hours a day—one-third of their life is gone. Sixty years is the average life. One-third of that, twenty to twenty-five years, is spent in unconsciousness. Thus only forty or thirty-five years are left. About five or ten years are spent in talking about nothing, and amusements. That brings it down to thirty—and out of that thirty years, what else do you do? Eat and do nothing, and of course attend to business. Business is necessary, business is for the purpose of keeping the bodily animal all right. That takes most of your time. Actually scrutinize your life—you live hardly ten years. In the morning you get up, and most of you wake with the consciousness of coffee and toast—first comes the breakfast consciousness—then rush to business. The day passes—hurry, worry, and at noon-time, coffee and doughnuts! You don't even eat right. Evening comes—movies and dancing. You come back late at night, go to bed, get up in the morning and start in again with the breakfast consciousness. This is the way you spend your life. Sometimes you read those books that are not worth while, and perhaps sickness comes and begins to shorten your life. This world is a vast school, and in your sixty years of life many things are necessary, but if you keep only the body vehicle all right, that is not the sole purpose of life. Don't think that just in order to be well-clothed and fed you have to have millions—you don't have to lead a sophisticated life in order to merely feed the bodily animal. Life's goal is much better. Ask yourself now this question—how many good books have I read in this life? Every day about two dozen new books are being printed in America on ethics, music, literature, botany, logic, science, the scriptures—how are you going to pack all this knowledge into your ten years of life? Then again, sixty years is not the life of every one; just the lucky ones have even that. What hope have you got? And yet you are idling and having bridge parties! I have no objection if you do it for a good cause. But are you going to waste your time standing on the sidewalk, watching the crowds pass by or looking through the windows at many things you don't need and want to buy?

Knowledge is Infinite

Are you going to waste your time by the wayside? How are you going to condense your experiences, how are you going to learn all the things you want to learn? The ordinary person does not think at all—just eats, sleeps and dies. Doesn't your heart throb to learn everything that is going on in the world? How is it possible for the average human being to know them all? How are you going to find time to read of Jesus, or Aristotle, of all the great poets? Life seems hopelessly short when you think of that. You read a few books, and think you know it all. In the cities you have wonderful libraries, but few people go there. Think of all the knowledge of all human beings; how, in these few years, are you going to pack it in your brain? Is it possible? As long as you live on this earth, as long as the power in the eye shall give you strength to see the stars, as long as you enjoy God's sunshine and breath His air, so long will you yearn for knowledge. Most human beings walk with an empty skull, and they think there is a brain there—they think it, that is all: they walk in emptiness. "Oh, yes, I have a wonderful library at home. Come on, I will show it to you." Beautiful but untouched! Music, poetry, science, everything is there. With all the things you want to learn you don't want to waste your time. You are filled with unhappiness most of the time because you don't keep the mind engaged. Think of Aristotle, Shakespeare, Maeterlinck, Lord Shankara and their works. Think of the privilege you have. You can converse with all of them at will through their wonderful books. Instead of that you are wondering all the time what show you are going to see next! It is good once in a while to be entertained, but if you spend your life gossiping about others, or being interested in others' faults, not your own faults, the loss is yours. You have lots of house-cleaning to do yourself—you are wasting priceless time when the treasures of God are around you, ready to be received. Wisdom comes, knocks at your gate, gently asking, "Let me in," but there is no answer, no thought, no response there. Cheap, sensational novels call you hoarsely with their grossness and your thoughts rush out to receive them with open hearts. You develop a taste for inferior things thus. If you develop a liking for unwholesome cheese, you lose your taste for the good, fresh cheese. As you develop a taste for inferior things you lose taste for better things and you think yourself unable to be otherwise because of bad habit. Cultivate the habit to pick up in this life more worthwhile things. Schedule your life, read the best books in the world, don't waste time reading this and that—pick up the best books. Read of medicine, astronomy, science, the scriptures. One thing that must be your first concern: you must find out your vocation. By contact with the Cosmic Vibration in meditation you will be led to the goal, you will be led to the thing you ought to do. Concentrate upon that thing, make yourself proficient in that. Many try ten kinds of business without getting really acquainted with any. You can't get everything of many things—learn everything of one thing.

Still, knowledge is so vast, spiritual wisdom and all things are so vast, and though this world is vast to us, it is but a speck in the universe. How is it possible in this life to know all the wisdom that many human beings have from time to time gathered from the school of life? There are lots of things to know. The world is becoming small—every day it is growing smaller, due to transportation facilities. Soon we will have to take a trip to other planets to have adventure in travels. Electricity goes anywhere in a second—why can't we? We are the makers of electricity. We are progressing in numerous ways, we are doing things quickly. The adoption of better methods in business and transportation, mass production by huge machinery, have quickened evolution. Think of the time of life used up just in weaving of cloth by hand in the past! That labor has been saved by modern machinery—so evolution has been quickened by the adoption of better methods. Machinery can do that. Machinery gives mass production, saves labor. How are we going to quickly weave lives into all-around success? Why can't we quicken human evolution as well as world evolution?

Luther Burbank's Methods

How is the human brain going to acquire in a lifetime all knowledge and wisdom? That is my question. When I met Luther Burbank he showed me a walnut tree, and he said, "I took off more than one hundred years form its usual period of growth. I grew that in twelve years." And you could see the tree bearing walnuts! He made almonds have soft shells,

Balancing East-West

made over the tomato and created the Shasta daisy from bulbs, and the cactus without thorns. In primitive times the different animals used to eat the cactus, so the cactus developed thorns. When one life begins to hurt another life, that life develops weapons of defense. Burbank went into the garden, looked at the cactus, and every day began to talk to the cactus. "Please, beloved Cactus, I am Luther Burbank, your friend. I don't mean to hurt you, I am not going to hurt you at all, so why develop thorns?" And so the thornless cactus was developed by talking, by attention, by his knowledge of nature's laws. You can impress certain vibrations on protoplasm. If the walnut tree can be made to grow in twelve years instead of one hundred and fifty years, there is a chance for human beings also. How is a human being within sixty years of existence to develop so that he can be the center of all knowledge? That is the point I want to drive home in your mind. I have shown how machinery quickened world evolution. Where did machinery come from? —from the factory of human minds. If man quickened evolution in business, man can quicken his evolution in all branches of life, including his own inner life.

In ordinary study there is a vast difference between the methods applied by teachers in India and in the West. In the West they pump into the brains of children the ideas, "How many books have you read; how many teachers have you had?" A man returned from college with a Ph.D. in making sugar from different fruits. He was asked if sugar could be made from the guava fruit. After some deep thought he said, "I did not study that. It was not in my curriculum." Using common sense was beyond him. It is not pumping from the outside in, that gives you knowledge. It is the power and largeness of receptivity within that determine how much and how quickly you can grasp knowledge. The man who has the power of receptivity quickly sees everything. An intelligent man lives far ahead of the idiot. All your experiences are measured in terms of the cup of your receptivity.

Prof. James of Harvard said that most of our habits come through heredity. Feeble-minded people, science says, cannot be helped. Scientists take measurements and believe in the stamp of heredity too much. They forget this: that by awakening the brain cells, man can quicken his evolution. The power of receptivity of the brain cells can become so great that a man can receive all the things he wants to absorb within himself, in a normal lifetime.

How can you quicken evolution? By consciously condensing all your experiences, by the power of concentration. By concentration you gather your attention, focusing it to a point. By condensation you again use your attention to quickly do a thing which ordinarily would take a long time. I will tell you of such an experience. A friend of mine said I was alright as spiritual man, but that I could not succeed in business. I replied, "I am going to make five thousand dollars in business for you, within two weeks." He said, "You will have to show me. I am from Missouri." I did not rush to invest money on unwise things. I used concentration, disengaged my mind of all disturbances, and focused my attention on one thing. (Most of us have the searchlight of our attention turned outside all the time instead of inside—we should turn the searchlight of the mind on the divine source. Every change in business, every change in the planetary system, in the physical system—everything is recorded there. We are living on one side of the universe; the other side is more tangible than this side.) So I touched that source. Ordinarily men do not concentrate—the mind is restless, and the restless mind jumps at conclusions and races for something that does not belong to it. You must obey the law. Remember, concentrate, and then ask Divine Power. Thus, as soon as I contacted that source, there were shown to me lots of houses. But I did not sit quietly in my room and say, "The Heavenly Father will open the ceiling and drop five thousand dollars in my lap," because I have favored Him with a fervent prayer. I bought the Sunday papers and looked at real estate advertisements. I picked out a few houses, and told my friend to invest his money in them. He said:

"Everything seems pretty shaky," and I said, "Never mind, doubting Thomas, don't try to spoil success by your doubts." In two weeks there was a real estate boom and prices of houses went way up high. He sold the houses and had a clear profit of five thousand dollars. I showed him that the power of God or mind works wherever we apply it with faith.

Concentration Is the Key

Concentration, when directed by Divine Power, does not allow you to ramble through wrong investments—you go straight to success. Hence, if that mind power can be applied in business it can be applied in other things, in music and writing, for example. I always start from within, out, and not from without, in. All the musical instruments

I play I learned that way. I was too proud to go to a teacher, and I thought, "Well, the first man that started to study about music, he did not learn from anybody; why can't I do the same?" Start from within, not from without. That's how anyone can get the experiences of many years within a short time. You have not to learn all the books in the library. You have not to learn everything. Knowledge, poetry, music and all knowledge come from the inner source, from the soul without limitation. How are you going to find out all the mysteries of the body and all the mystery of divine things in one short span of human life if you do not tap your inner source, which is omniscient?

Story of an Ignorant Devotee

There was a Hindu devotee. He was puzzled to decide what kind of scriptures he should read, and what kind of idol he should worship. (Idols are used to help fix the mind in concentration, and are kept covered in a temple so that the birds and weather will not destroy them. So he said, "Which god shall I worship?" He bought one idol, and then he would be afraid the others would get angry. He would buy another. He had two big trunks which he used to carry with him, suspended from his shoulders on a pole. Every day somebody would say, "You had better worship this idol god and that idol god, read this or that holy book,"—so heavier and heavier the trunks grew. He thought he would have to buy a third trunk. Then he thought it was not possible to have three trunks and carry those himself, so he sat by the side of a pond and began to weep; "Heavenly Father, tell me which book to read, and which idol to worship. As soon as I worship one god I think the others are getting angry." It so happened that a saint passed by that way, and seeing the crying man, said: "Son, why are you weeping? What is the matter?" "Saint, I don't know which book to read, and look at these hundreds of idols; I don't know which one to please." The saint said, "Close your eyes and pick up any book, and follow that book through life, and drop the idols on a rock and break them one by one. The one that does not break, worship that one." So he picked up one book. Most of the idols were made of earth, and all broke except one which was made of solid stone. Then the saint suddenly came back and said, "I forgot to tell you something. Now that you have found your god, go back home. But if you find a more powerful god than this one, worship him. Always worship the more powerful god." So the man went home and on a little altar which he had there, he put the stone idol, worshipping and offering fruits. Every day he discovered the fruit was gone, so he thought, "The saint certainly told me of the right idol god. Since he has eaten the fruits he must be a living god." One day, overcome by curiosity, he thought her would watch how a god eats. He just opened his eyes a little, and while he was praying he saw a great big mouse come and eat the fruit. The he said, 'Look at that same idol. It cannot eat the fruit, but the mouse can, so it is a more powerful god." No sooner had he thought this than he caught the mouse by the tail and tied it on the altar. His wife said, "You have gone crazy." "No, I have not gone crazy. I am just following the instructions of the saint to worship more and more powerful gods." So he threw the stone away and began to worship the mouse there. One day he was meditating when suddenly he heard a great noise, and opening his eyes he saw a pussycat eating the mouse. He thought, "That is interesting. The pussycat is more powerful than the mouse. So I must worship the cat." Thus he got hold of the cat and put it on the altar. The cat did not have to catch mice any more, and she got fat getting milk every day without any labor of stealing. Day after day the man's meditation grew deeper and the cat got fatter. Every day when the man waked up he used to drink a bowl of milk. The pussycat was not satisfied with what she got, so she concentrated on the bowl of milk. One day she drank it up and went back and sat on the altar. The wife came in, saw the milk gone, looked at the innocent-looking cat sitting on the altar, and went and got the broom. Her husband's meditation broke with the noise of the broom-stick falling on the cat. He looked at his wife pounding the cat, and he thought, "That is interesting. My wife is more powerful than the pussycat, so she is a better god than the cat." Then he demanded that his wife sit on the altar. So she sat, and every day he meditated on her. Of course the wife used to cook some food for her husband, and after he finished worshipping her he would eat his meal. It so happened that one day he found a piece of charcoal in the rice. "Why did you put charcoal in the rice? Why did you do that?" the man shouted at his wife. To which the wife promptly replied, "Master, I did not deliberately put charcoal in the rice. Master, forgive me, I am thy servant." Then he said, "Ah, that's interesting. So you are my servant, you like to serve me. Then I am more powerful than you are. Then I am the most powerful god. God is in me. I have found Him now within myself."

If you find Him in the temple of your soul, you find Him in all temples and churches. Find Him within, you find Him without. You won't find Him anywhere unless you find Him within.

Making Brain Cells Receptive

It is impossible in this life to read all the Vedas and bibles, and to follow all the systems given, to be God-like. How are you going to do it? Search within just as the devotee in the above story did. Everything depends upon the receptivity of your mind, brain cells and spinal column. This body changes every twelve years, and that is why at twelve, twenty-four and thirty-six years we find distinct changes occur. With the change of years and change of body without the obstruction of disease, the mind changes correspondingly. Disease, wrong living, will retard that evolution. In twelve years your brain develops in such a way that it displays a certain kind of mentality. If it takes twelve years of growth and change of tissues to manifest certain thoughts, how are you going to wait indefinitely to make the brain receptive to all wisdom? You cannot have all wisdom unless your brain is evolved accordingly. So there is a method which the master minds of India have taught of revolving certain kinds of vital currents around the spine and brain. By twelve times of practicing this method you can gain the result of one year's ordinary physical evolution. That is how many saints quickly get their spiritual knowledge, far beyond that of theoretical theologians. Things which they perceive in a second amount to years of ordinary experience. Revolving this current around the spinal column and brain develops their receptivity. Experiences come through the channel of the senses, but he senses don't give you more than the knowledge of the phenomena or the appearances of the real substance. When by concentration all the fine spinal and brain cells can be turned on to the cosmic source, they become highly magnetized. Your body is made up of 27,000,000,000,000 cells. Every cell is like an intelligent being. You are not alone—you have to educate each cell in order to know all the things that are going on in the world. You never trained those cells. That is why you are all the time full of melancholia and of passing fancies and suffering from lack of understanding.

In twenty minutes of this spinal practice you can attain the result of one solar year's living on earth, so that in a year of such practices you get the result of many years of evolution. Jesus Christ did not go to college, and not one of all the scientists of the world knows of God and nature's laws as he knew. Whenever you want to know something don't start with data—go and retire and concentrate. When the mind is receptive, then bring the data; start the business or mental solution. Don't be filled with discouragement and say it cannot be done. The world starts with books and outside methods—you should start with increasing the receptivity of your intuition—in you lies the infinite seat of all knowledge. Calmness, concentration, condensation of experiences by intuitional perception, will make you master of all knowledge. Don't do anything in a haphazard way—do everything with full attention, but don't do too many things. Pick up the more important things, and do them with all your heart. Don't swallow useless things. Potentially, all knowledge is within you. Why should you walk in dead men's shoes? Don't let yourself act like an intellectual victrola. Everyone represents infinite power and should manifest this in everything. Whenever you want to produce something, do not depend upon the outside source. Go deep and seek the infinite source. All methods of business success, inventions, vibrations of music and inspirational thoughts and writings, are recorded in the office of God. First find out what you want, ask the divine aid to direct you to right action, whereby your want will be fulfilled; then retire within yourself. Act according to the inner direction you receive; you will find what you want. When the mind is calm, how quickly, how smoothly, how beautifully will you perceive everything. Success in everything will come to pass in a short time, for cosmic power can be proved by the application of the right law. Last of all, don't concentrate without, don't do things in a haphazard way. Start everything from within, no matter what it is, writing or anything else. Seek guidance within. The scientific man would accomplish more if he concentrates on increasing the receptive quality of his brain cells, instead of just depending on books and college work for his progress. Some say that our brain cells at birth come already saturated with fixed habits, and, therefore, cannot be remoulded. This is false. Since God made us in His image we cannot have limitation, if we probe deeply enough within ourselves.

Man Superior to Heredity

Even in the feeble-minded, God's power shines as much as in the greatest man. The sun shines equally on the charcoal and the diamond, but it is the charcoal which is responsible for not reflecting the sunlight like the diamond. All congenital limitations come through man's own transgression of a law sometime in the past. And what has been done can be undone. If the brain cells of a feeble-minded man are scrubbed with the search light of concentration thrown within, he will display the eclipsed intelligence the same as the intelligent man.

The last great scientific method is to magnetize and to send the current around the brain and spinal column, and thereby secure one year's health by twenty minutes of this practice. In connection with mentality, when you have cleansed the brain cells, when the divine magnetism touches them, every cell becomes a vibrant brain, and you will find within yourself myriads of awakened brains ready to grasp all knowledge.

With the awakened brains, myriad mentalities will awake and all things will be apprehended by you. You will study the vast book of Nature and Truth with twenty-seven thousand billion awakened and spiritualized microscopic brains and mentalities. Why be satisfied in half-educating a small part of your brain only?

Where are you seeking, my friends? Prayers have been asked, but god has not answered. But with the awakened brain cells for intelligent beings whom you have kept uneducated, vibrant with the joy of God, all knowledge can be had in this life; Eternity realized now; AWAKE!

Paramhansa Yogananda

FOUNTAIN OF SMILES

Behold not the sarcastic smiles
Which are born
From the womb of dark hate.
Welcome not the bandit smiles
Which rob thy trueness,
Wear not serpent smiles
Which hide their venom
Behind the sting of laughter.
Banish the volcanic smiles
Of subterranean wrath.
Bedim not the mirror of Soul—
Thy face—with shades of pitying smiles.
Let no witless, noisy, muscle-contorting laughs,
Like rowdies,
Echo the emptiness of thy soul.
A fountain of joy
Must gush out of the soil of thy mind
And spread sprays of fine smiles
Running in all directions,
Spreading their vital veins
Through laugh-thirsty hearts.
Let the lake of thy smiles break its embankment
And spread to territories of Infinitude.
Let thy smiles
Rush thru lonely stars
To brighten their twinkles.

Balancing East-West

The flood of thy laughter
Will inundate the drought of dry minds
Sweeping away the barriers of cold formalities.
Spread thy smile like the dawn
To vanish the gloom of minds.
Paint thy golden smiles on every dark spot,
Brightening cloudy days.
Command thy smiles to resurrect life
Into the walking dead.
Smile for the dear,
For their grim peace
Bespeaks their victory o'er pain.
Let thy smiles
Pulverize the rocks of sorrow to atoms.
Let thy smiles meander
Thru desert-souls and oasis-hearts alike.
Let the deluge of thy fearless smiles
Sweep thru all minds and every place,
Drowning, washing away
All barriers for miles and miles.
When God laughs thru the soul
And the soul gleams thru the heart
And the heart smiles thru the eyes,
Then that prince of smiles
Is enthroned beneath the canopy
of thycelestial brow.
Protect thy Prince of Smiles
in the Castle of Sincerity,
Let no rebel hypocrisy lurk to destroy it.
Spread the gospel of Smile,

Purify all homes with thy healthy smiles,
Let loose the wild fire of thy smile
And blaze the thickets of melancholia.
Open the long-bottled-up musk of smile.
Unloosen its perfume in all directions,
Intoxicate all with the wine of thy smiles.
Take the rich smiles form every joyous soul,
And from the mine of all true mirth.
North, south, east, west, wherever you go.
Thou smile millionaire,
Scatter thy golden smiles
Freely, freely everywhere.

THE MEANING OF LENT

Actions represent thoughts. Thoughts manifest themselves in actions. Ceremonies represent some spiritual or disciplinary actions. Religious ceremonies are symbols of wisdom. To idolize the symbol by the mechanical performance of ceremonies without understanding their significance is of little use. Mechanical ceremonies, worship of forms without understanding their spiritual essence, is idol worship and creates ignorance. That is why the worship of symbols and the performance of religious ceremonies must be done with perfect spiritual understanding and devotion.

The holy observances during Lent, spiritually understood and practiced, will certainly produce many good results. Just as Jesus prepared his divinely and humanly struggling mind for ultimate union with God, so all people should also prepare their minds and bodies by discipline and sacrifice during Lent in order to understand its spiritual significance. The body overgorged with meat and the mind engrossed in short-lasting frivolities cannot be a fit receptacle to receive the deep message for which Jesus prepared himself and ultimately died to glorify.

So every year, Lent is a good reminder of the duties of mankind so that they may keep themselves in readiness by disciplining their bodies and minds by prayer, fasting and service to receive the Divine Christ wisdom.

To the man of deep discipline Lenten ceremonies are a part of his life; to the forgetful they are a spiritual reminder.

Let us celebrate Lent with a full realization of its significance and spirit.

RECIPE MESSAGES January 1929

Prosperity Recipe

It seems that making money honestly is the most difficult of all life's undertakings, next to finding God. Those who inherit vast fortunes never know this. Making money to support your family or to maintain your God's family of a spiritual organization, is full of trials and romance. It is not the man who is over-eager for success who succeeds. Many want success, a few act for it, and a very few perseveringly and wisely act to find it. Mental laziness, lack of initiative, lack of perseverance are the greatest enemies of success. The poor want money, the rich feel safe in prosperity, only to find they often die poor.

If the poor win victories by satisfying the demands of real necessities, they receive contentment and may live and die rich. That is real prosperity. But to live in poor contentment and die spiritually poor in spite of material riches, is real poverty. Be prosperous by smiling, no matter what happens. Do not be afraid to sell the bonds of smiles when the market of happiness is low. Keep smiling while planning and acting for success, and your smiles will fetch priceless treasures in the end. Wise, persevering activity with unfading smiles bring sure success.

Earn rightly, spend less than your income, invest your money in absolutely secure things, and prosperity will seek you.

Intellectual Recipe

Everyone likes to think he can understand the minds of others. Since Mr. John, an average intelligent man, can understand the mind of his inferior, he thinks he can likewise measure everyone's intelligence. He forgets that another more intelligent man can measure his intelligence just as he can that of his inferior. Thus in an endless way the more intelligent discover the boundaries of the less intelligent ones. To be wise is not to be self-sufficient nor all-knowing. To know, you must be receptive. The humbler, attentive person quickly drinks in knowledge from everyone, everything.

There are two kinds of learned men. The one is a moving library, always collecting books on the shelf of memory. The other is always busy expanding his powers of introspection and of assimilating ideas into his own wisdom. One should never read without assimilation. If you can assimilate, you will know much with little reading. Read every day some good book and keep busy and thus free from getting into mischief. Good books are your most civil, silent friends. Don't forget them in the moments of your adversity. They will never forsake you when other worldly friends may.

The two new books by Brahmacharee Nerode, reviewed in this issue, are very inspiring and full of spiritual food for the hungry.

Spiritual Recipe

We read about God in the various Scriptures differently described. Of His presence and praise we hear in the sermons of professional religious men or in the voices of saints. We imagine His presence behind the veil of beautiful Nature. We think about His existence through the logic within us. All these windows through which we try to look into God are fitted with opaque glass of uncertain inferences drawn from untested, unscrutinized data.

The greatest proof of the existence of God can only be found within by deeply, daily practising some right method of meditation learnt from a competent Guru or preceptor. Salvation, self-realization, will never come through unexamined beliefs. God's light never can shine through the closed doors of blind sentiments. Through the open windows of logical seeking, God can manifest. Satisfaction in a belief about God without actually contacting Him is the death of wisdom and divine acquaintanceship. Remember your outward satisfaction and religious trade-mark of being a Christian or a Hindu Brahmin will not redeem you. Do not remain idle and hidden behind the cloak of a denominational religion and thus stop from making a real unceasing effort to know God in this life. Do not die ignorant, but die in wisdom to live forever in God. Right meditation balanced with activity must be the cry of Christians, Hindus and all religionists, all churches, as the only saviour. Your question of redemption from the self-created prison of ignorance must be settled directly by yourself with God. If you mean business with God, He will surely answer you. Only be persistent, deep, unbaffled in your demands from God.

Find Him in the grotto of your heart's silent craving and you will find Him in the jungles of Hindustan or the jungles of a modern city where the roaring, death-dealing tigers of automobiles and fierce trucks prowl.

Find Him not within and you will find Him not in the holiest of holy places. Find him within and you will find Him everywhere.

One hour's deep meditation will make you directly feel Truth more than a lifetime's theoretical study of scriptures. Churches and ministers should hold their people not just for big donations nor for erecting big edifices merely, but for their own real good. The religious institutions should hold their followers not by dances and festivities only, but by their own self-realizations won by deep meditation.

Seek until you find the real technique of salvation, but when you find it, stick to it. Do not spend your life in listening about spiritual menus through lectures, but rather get busy practicing the real method of meditation. Remember, you cannot join five universities at the same time nor skip from one university to another every day. So do not skip from one religion to another all the time to find Truth. With reason be loyal to the path you have taken, and above all keep traveling, running, racing in it until you have reached the goal of peace.

The surest sign that God exists is felt through the increasing heart-bursting Joy felt in meditation. When your mind is free from prejudice, when little narrow-mindednesses vanish, when you unreservedly sympathize with everybody, when your tears flow when others weep, when you hear the one voice of God in the chorus of churches, tabernacles, temples and mosques, when you realize life is a joyous battle of duty and at the same time a passing dream or a temporary motion picture performance, and above all, when you become increasingly intoxicated with the joy of meditation and in making others happy by giving them God-peace, then you will know God is with you always and you in Him.

RESURRECTION

Thought is infinite. Every word represents an ideal conception of the Infinite, because behind every word and thought is a manifestation of the Infinite. Many waves of thought are dancing in the waves of consciousness, but behind that there is the great unceasing ocean of Truth. Our expressions are waves of the ocean of understanding.

Resurrection—what is its meaning? It is life! To rise again! To rise to life! To rise—what and how? We must understand that resurrection means to live again. Every thing is undergoing a process of change. Then changes are either detrimental to the object which changes or are beneficial to it. For example, if I take this glass and strike it on the floor it would be changed, would it not? It would not be a beneficial change; it would be harmful to this object. But if I polish it up and make it shine, and clean it from bacteria, then that change is beneficial. Resurrection means any beneficial change that happens to an object or to a human being.

Now we are talking about human beings. You can resurrect your old furniture in the carpenter shop. You can resurrect your house through architects. We are talking of resurrecting the human body, and resurrection means any uplifting change. You cannot sit still because you must either go backward or forward. Isn't that a great thing—a marvelous truth that in this life you cannot remain stationary? Either you must accept changes which are harmful to yourself or which are beneficial to yourself.

We say that every human being is an expression of the great vast Spirit. Isn't it marvelous when we see how we human beings, without any motors, without any wires, without any visible electricity, run smoothly? The human machine wakes up in the morning, eats breakfast, goes to work, goes to lunch and eats again; goes back to the office, has dinner, then it goes to the movies, then goes to sleep, then it wakes up again and does the same thing all over again day in and day out.

We are controlled by something like radio-active and vito-active energy let loose by God! Just as ships are radio-operated, so we are controlled by the Infinite Spirit which is present everywhere. But the thing is this—just as the sunlight falling on the water in a glass which I keep moving becomes divided into a million suns, so the Spirit reflected in each human body and mind has been reflected as individualized Spirits or souls. Now though this soul reflects spirit, still, being identified with the body, it is trying very hard through processes of evolution to resurrect itself from the cage of the body, from the thralldom of the body and mind. The soul wants to return to the Spirit. If I had a cup filled with water and I held it under the lamp and moved the water, I have only a distorted reflection of the light in it. That is not the real light, but it may delude you into thinking that the light is real. Resurrecting the reflected image signifies taking it away from the moving cup of restless consciousness and reuniting it with the original all-pervading light.

Soul is reflected from the Spirit in the body and it is caged by the body, so it has all the limitations of the body and the mind. We must resurrect the soul from the thralldom of the body and the mind and unite it with the Spirit. It is easier said than done, isn't it?

Theory and Practice

There is a story that Bernard Shaw met God in Heaven and said to Him, "Don't you remember me? I introduced You to crowds in big halls and sent them up to heaven by the carloads." Than God said, "You sent them all right, but none arrived here." The thing is, sometimes we pray theoretically. We have resurrected ourselves from our blemishes according to our imagination, but facts are different. Resurrect yourself! It must be not only theoretically but practically. Even theoretical prayer is better than nothing at all, but sometimes it is a detriment to practical understanding.

Let us study first about mental resurrection. In the beginning of our life the soul begins to play with the body and gradually becomes the slave of the body. We must learn to live the life above the physical. Mental development is the by-product of physical development. We find according to natural evolution that the soul resurrects itself to the plane of intellect or plane of prosperity, and then rises to the plane of spiritual realization which gives a meaning to all prosperous development and intellectual attainment. Intellectual attainments are undoubtedly helpful—all good things help. Gradually we understand the way how to resurrect the body into the Spirit.

Resurrection means to resurrect the soul from the cage of ignorance; to lift it, to release the soul from the bondage of human life. Human life may be very beautiful, but it is just like a bird of paradise in a cage. You open the bird's cage but due to love it may stay in—it does not want to fly away; but is that not a pity not to want to go out into the open from whence it came? It is afraid—and we, in meditation, say, "I am slipping—will I slip into the Infinite and never come back?" We are afraid of the skies. We have lived too long identified with the body. That is why we are afraid of our own infinite omnipresence—afraid to resurrect our omnipotence—afraid to resurrect our omniscience.

Bodily Freedom Not Real Freedom

To resurrect our wisdom from the bondage of body is spiritual resurrection. I will talk of body resurrection now. The next thing I have to say is about living dead people walking on the streets. So many think they are free because their hands and feet are free and they walk on the streets of a city free. They think they are free, but they are not free. They are in bondage—in chains—like men walking in sleep. If you have not been able to resurrect yourself form the bondage of sickness you are still imprisoned behind the bars of matter. To resurrect yourself from disease by right living is extremely necessary. By deep study, after many years, I have found out in a nutshell how to express health—by contacting Cosmic Energy.

We must also understand about food values. Carrots contain valuable vitamins. Wash them but do not do anything else to them. I ordered some raw carrots at a place I was visiting and when they were brought in they didn't have any heads or feet. The tops and bottoms contain the vitamins. Meat is not worse than a cooked vegetable dinner of killed vitamins. Resurrect your mind from the bad habits of wrong eating. Start with the carrots. Don't forget them. They are hard and nice—you have not to chew bones to get strength. When you chew carrots they give power to the teeth. The vitamins are in the top. Vitamins are sparks which set the gunpowder of chemicals in motion. Vitamins are absolutely necessary to the system for the harmonious development of physical strength. Vitamins are the brains of the food. Vitamins are rearranged in the system to give vitality to the body.

A lemon a day; an apple a day; an orange a day; half a glass of orange juice with two tablespoonsful of ground nuts; eight leaves of raw spinach. My mind said I must eat it but my palate rebelled against it. I am a believer in facts, so I chopped the spinach leaves very fine and added orange juice, and it makes a wonderful dish. Then you will know you are eating spinach. When you cook it the vitamins are all gone. I have never felt better in my life. I have very strong muscles now and of course Yogoda and not only food helps that. Grapefruit is very good. Then a little piece of banana—about one-fourth. Then unsulphured figs and raisins. Eat these things every day.

Right Food Must Be Taken

I recently met a man called Uncle Billy Ries—79 years old. He has grown a head of hair on a perfectly bald head. He said that he had been for years carrying a bay-window in front and was given up to die at 25 years of age. He resurrected himself—he began to think if there is a God ...He has no business in making me sick—then to think it ....must be his own fault. You see, he was resurrecting himself form the disease which had been constantly coming to him ....through his own fault. He found that sixteen elements are necessary to the body. You have a whole meal often but a starvation diet; whole meals of white bread and sugar and pies might satisfy but would kill in a few months. When you have to eat why not eat rightly? So he dieted and got back his health completely. He kicks way up high in the air and he successfully wrestled with me. We are great friends. Much valuable health information I owe to him.

The ordinary figs and raisins are mummies. They are so fixed that they do not decay, but have no life. These figs and raisins you can write in your will and leave to future generations as heirlooms. sun-dried figs only live three months. In the mummy kind the sulfur fumes are passed through them and kill all the vitamins. Isn't it too bad to preserve things and kill the good part? Four unsulphured figs and prunes and a few raisins a day are good. Then you need a half or a fourth glass of milk or a boiled egg. It is good to boil eggs hard because there may be germs through the hen's being sick. One-half glass of orange juice with ground nuts. Then one-fourth glass of buttermilk, a little piece of cheese, a piece of whole-wheat bread with butter or nut margarine. Nut margarine is very good. I do not mean that you shall live only on this, but you may eat more or less. But if you remember these rules you will not be making any transgression on nature. This has been only after years of experiment I have found all this out. I shall broadcast this information. Nature will not listen to excuses of your years of transgression against her health rules. If you eat sensibly, then if you are in the habit of breaking some laws occasionally, it will not so much hurt you.

So resurrect yourself from the bad habit of eating wrongly. A rattlesnake gives you warning—but gravy and white flour don't tell you. The gravy and white flour look very nice. Everything white is not always good—sometimes brown things are very nice. We used to have unprocessed cereals until the mills came and we began to refine things, and now by a round-about way the best is taken out of the grains. Colonic poisoning comes with white bread. You cannot afford to have constipation. Stomach exercise of Yogoda is marvelously efficient.

The Wisdom of Fasting

Another thing, every week you must fast one day on orange juice to rest the organs. You won't die—you will LIVE! Each month fast two or three days consecutively, living only on orange juice. There is so much bondage to matter—of fear to miss a meal. It is so evident we are not living by the Spirit of God. Jesus Christ talks about living by the Spirit of God. Resurrect yourself from this bad mental habit of overeating and palate slavery. When you fast on orange juice it scrubs every cell. At least every month you should give a thorough house-cleaning to your body by fasting. Do not let poison accumulate in your system. When you are suddenly sick you begin to pray to God. Don't let yourself get sick. The greatest way of health and the simplest is, every week fast one day on orange juice and two or three days consecutively a month.

Resurrect your soul from the hypnosis of bad habits in eating. You must do lots of resurrecting in order to get to God. Not only right eating but moderation in all things and sunlight and exercise are just as important. Then comes the question of resurrecting yourself from the consciousness of disease. That is more important than even meditating or trying to seek a remedy when you are sick. According to experiments of German scientists, many people are better because they do not analyze themselves or suffer from mental discouragement. There is a close relation between the mind and the body, and destroying the consciousness of disease is important. Many times diseases have left us and our consciousness of disease brings them back again.

The Ghost Explains

In a village a saint lived. He was meditating in the night, when he saw a ghost of smallpox entering the village. He said, "Stop, Mr. Ghost, go away. You cannot molest a town in which I worship God." But the ghost said, "I will take only three people according to my cosmic karmic duty." The saint unwillingly had to nod assent. The next day three died, but the day after more died, and so on, more and more, until hundreds had died. The savant, thinking of the deception played on him, meditated, and the ghost came. The saint said, "Mr. Ghost, you deceived me and did not speak the truth." But the ghost said, "By the Great Spirit, I did speak the truth to you." Then the saint said, "You promised to take only three and your have taken hundreds." The ghost said, "I took only three, but the rest killed themselves with fear."

You must resurrect your mind from the consciousness of disease—from the thought of disease. You are reflecting invulnerable spirit. The body rules the mind but the mind must rule the body and then the body will not accept suggestions of environment and suggestions of heredity. Wrong ways of physical living have been handed down to posterity. Diseases exist only when you stimulate the thought of the forefathers and thereby reinforce their ignorance. You must always remember that if the Spirit takes away the radio-active energy then you would drop just like that. So if God takes away the energy, with all your dinners and all your society and money, you cannot live; so remember that you are living by the power of God. You must give the whole credit to God that you are directly living by His power. You do not care about difficulties—you are not afraid. Resurrect yourself for the consciousness of diseases that have been handed down by your forefathers. God never created disease. These are the truths which have been preached in India ages ago. Truth that shall make you free!

Then comes resurrection from our own mental habits. You know that the silk worm weaves threads around itself into a cocoon. Before it slips out of the cocoon into a butterfly, the silk man gets hold of him and the silk worm finds its death in the prison created by itself. We do just like that. Before the wings of spirituality grow, we foolishly weave the threads of fear, worry and ignorance around ourselves until disease and death come and destroy us. We find ourselves in the bondage created by ourselves. What is most destructive? Our own thoughts, our own wrong ways of living, thinking first and then doing. We must resurrect ourselves from the thought of anger, from the thought of selfishness, from the clamor of inharmonious living.

"Let the Dead Bury Their Dead"

Many people think they are awake, but they are not. Mostly they are walking deads. Have you ever heard of people walking in sleep, crying fire or lecturing? Most people are like that. I don't mean Yogoda students or those who are living the life of truth. Jesus said, "Let the dead bury their dead." Because one was to be buried beneath the soil and one was already buried beneath the soil of ignorance. So the thing is this—resurrect those who have buried themselves under their wrong living. You must be able to smile in order to do that. Not like this: "I am DEElighted to meet you," not that kind of smile. When you smile—when God smiles through the heart, through the soul, when the soul smiles through the heart and the heart smiles through the eyes, then the prince of smiles is enthroned beneath the canopy of your celestial brow. Let no rebel hypocrisy ever destroy it. Smile when the storms of suffering shock themselves around you. Say, "I have launched my boat on a dark sea, I have heard Thy call, Thou knowest that I am coming." He knows that you are on the sea of trials; He knows that you are moving your bark. He knows that you must battle these storms that are around. You are clouded through self-ignorance because you don't see the Spirit around everything. That is why you must resurrect yourselves, your souls, from the trials around you. You must always say, "I have launched my boat on the sea of sunshine. I, through my mental radio, am sending the vibration that I am coming." You must battle even when the hands seem to break, you must battle, you must not give up. Then, when the clouds will finish and the life of happiness and prosperity will be back again, you will forget your trials.

Trials are not sent to you to destroy you but come that you may appreciate God better. God does not send those trials; they are of our own making. All we have to do is to resurrect our consciousness form the environment of ignorance. Environmental troubles, which we consciously or unconsciously have been creating in the past somewhere, some time, we must blame ourselves for. There must not be an inferiority complex. You must say, "I know You are coming! I will see Thy silver lining. In this tumultuous sea of trial Thou art the pole star of my shipwrecked thoughts." What are you afraid of? You are not a man. You are not what you think you are; you are the immortal. Not immortality identified with human habits—habits are your deadliest enemies. In crucifixion Jesus could keep His love and say, "Father, forgive them, for they know not what they do." So forgive your trials and say, "My soul is resurrected; my power is greater than all my trials, because I am the child of God." All those who receive God develop their mental powers by serious application. Your mental powers will expand, your cup of realization will be big enough to hold the ocean of knowledge. Then you have resurrected yourself.

Give and Forget

Resurrection was celebrated last Easter. Jesus gave a great example. People that you do good to turn around and slap you. Expectation is meanness, is littleness. Give and forget. If your neighbor slaps you, just say he does not know any better, but don't say it loudly. Resurrect yourself from the littleness of life, little things that disturb you. Do you think you are completely unbalanced, ruffled, shattered, whipped, lacking power? No. You have power; you don't use it. You have all the power you want. There is nothing greater than the power of the mind. Resurrect your mind from the little habits that all the time keep you worldly. Smile that perpetual smile—smile of God. Smile that strong smile of balanced restfulness—that billion-dollar smile that no one can take from you.

I was on my way to Los Angeles once and met a man for whom I felt sorry. I thought, "What is the matter with this man? I must resurrect him. He has buried himself beneath this artificial habit of gloom." I said, looking at him, "Are you happy?" He tried to kill me with a gaze. I looked straight at him. What have I to fear? Nothing. He said, "Is that your business?" I thought, he had killed me in his mind and he could not kill me more. He said, "Yes, I am happy." I said, "No, I can tell what is in the mind." I call a spade a spade. He said, "Why shouldn't' I be happy? I put fifty to sixty thousand dollars a month in the bank." I thought, "Poor soul!" I said, "Tomorrow you may not be here to carry a cent. Have you opened your bank book with God?" Later he invited me to lunch, but he was inwardly antagonistic to me. Then we talked and he loosened up. I said, "Don't rely on riches. You may die and not have even a chance to make a will. These material riches are not yours. Open your bank book with God." He said, "Meet me in Boston." I said, "Meet me in Los Angeles." but he did not have time. Then in Boston I was at the hotel where he stopped and the hotel manager said, "Don't you know what happened to him? He was coming from a hockey match and was struck down by a truck and never regained consciousness." I felt very badly. See, he waked up a little bit but not enough.

The Lap of Immortality

If you have assurance with the Infinite, you will know, whether or not nature shatters your body, you are still on the lap of immortality, still on the lap of that Infinite assurance. Resurrect yourself from the consciousness of human habits and the human thoughts thereof. Every second live in that consciousness—it is the last thing, that which alone will live forever. This is not to frighten you but to quicken your understanding, quicken your efforts—that you do not keep your soul buried under false satisfaction.

Open your bank book with Him—it shall never be lost. You can use it through all your travels in eternity, whether in an airplane or an astral plane. You should say to yourself: "From star to star I will fly, whether on this side of eternity or the other side of eternity, or surging thru the waves of life, from atom to atom—flying with the lights—whirling with the stars or dancing with human lives! I am the immortal! I have resurrected myself from the consciousness of death."

Resurrect yourself from anger, from melancholy, from failures. You must succeed to know that you are God's child. Success is not limited to spiritual matters. Success must come in everything. Resurrect yourself from the consciousness of disease, from mental habits and weakness. Have a strong smile which shall never be shattered by the trials of your circumstances. Then comes spiritual resurrection. Resurrection means relaxation—to relax yourself from your body. As you relax yourself from your mental body in meditation, so you must relax yourself from the internal organs, and body consciousness. Then you become free; your soul knows that you can live without the body though living in the body; it can say it is separate. Resurrection does not mean a change only after this mortal change. You must resurrect yourself while in this body. You resurrect yourself every night in sleep. Sleep is unconscious resurrection. You must do that consciously in meditation—meditation is conscious resurrection. Some of our saints in India have been buried and brought back alive after several days under the ground. They have proved that resurrection is possible. To do without food and still live, that is conscious resurrection. Resurrection of Jesus Christ is different. It is still higher. Resurrection means you understand creation—how to free the soul from the bondage of ignorance.

Right Understanding is Necessary

We have no existence but in the universal. The body you see is nothing but materialized electricity. How could electricity be sick? It is a delusion. But simply saying it is delusion is not enough. If in a dream you see a wall and you see your body strike the wall, you will have a broken skull in dream. Yogoda says it is only by coming in contact with God that one sees that God is the universe and that the body is nothing but condensed electricity. Science has said that electricity is nothing but energy or frozen cosmic consciousness. We must not call it mind. Mind is different. To say everything is mind is wrong. It is cosmic consciousness which makes us feel different things; consciousness of matter and consciousness of spirit. I have written plainly in joy "Scientific Healing Affirmations" why it is we do not see Spirit in matter. Jesus Christ had the power to see it. Resurrection means not only to resurrect body and soul to another sphere of existence, but to change the atoms of the body as well as spiritualize them and release them along with the mind. Everything—skin, hair, eyes—is nothing but frozen energy and frozen consciousness of God. Peter took off the ear of the centurion and Jesus healed him. Why? Because he knew that the atoms were controlled by the Consciousness of God and atoms obey Him. They do not obey you—why? Because you are not controlling that cosmic consciousness which is holding this flower together as a flower. You have the illusion of solids. By meditation you will first be able to separate the soul from the body. The cosmic golden cord that binds the atoms is the tender Spirit. It is His cord with which He binds the atoms and they become the flower, or the human body. He takes lots of electrons like a child modeling in clay models, and He throws them into eternity and they are stars or universes. We are very little to

Him—I think nothing more than bacteria. We are very small but we are very big!

A little story—about bigness. It is that though we think our things are marvelous they are not big to God at all. I saw a big pile of snow and a very little ant crawling along. I thought it must be thinking of scaling the Himalayas. It was Himalayas to the ant but not to me. A million of our years may be a couple of years in the mind of God. We must think everything in terms of bigness—eternity—space.

The Crucifixion of Self-Sufficiency

Last of all, resurrect your mind from formal faith—faith which may have given you a little satisfaction but which you have outgrown; religions which you lived with under the conviction that you know—while you don't know. The greatest crucifixion of the soul is the crucifixion of self-sufficiency—when we are thinking of how wonderfully big we are. Your soul must be relaxed from the bondage, the littleness of the body and the sufferings that the body is subject to. When you think of these diseases you think of the injustice of God, but KNOW you are immortal—not to be crushed by the mortal lessons but to learn and show your immortality and SMILE. Say: "I am immortal, sent to an immortal school. I am challenged by all the fires of the earth—I cannot be destroyed. Fire cannot burn me; water cannot wet me; breezes cannot blow me; atoms cannot shatter me; I am the immortal dreaming the lessons of immortality—not to be crushed but to be entertained." In the dreamland, sickness and health are the same—prosperity and failure are the same. A dream of prosperity is better than a dream of failure. Why not dream prosperity if you have to have dreams? You must have good dreams in this life. If you have too many bad dreams you will be very busy crying and not have time to know that it is all a dream. The dreams of health and prosperity and wisdom are better.

Never Acknowledge Defeat

Resurrect your soul from the dreams of frailties. Resurrect your soul in eternal wisdom. What is the method? Relaxation! Self-control; right diet; right fortitude; undaunted attitude of the mind. Refuse to be defeated. Don't acknowledge defeat. To acknowledge defeat is greater defeat. You have unlimited power—you must cultivate that power, that is all. Meditation is the greatest way of resurrecting your soul from the bondage of body and all your trials. Meditation! Meditate at the feet of the Infinite. Learn to saturate yourself with Him. Your trials may be heavy, may be great, but the greatest enemy of yourself is yourself! You are immortal, your trials are mortal; they are changeable, you are unchangeable. You can unleash the eternal powers and shatter your trials.

Two frogs—one a big one and the other a small one, feel into a pail of milk. The sides of the pail were shiny and smooth. The frogs were battling—every time they lifted their mouths to catch a little oxygen, down they went. They kept on battling. After a while the big frog gave up and was dying but the little frog said, "Well, life is too sweet. I don't like to die. I will keep battling no matter if my little feet fall off". So it was battling for hours, when suddenly it found something solid under its feet—the milk was churned to butter! Out jumped the little frog! That is just how life is! After battling insufficiently like the big frog, you deserve dying; but if you keep on battling with determination, your difficulty will burn up—some answer from the Infinite will come and you will hop out of your difficulties. Be like the little frog. By all means keep battling. Determination! Resurrect yourself form weakness, disease, ignorance, consciousness of disease, and above all from frailties of habits that beset your life.

RECIPE MESSAGES February 1929

Health and Food Recipe

You may eat a whole dinner, very palatable, very satisfying and filling, and yet you may be eating a dead meal.

Experiments show that mice can live eight weeks on water alone, but only six weeks on white bread.

Without the presence of vitamines in food, your meal is dead. It is a meal which you eat to deceive yourself. For instead of nourishment you invite disease.

Diseases are born of our ignorance of the laws of the body and mind. Right eating, moderation and exercise will practically banish disease from the face of the earth. Vitamines are the brains of the food you eat. They direct the digestion and absorption of food while the food builds the different tissues. No matter what you eat, never forget to include vitamines in your menu. Vitamines are condensed life force. They are subtle electricity stored to replete the body battery with fresh energy. They are tabloids of energy. Do not eat vitamine-killed boiled dinners. Vegetables have been ripened and cooked in Nature's kitchen with cosmic fire—ultra-violet rays. Why do you want to cook them again? Scientific experiments show beyond question that cooking destroys the vitamines. Without vitamines, the swallowed food goes into the stomach without direction. Vitamines direct the building of various tissues from food. Therefore, make it a point to remember the following articles to include in your daily food, and you will say goodbye to disease. The following are the garland of pearls of health laws gathered from beneath the vast ocean of study on dietetics:

1. A carrot a day (with a part of stem and roots—unscraped—only thoroughly washed). Chew it well. Nature made it hard to strengthen your teeth by chewing. It is sweet and luscious once you get used to the taste. You will soon find cooked carrots absolutely tasteless, in addition to their being only the corpse of the carrot from which the vitamine soul has departed.

2. A lemon a day.

3. An orange a day.

4. An apple a day.

5. A glass of almond milk or any nut milk.

(Grind two tablespoonfuls of nuts thoroughly and mix with water).

6. Chopped green-leafed vegetable daily.

7. Unsulphured dates and raisins—one handful daily.

8. Avoid white flour and over-eating.

9. Keep colon clean.

10. Whole wheat bread, fresh cheese and a glass of milk are beneficial if you work hard during the day.

One should not have a starvation meal or eat less than one needs of the right articles of food. A man of sedentary habits like a writer or office worker should eat small quantities several times a day rather than a few large meals a day—and should fast occasionally. A man working in the mines should eat more, of meat substitutes, nuts, milk, etc. Adding one or two boiled eggs or one quart of milk a day or six tablespoonsful of almonds with water or milk, would help the gathering of strength to fight hard work. Drink a glass of orange juice and nuts whenever you can if you want more tissue.

A common blunder of vegetarians is to eat an insufficient amount or to eat a "dead meal" of cooked vegetables, minus all the vitamines. Eating meat is not worse than eating just a boiled disintegrated hash of vegetable corpses. By eating boiled vegetable dinners, vegetarians lose strength and inwardly want to go back to a meat diet. The menu I have outlined above contains the minimum food for an individual. Distribute the articles of food during breakfast, lunch and dinner, but do not omit any one of the kinds of food mentioned in it. Following this menu saves one from the trouble of reading elaborate diet books and from the invasion of sudden diseases arising from the omission of one or more of the sixteen elements and vitamines which the body requires for sustenance.

Avoid wrong combinations of starch and meat, or starch and milk.

Rules for happy, healthy living include (besides exercise, pure air, sunshine and right eating) the mental habits of heartfelt smiles, creative ability, concentration, good character, conversation of sex energy, and keeping of good company.

Royal Spinach Salad

Wash raw spinach leaves thoroughly, then chop them finely with a knife. Mix the juice of an orange and sprinkle with a tablespoonful of ground nuts. Delicious.

Treat tender raw asparagus tips likewise.

Carrot Salad

Put two carrots through a meat-chopper. Mix with four tablespoonsful of orange juice and a few pieces of shredded pineapple and a tablespoonful of soaked seedless raisins. Serve on lettuce leaves with whipped cream on top. (Very delicious.)

Hot Nut-Meat Soup

Mix two tablespoonsful of finely ground nuts (almond or peanut butter or any nut) with half a glass of hot water. Add a little salt, 1/2 teaspoonful of sugar, a pinch of black pepper and a teaspoonful of fried onions. One tablespoonful of cream. Three drops of lemon. Put little square pieces of whole-wheat toasted bread floating on top of soup served in soup-plates.

Prosperity Recipe

Success is for the hard working man.

Success is for the man of creative ability.

Success is for the man who knows how to economize.

Success is for the man who thinks and asks opinions of financial experts before he invests his money.

Success is for the man who tries harder to make money after each failure.

Success is for the man of incessant working ability.

Success comes to the man of character.

Success comes to the man of regularity.

Success comes to the man who seeks for more with dissatisfied satisfaction—who does not rest on his laurels.

Success comes to the man who does little accomplishments very well.

Success comes to the undaunted rational plunger.

Success comes to the man who advertises his business rightly and sells the best articles.

Success comes to the man who spends less than his income and not more.

Success comes to those who make money by making others more prosperous.

Success comes to those who spend for God's work with as much spontaneity, naturalness and pleasure as they do for themselves or their own families.

Spiritual Recipe

"All those that received Him, to them He gave the power to be the sons of God."—St. John I:12.

All those who know the methods of enlarging the capacity of their consciousness by right meditation will be able to receive or comprehend the vast Spirit and, being identified with spirit, would become reflected spirits or Song of God.

The above passage in the Bible is a message bearer of the impartiality of God. It declares an undeniable Truth. God is Infinite Omnipresence. He is present in everything equally. His light shines equally in wisdom-sparkling-diamond-souls as well as in charcoal mentalities dark with ignorance. Because God has given us independence to choose between error or Truth, we can keep our minds transparent with purity of knowledge and love, or dark with dogma and inharmony.

But the point is, though the light shines equally on everything, yet diamond souls, by their own creative quality, appreciate or receive the light that flows through them, whereas the sooty souls do not allow the rays to pass through them. Though God made us in His image still it is up to us whether we veil that image with ignorance or let it shine freely through us.

The great point is that though God made us all, the yellow, the white, black and olive-colored, in His image, still some receive and reflect His rays more than others. God has so endowed man with His own power of liberty that man can shut God out or receive Him through his logic and right struggle of life. That some know less than others is not due to God's limiting the flow of His power through man, but to man's not allowing His Light to pass through.

This view alone can make man and not God responsible for all the apparent injustices of the world.

At the same time this view holds out the eternal hand of mighty certainty that everybody is a Son of God, even though he does not know it. God is equally present in every man, and those who receive His Light through their self-created transparent purity can surely be a Son of god. Jesus the man by discipline made himself pure and became God-like, a Son of God. Such a self-made Christ can be the ideal example of ordinary beings. Ignorance-stricken people may be healed of delusion's diseases by contacting the Christ Consciousness of meditation and faith.

The Ideal Example of Jesus

A Jesus redeeming his lost consciousness as a Son of God can alone be the example of other spiritual aspirants who are trying to actually remember their forgotten images as Sons of God. There were Sons of God before Jesus and there will be Sons of God after him. Jesus was one of the greatest ideals who knew how to receive the impartial Light of God within him and thus show others how to receive God's Light through them and become Sons of God.

The Hindu Scriptures say, of each soul, "Thou art That." This idea of identifying one's self with God is not blasphemy, as some suppose. On the other hand it is wrong to say we are mortals, whereas we are essentially made of immortal stuff. It is the Truth that we are Gods and it is wrong to call ourselves weaklings.

The dream of error has become a reality with man. The dream of a soul of being a mortal being must be broken. The thought of one's being an immortal soul if properly cultivated can make one realize his vastness instead of smallness.

It is only by realizing our oneness with God that we can completely break our self-created imaginary limitations of accidents, failure, lack, disease and death. God has everything, health, efficiency and wisdom, and to be one with Him is to have claim over everything which He has, as His own Son.

VISIONS OF INDIA

India is the epitome of the world in everything—a land of all kinds of climates, religions, commerce, arts, peoples, sceneries, stages of civilizations, languages.

Her civilization dates back many thousands of years. Her great seers, prophets and rulers left records behind them that prove the great antiquity of the Aryan civilization in India.

Many European travelers visit India, see a few of the street magicians, sword-swallowers or snake-charmers, and they think that is the highest India has to offer them. They do not realize that these men do not represent India. The real life and secret of India's vitality is her spiritual culture, which has made her the motherland of religions since time immemorial. Although the West can teach India much about sanitation, business methods and development of resources—although India needs business missionaries like Henry Ford and Thomas Edison, yet the Western lands, too, are thirsty, consciously or unconsciously, for the practical spiritual lessons that India has specialized in for centuries.

In the Western cities, science has progressed so far that the physical man is usually well taken care of, fed and clothed and sheltered. Yet physical and material comfort without mental and spiritual peace and solace is not enough. India has been the unproclaimed reformer, the grand inspirer of human minds and souls. She has been the spiritual model of all religions. Her greatest and richest legacy to mankind has been the techniques discovered and handed down for centuries by her saints and seers for the scientific spiritual culture of man.

India is a land of mystery, but of mystery that reveals itself to the sympathetic inquirer and seeker. India has the grandest and highest mountains—the Himalayas—in the world. Darjeeling, in the north of India, is the Switzerland of that country. The unique ruins of ancient castles and vast palaces of princes in Delhi; the vast Ganges made sacred by the centuries of meditation near its banks by many God-realized saints; the sun-gilded teeth of the Himalaya mountain-ridges; the ancient places and caves of meditation where Yogis and Swamis saw the faggots of ignorance blaze with the wisdom of God; the Taj Mahal at Agra, the finest dream of architecture ever materialized in marble to symbolize the ideal of human love; the dark forests and jungles where the distant tigers roam, the blueness of the Indian skies and the bright sunshine, the innumerable varieties of Oriental fruits and vegetables; the many various types of people—all these tend to make India different, fascinating, romantic, never-to-be-forgotten.

A Land of Great Contrasts

India is a land of great contrasts—untold riches and utmost poverty, the highest mental purity and coarse, plain living, Rolls Royces and bullock carts, gaily-caparisoned elephants and quaint horse-wagons.

In the north, we find blue-eyed and blonde-haired Hindus, and in the hotter south, we find the dark sun-kissed skins of the tropics. From start to finish, India is a land of surprises, of contrasts and extremes. Life becomes prosaic with too much business, too many dull certainties; so in India one feels that life is a great adventure, a thing of mystery and surprise.

India may not have material skyscrapers and all the sometimes spiritually-enervating comforts of modern life—she has her faults, as all nations have—but India shelters many unassuming, Christ-like spiritual "skyscrapers" who could teach the Western brothers and sisters how to get the fullest spiritual joy out of any condition of life. Those scientific mystics and seers, who have known Truth by their own effort and experience, and not through ordinary, personally-unverified beliefs, can show others how to develop their own intuition and open the fountain of peace and satisfaction from beneath the soil of mysteries.

Though I have had the advantage of some Western education, yet I feel that in India alone I found the true solution to the mysteries of life. This feeling inspired the following poem to India, which I wrote recently:

My Mother India

Not where the musk of happiness blows,
Not in the land

Balancing East-West

Where darkness and fears never tread,
Not in the homes of perpetual smiles,
Not in the heaven or Land of Prosperity
Would I be born
If I have to put on a mortal garb again,
A thousand famines may prowl
And tear my flesh,
Yet would I love to be again
In my Hindustan.
A million thieves of disease
May try to steal the fleeting health of flesh,
Or the clouds of Fate
May shower scalding drops of searing sorrow,
Yet would I there
In India love to re-appear.
Is this, my love, a blind sentiment
Which beholds not the pathways of reason?
Ah no! I love India,
For I learned first to love God and all
beautiful things there.
Some teach to seize the fickle dew-drop—Life—
Sliding down the lotus leaf of Time.
Some build stubborn hopes
Around the gilded brittle body-bubble.
But India taught me to love
The soul of deathless beauty
In the dew-drop or the bubble,
Not their fragile frame.
Her sages taught me to find my Self

Paramhansa Yogananda

Buried beneath the ash heaps
Of incarnations and ignorance.
Through many a land
Of power, plenty and science,
My soul, garbed as an oriental
Or an occidental, traveled far and wide
Seeking Itself—
At last in India to find Itself.
If mortal fires blaze all her homes
And golden paddy fields
Yet to sleep on her ashes and dream immortality,
O, India, I will be there!
The guns of science and matter
Have boomed on her shores,
Yet she is unconquered,
Her soul is free evermore.
Her soldier saints are away
To rout with Realization's ray
The bandits of Hate, Prejudice,
Patriotic Selfishness,
And burn the walls of Separation dark
Which lie 'tween children of the One,
One Father.
The Western brothers by matter's might
Have conquered my land;
Blow, blow aloud her conch-shells all!
India now invades with love
to conquer their souls.
Better than Heaven or Arcadia.

Balancing East-West

I love Thee, O my Mother India,
And thy love I shall give
To every brother nation that lives.
God made the earth,
And man made his confining countries,
And their fancy-frozen boundaries.
But with the new found love I behold
The borderland of my India
Expand into the world.
Hail, mother of religions, lotus,
Scenic beauty and Sages,
Thy wide doors are open
Welcoming God's true songs
Through all the ages.
Where Ganges, woods,
Himalayan caves and men dream God,
I am allowed; my body touched that sod.

Visions of India's Life-Giving Philosophy

From time immemorial, India's greatest minds have specialized in discovering and understanding the philosophy and mystery of life. One of the oft-disputed questions in philosophy is whether the goal of human life is service or selfishness. Once I had a great controversy with a European who repeatedly and blindly affirmed that the goal of life was service, while I maintained that it was higher selfishness. I asked him again and again for his reasons in believing in "service", but instead of satisfying my discrimination, he kept on reiterating, "Service is the goal of life. It is blasphemous to doubt that." Finding him so dogmatic, I asked him, "Is service the goal of life because the Scriptures have declared it?" "Yes," he vehemently replied. "Do you believe everything literally in Scripture?" I questioned him. "Do you think Jonah was swallowed by a whale and came out alive after a few days? How do you account for it?" "No. I do not understand how he could do that," my friend said. That was just the point. In order to really know the truth contained in Scriptural stories, and in order to understand what is erroneous, or right, literal or metaphorical, in Scriptural writings, one must use his own reason, discrimination and power of intuitional verification developed thru meditation.

Scriptures Not Always Infallible

Many people think that what is printed in black and white is right. Above all, most people believe that anything wearing the robe of Scriptural authority is absolutely beyond question. But putting on an outward garb cannot make one infallible. Writers of Scriptures can also make mistakes. In order to know the truth of a doctrine, we must live it and find out if it works or not—give it the acid test of experience. Let us get out into the world and compare our religious beliefs with the religious experiences of true teachers. Let us be iconoclastic of our own errors that need to be destroyed within us. We must not harbor an undigested mass of theology and thus suffer from chronic theological indigestion.

Service a Form of Selfishness

The law of service to others is secondary to, and born out of the law of self-interest and self-preservation and selfishness. Man never in his sane mind does anything without a reason. All religious doctrines and instructions are based either on blind superstition or on real religious experience. The real reason behind the Scriptural injunctions to "Serve thy fellow-men", and "Love thy neighbor as thyself" is that the law of service to others is to be obeyed by all devotees who would, thru others, expand the limits of their own self.

No action is performed without reference to a direct or indirect thought of selfishness. Giving service is indispensable to receiving service. To serve others by financial, mental, or moral help is to find self-satisfaction. Besides, if any one knew beyond doubt that by service to others, his own soul would be lost, would he serve? If Jesus knew that by sacrificing his life on the altar of ignorance, He would displease God or lose His favor, would He have acted as he did? No, He knew that though he had to lose the body, He was gaining His Father's favor and His own Soul. Such immortal sons of God and all the martyrs and saints, make a good investment—they spend the little mortal body to gain immortal life.

There is nothing worth-while gained without paying a price. Thus even the most self-sacrificing act of service to others can be shown to be done not without any thought of self. It is logical, therefore, to say that the higher selfishness, or the good of the Higher Self, is the motive of life instead of service to others without thought of self.

Must be Given Because Received

In giving service to others, a man knows also that otherwise he cannot rightly receive service from them. If the farmers give up agricultural work, and the business men give up their business of transportation and distribution, then how could even the renunciate maintain himself? Nowadays, with increased population and wealth, even forests are divided off and owned by big landowners, who placard the trees with signs warning the trespasser that he will be prosecuted for coming into another man's property. So the renunciate cannot logically say, "I will not work or earn my living—I will live on the wild fruits of the forest". Hence, services given and received have reference to the goal of a lower or higher selfishness.

Three Kinds — Evil, Good and Sacred Selfishness

We must, however, clearly distinguish between the three kinds of evil, good and sacred selfishness. The evil kind is that which actuates a man to seek his own comfort by destroying the comforts of others. To be rich at the cost of others' loss is sin, and against the interests of the higher individual self of the person who does it. To delight in hurting others' feelings by carping criticism is evil selfishness. This malignant pleasure is not conducive to any lasting good. True and good selfishness is the kind which makes a man seek his own comfort, prosperity and happiness by also making others more prosperous and happy. Evil selfishness hides its many destructive teeth of suffering beneath the apparently innocent looks of comfort-assurances. Evil selfishness shuts one in a small circle and shuts all humanity out beyond it. Good selfishness takes everybody, including one's own self, into the circle of brotherhood. Good selfishness brings many harvests—return services from others, self-expansion, divine sympathy, lasting happiness and self-realization.

Good selfishness should be followed by the business man, who, by sincere, honest, wholesome, constructive actions and labors, enables himself to look after his own and his family's needs. Such a business man is far superior to the business man who thinks and acts only for himself, thinking neither of the ones he serves or of those dependent on him for support. He is then acting against his own best selfish interests, for he will suffer in time. Many misers die, leaving their wealth to relatives who often squander it on wrong self-indulgences. Such selfishness helps neither the giver nor the receiver, in the end.

To avoid the pitfalls of evil selfishness, one should first follow and establish himself in the good forms of selfishness, where one thinks of his family and those whom he serves, as part of himself. From that attainment, one can then advance to a practice of the sacred selfishness, (or unselfishness, as ordinary understanding would term it), where one sees all the universe as himself.

Being Sacredly Selfish

Feeling the sorrows of others in order to make them free from further suffering, seeking happiness in the joy of others, and constantly trying to remove the wants of bigger and bigger groups of people is being sacredly selfish. The man of sacred selfishness counts all his earthly losses as deliberately brought about by himself for others' good, and for his own great and ultimate gain. He lives to love his brethren, for he knows they are all children of the one God. His entire selfishness is sacred, for whenever he thinks of himself, he thinks, not of the small body and mind of ordinary understanding, but of the needs of all bodies and minds (within the range of his acquaintance or influence). His "self" then becomes the Self of all. He becomes the mind and feeling of all creatures. So when he does anything for himself, he can only do that which is good for all. He who considers himself as the one whose body and limbs consists of all humanity and all creatures—certainly finds the Universal, All-Pervading Spirit as Himself.

Act Without Expectation

He does not act with expectation but, with his best judgment and intuition, goes on helping himself as the many, with health, food, work, success and spiritual emancipation.

Working with good selfishness and sacred selfishness brings one in touch with God, resting on the altar of all-expanding goodness. One who realizes this, works conscientiously only to please the ever-directing God-peace within.

Paramhansa Yogananda

ODE TO LAKE CHAPALA

O Chapala!
Like the flickering flame of Indo-skies,
Thy moods of limpid waters
Boisterously play with fitful gleaming storm,
Or rest on thy shining forehead
without a ripply wrinkle!
'This then thy silver, shining mind,
Free of ruffling causes,
A transparent mirror—
Reflects just noble images
Of the green-dressed young and old hills,
Like tableaux of drilling soldiers
Standing hand in hand, with dwarf and tall heads,
Crowned with sliver skies or fleecy clouds.
I beheld the starry damsels
Beautifying their twinkling faces
In the mirror of thy waters.
How I watched in the flickering hall of lightning
Thy furious fight with the gunning clouds.
Showering torrential bullets of spattering rain,
O! what wild cloud-churned skies
and bounding winds,
Rolling thunder peals,
bursting vapour embankments,
Have flooded thy territory of waters
And have lashed thy spirit

Balancing East-West

to rouse thy resting soldier-waves
To leap to furious fightings!
Then again, when truce is signed with storm gods
And warring fury of the skies,
I find a stray white sail
Charged with a vital breeze,
Racing to thy horizon's hidden unknown shores.
Thy nocturnal silence,
Oft rocked to sleep
By the lullaby of thy gentle breakers,
Is rudely roused at dawn
By those busy silence-shattering, droning sounds
Of man-made, horrid watery ploughs
Which encroach upon
Thy private fields of silence,
O! Changing Chapala
—The gleaming lightning of my feeling's skies!
I love thee as never before!
Here's hill-ramparted lake—
Which can allay
The scenic-beauty thirst of yearning minds.
When comes such another? Where?
Alas, Chapala!
Thy beauty will be snatched
Form my adoring skies
By cruel duties of exacting life,—
But they will fail to take away
Thy beauty enthroned in me as joy for e'er.
The stony arms of the palace by thy banks
Enclosed a tract of thy loved waters,

Paramhansa Yogananda

And 'neath the lone, shady tree,
Standing on the spot 'tween two sheets of water,
Oft I sat with those unforgettable hours—
When I beheld the Infinite
Emerge from pale unanswering walls of blue—
And unite my soul with thee,
Mounts, skies, and me!

RECIPE MESSAGES March 1929

Worshipping God Through Sunset

The Sunset City of Dreams at Guadalajara, Mexico.

From the balcony, I gazed westward. On wings of fancy I was carried far. I stood on the shores of the horizon. To the left and right were two mountain ranges which turned mystic violet. When I looked again some fairy hand had already dressed them in intense blue. Behind me lay the twilight-bathed man-made mystic city of Guadalajara. The eastern sky was daubed with deep-rose, fluffy colors. All around, strata of pale clouds lay stacked here and there. As I looked in front, my eyes beheld a magic city of blue islands floating in a lake of gold.

In this archipelago of magic blue isles lay one with a huge peak of blue chalk. This king's peak was crowned with a volcano of gray-white fumes belching a fountain of golden-red lava, which fell arched like a rainbow into the still lake of gold. These golden-red flames swam thick and close like moving, burning aureole-garlands around the blue isles. The blue peak and its crown of flames were mirrored as twins in that silent sheet of the golden lake. To the extreme right, a little quiet lake lay silently sparkling on the bosom of one of the blue isles like a half-veiled moon resting on the billowing clouds.

I long roamed in the mirage city of sunset and clouds, floating in the lake of limpid golden light. O! What wilderness of golden waters, studded with red icebergs of light, spreading directionless to the brink of Eternity!

Methought little fairies of light who were once good souls on earth, after successfully passing through this final test of life, were prompted to play there with their fancies. Methought every day during sunset hour, they turned celestial architects and conjured up mirage cities circled by golden lakes and golden seas. There beyond the gaps of sorrow, beyond the trap of this troubled, hurt-making world, there beyond the hedge of unfulfillment, they breathed red lights, drank orange flames, played and swam on multi-colored lights. There these fairies build a dream-mint where they coined their fancies promptly into realities and remelted them variously as they desired. Here they rolled in wealth of satisfaction and lavished fulfillment on all who could meet them on these dream shores.

Here they did not, like earth folks, have to wait for dreams to come true. Here the fairies dreamt as they wanted and made all those dreams come true by the mere wishing.

This sunset city of dream-isles is the long-past, hidden dream of my fairy fancy come true to-day. I beheld the long-buried treasure of my Soul brought out to dazzle my longing gaze.

Avocado Recipe

Mash up one-half avocado; add to it half a mashed raw tomato, one-quarter of a finely-chopped raw onion, half a finely chopped raw green pepper. Add the juice of one-quarter of a lemon. Mix them and serve on lettuce leaves. This raw-food dish has food value superior to that of meat, and lacks the latter's impurities.

Raw Tomato Cream Soup

The following recipe is taken from "Mrs. Richter's Cookless Book" (published by The Eutropheons, 833 So, Olive St., Los Angeles, California—$1.00) which contains a veritable mine of valuable recipes for raw-food enthusiasts and those who see the health value of eating nature's products in their natural state:

"Put tomatoes and celery through food chopper, proportion being three cups tomato pulp to one cup each of celery and peanut butter. Put the ground tomato pulp and celery through sieve, then add peanut butter, creaming it into the liquid until smooth and without lumps. Now add two tablespoonsful parsley and one large clove of garlic, very finely minced, two tablespoonsful of oil, and beat all ingredients well together."

WHAT IS LOVE?

Love is the scent with the lotus born.
It is the silent choirs of petals
Singing the winter's harmony of uniform beauty.
Love is the song of the Soul, singing to God.
It is the balanced rhythmic dance of planets,
Sun and moon lit,
In the Skiey Hall, festooned with fleecy clouds
Around the Sovereign, Silent Will.
It is the thirst of the rose to drink the sunrays
And blush red with life.
'Tis the Mother-Earth's promptings
To feed her milk to the tender, thirsty roots,
And to nurse all life.
It is the urge of the Sun to keep all things alive.
It is the unseen craving of the Mother Divine,
Which took the protecting Father's form
And the milk of Mother's tenderness
To feed helpless mouths.
It is the babies' sweetness,
Coaxing the rain of parental sympathy
To shower upon them.
It is the lover's unenslaved surrender
To the beloved
To serve and solace.
It is the elixir of friendship,
Reviving broken and bruised Souls.

Paramhansa Yogananda

It is the martyr's zeal to scatter his blood
For well-beloved Fatherland.
It is the ineffable,
Silent call of heart to another heart.
It is the God-drunk Poet's heart-aches
For every creature's groans.
It is to enjoy the family rose of petalled beings,
And thence to move to spacious fields—
Passing by the portals
Of social, national, international sympathy,
On to the limitless Cosmic Home—
To gaze with looks of wonderment and to serve
All that lives—still or moving
This is to know what love is—
He who knows who lives it.
Love is evolution's ameliorative call
To the far-strayed sons
To return to Perfection's home.
It is the call of the beauty-robed ones
To worship the Great Beauty.
It is the call of God—
Through silent intelligences
And star-burst of feelings.
Love is the Heaven
Where the flowers,
Rivers, nations, atoms, creatures—you and I,
Are rushing by the straight path of action right,
Or winding laboriously through error's path,
All to reach haven there at last.

ORIENTAL CHRIST

(LECTURE DELIVERED AT MT WASHINGTON)

Jesus Christ was an Oriental. Therefore, His teachings were derived from Oriental environment and heredity. Truth is not a monopoly of the Orient or the Occident. The sunlight, though pure silver, appears to be red or blue when looked upon through red or blue glasses: so, also, does pure, undiluted Truth appear to be different when expressed through Oriental or Occidental civilization.

The original simple teachings of Jesus have undergone many changes, because of divers translations from language to language, and divers translations of translations. But all of the Great Ones have expressed Themselves simply, and I can find very little difference in the message of Jesus Christ and the other Great Teachers.

Now, I want to tell you something in the beginning, lest there be any doubt in your minds: What I received from the Great Oriental Masters, that same have I received from the teachings of Jesus, the Christ!

The Great Ones, like waves, bathe in the Eternal Sea, and become One with It. Disciples make all the trouble and differences. They begin to create narrowness and bigotry. The pure Message becomes diluted with ignorance. Humanity drinks of the polluted waters and then cannot understand why the thirst remains. Only pure waters can quench thirst. The time has come to separate truth from falsehood, knowledge from ignorance. All truth and knowledge must be sued to combat the black doubts and superstitions hedging humanity in the prison of unhappiness, that the mighty flood of Truth may inundate the gathered darkness of the ages, setting the soul of humanity free.

It amuses me when I hear my Western brothers say—"Do you believe in Christ?" I always say "Jesus Christ." And I picture Him in my mind as He really was—Oriental Christ. Many painters have tried to give Him blue eyes and light hair, but He was a pure Oriental. And you of the West have taken from an enslaved nation, Jesus Christ as your Preceptor, and the greatest gift of all—spiritual freedom, taught by this great Oriental.

Every human being is a product of his climatic conditions, heredity, family characteristics, and the pre-natal and post-natal actions performed by him, as influenced by right or wrong will, right or wrong judgment, right or wrong habits, right or wrong feelings, and by the soul's intuitive guidance. No matter what Jesus Christ was Himself, as regards His own Soul—none can deny that He, being born in the Orient, had to use the medium of Oriental civilization, customs, mannerisms, language, parables, etc., in spreading His message. Hence, the teachings of Jesus Christ, no matter how universal they may be, are saturated with the essence of Oriental civilization.

Jesus was an Oriental, by birth and blood and training. The Wise-Men of the East, or East India, came to confer about Him when He was born, knowing Him to be one of the greatest message-bearers of Truth.

I am not saying that Jesus Christ learned everything from the Great Masters of India, because God never teaches directly through human vehicles. But it has been definitely proven that Jesus was connected with the High Initiates and the Masters of India. In the "Unknown Life of Christ," by Nicholas Notovitch,—the Russian author tells how he went to Tibet, hoping to study Tibetan literature, hand-written on papyrus scroll. Because of the secretiveness of the Lamas, it was impossible to find a trace of what he wanted; but a strange miracle happened. Just when he was returning fruitlessly to India, he fell from a cliff and broke his leg, and was taken back to the Monastery to receive the necessary care! The Tibetans are very hospitable to their invited or stricken guests. While the injured man was recovering, the had Lama asked him what he wanted. He said—"Read to me the papyrus scrolls!" From these sacred scrolls, he secured conclusive evidence that Jesus Christs's name was Isa—meaning Lord, which afterwards was pronounced as Jesus. He conferred with the Masters on Yoga and great problems of human upliftment, living with them at the Monastery; but at the age of fifteen, it is said, they tried to get Him married, so he fled. I don't blame him. But, alas, those who do not marry, repent; and those who do marry, repent. That is why I am glad I am married to the Infinite Nature and Spirit. There is never any hurt and disappointment in that kind of marriage.

The sacred scrolls further revealed that as Jesus Christ was visited by the Wise-Men of the East, so He paid them a return visit to Tibet, and conferred with the Great Masters. Jesus then went to India to commune with the Masters there; and after preaching the Message in India, he went to Asia Minor. He wanted to spread His message universally. Mr. Nicholas Notovitch, in order to prove the above fact about the trip of Jesus, challenged many missionaries to go with him to Tibet. But they did not want to do so. Jesus Christ gave His secret message in India, first of all. If you love Jesus, you must have some consideration for the Orientals. Do not give them nicknames, for you do not know what nicknames they will give you in return. An exchange of nicknames will not enrich you spiritually. Give wisdom, and wisdom will come to you. Give kindness and love, and kindness and love will be returned to you. You always get back what you give out.

Now, to come back. Jesus Christ was an Oriental. His teachings were Oriental, expressed in Oriental language. The Occidental tries to monopolize Jesus Christ, but completely ignores the influence of Eastern customs, culture, and Eastern lessons in Christianity, and thus becomes one-sided. It is not possible to separate the Teacher from His nationality, without causing great misunderstanding and confusion.

I shall tell you a few things which will help you. I am going to tell you frankly, openly,

without any prejudice or partiality, about the Western adaptation of the teachings of Jesus Christ—its defects and its merits. The Western adaptation emphasizes brotherhood; yet, whenever you think of a Church, you think of a band of secretaries collecting money, instead of thinking of their deeds of mercy and good. You think of sermons about Jesus, not sermons giving the revealed message of Jesus Christ, the Great Master. The Western spirit lacks much which the spirit of the East can supply. Granted, that the East is not practical enough! The West is too practical to be spiritually practical. That is why I am trying to unite the two. They need each other.

The pride of materialism should be destroyed, though material efficiency is necessary and right. This is a lesson for the West to learn. Not the complete ignoring of the practical, though the philosophy of idealism should be continually practiced, blended with enough practical commercialism to avoid hardship and suffering—this is the lesson to be learned by the East.

To understand Jesus Christ and his teachings, one must sympathetically study the Orientals—their ancient and present civilization, religious scriptures, traditions, philosophies, spiritual beliefs, and intuitive metaphysical experiences. Though the teachings of Jesus are universal and have been made adaptable to Western environment,—still, in order to understand Christianity, one must first take away its Western veil, and then its Oriental veil. Behind the two opaque veils, real Christianity hides. Western Christianity is the outer crust and Eastern Christianity is the inner crust. The Oriental Christ always emphasized: Take no heed for the body,—what ye shall eat, what ye shall wear. Bread, the men of the world seek after; seek ye the Kingdom of God, and all these things will be added unto you. The Occidental Christian might say instead: Take heed of the body first, that in a healthy body temple ye may find god. Bread, ye men of the world, seek first,—and afterwards, seek ye the Kingdom of God.

In the warm Oriental climate, in a by-gone age, it was easy to get bread without much thinking or much laboring, and thus it was easy to meditate on God in leisure and solitude; whereas, in the Occident, one has to think of bread, hard and fast and successfully, or he will not have time at all, or strength, to seek the Kingdom of God.

Oriental Christ and His teachings are suited to the Orientals and the Oriental climatic conditions. Therefore, the teachings of Jesus must be so judiciously adapted, that they may become possible for the Occidental to follow. Otherwise, it would happen that, as some doctors say, "the operation was successful," but the patient peacefully died on the table. The universal teachings of Jesus Christ should be adapted according to the needs of the Oriental and Occidental—emphasizing the principles of Christian religion, and omitting the non-essential forms added to them from time to time.

Great care should be taken, however, to embody the essential, living principles of Christianity, while it is being transplanted from Oriental atmosphere to Occidental environment. No difference must be made between Oriental Christian religious methods of salvation and Occidental Christian religious technique of salvation. Rather, the distinction should be made between true Christian principles and false, formal, dogmatic Christian creed-bound beliefs. Eastern Christianity considers church-going and intellectual study of scriptures, as spiritual kindergarten work, these only emphasizing the necessity of testing out religious beliefs in the laboratory of meditation, under the guidance of a real man of self-realization, who has found God in the light of his intuition, through deep and unceasing scientific spiritual efforts.

Occidental Christianity advocates formal but beneficial moral and religious welfare and organization work. Western Christianity appears satisfied with theological beliefs and the production of victrola-record, cut-and-dried sermons, and the erection of huge edifices and churches, with a wonderful business system to run them. But while Western Christianity has saved Western civilization from Atheism and immorality, it has failed to awaken the desire to obtain intuitional metaphysical experiences about God, evolved out of the self-created efforts of meditation. Occidental Christianity advocates too much formal, congregational worshiping of God. Oriental Christianity emphasizes individual contact of God, but is utterly lacking in philanthropic organization and social welfare work.

That is why the West, with all the wonderful devices of the practical Occidental mind, is in the East today, dominating it. But mark you, the Eastern soldiers are not silent. The West has power and strength; but the East is armed with silent philosophy—not to conquer lands, but to conquer souls, with love, service and kindliness. We are all children of God,—we have always been,—and will be always. The differences come from prejudices, and prejudice is the child of ignorance. We should not be proud of being Americans, or Indians, or Italians, or any other nationality, for that is but an accident of birth. Above all else, we should be proud that we are children of God, made in His Image. Isn't that the message of Christ?

The East must learn from the West, and the West must learn from the East. The West preaches practicality! The East teaches spirituality! Without idealism, material practicality is the harbinger of selfishness, sin, competition and wars. Without practicality combined with idealism, there is confusion and suffering and lack of natural progress. Let us combine forces and conquer together, instead of one nation conquering the other.

The Orientals revere and acknowledge Jesus as Leader of humanity, Son of God and Truth,—only, they interpret Him differently. The community religious service of the West is marvelous, but that is not enough—for the Western service lacks metaphysical meditation and the knowledge of the methods of direct communion with God. On the other hand, the East lacks organization, but emphasizes direct, first-hand knowledge from God. Therefore, in order to understand Jesus Christ's doctrines, it is necessary to combine the organization efficiency and social welfare philanthropy with personal verification of Christ's teachings by metaphysical study and contacting God individually in the temple of meditation. Then each one can, himself, understand what Jesus Christ was, through the intuitive self-verification of His teachings.

Both organization and spirituality are necessary for normal and satisfactory human progress. I shall give you a picture:

In one place, a ten million dollar temple with marble decorations and a sky-scraper golden dome, allowing ten thousand to be seated comfortably, with a million dollar organ and famous choir chanting hymns to God. It is all impressive and enjoyable, and I appreciate and admire such. But, mind you—God cannot be bribed by big churches, by wealthy people, nor by sermons, songs and formal prayers.

Now, behold: sitting under a tree, beneath a canopy of free skies, a Christ-like man, with only three disciples—but all in conscious contact with God! Would you not prefer to be there, to feel God, and not be overpowered by admiration of the evanescent glory of a gorgeous church? That does not mean that God is not in the churches. God is in the temple, and He is under the tree. But only by earnest, scientific meditation, by spiritual strength, by unceasing desire—can the closed spiritual door of inner Silence be opened to the congregation in the temple or to the devotees under the tree. Pomp and show are not able to open that door, nor is hardship of any kind necessary. It swings on magical hinges, only when the seeking soul's high vibration turns the fairy key. And behind the unseen door lies REALIZATION, the Divine Realization of Jesus Christ.

Hidden away in a Monastery of Tibet, priceless records lie. The world is not yet ready for them. Religious fanatics would only destroy them, should they be given too soon to the world. But no other history of the life of Jesus between the ages of fifteen and thirty, has ever been found. Because of the custom in Tibet, that a sick guest may have his desire granted when possible, the hospitable Tibetan Priests or Lamas have shown the Sacred

Scrolls to one man who is living today. They will belong to the world eventually, when the world is ready for them.

Meantime, the Great Message of Jesus Christ is living and thriving, in both East and West. The West has been perfecting the physical man, and the East has been developing the spiritual man. Both East and West are one-sided. And is it not strange to note that, perhaps due to God's secret Plan,—since the East needs material development, it has been invaded by Western material civilization! And since the West needs spiritual balance, it has been silently, but surely, invaded by Hindu philosophy!

Verily, the West invaded the East to conquer its lands with guns and material force. But the East, in return, has invaded the West with love and philosophy, to conquer souls.

Jesus Christ is the model for both East and West to follow. God's stamp, as Son of God, is hidden in every soul. Do away with masks! Come out openly as Sons of God! Not by talk and learned-by-heart prayer, intellectual fireworks of worded-sermons to please God, but by REALIZATION! Indentify yourself with Christ-consciousness, not with narrow bigotry, masked as wisdom. Identify yourself with Universal Love, by serving all, both materially and spiritually; and then you will know who Jesus Christ was, and can say in your soul that we are all one ban, all Sons of the One God!

Peace! Bliss! Peace!

HOW TO ACQUIRE INITIATIVE

When you look at the vast panorama of this world, when you look at the vast crowds of humanity rushing hot-haste throughout their string of life, you wonder what this is all about. Where are we going, what is the motive, what the best way to get to our destination? Most of us rush aimlessly, regardless of our destination, like a runaway automobile, driving heedlessly in the pathway of life, never realizing the purpose of the path, the winding ways and straight paths that lead to our destination. How can you find your destination, if you never think of it? Many people, though they don't know their destination, still have initiative enough to find out and seek the thing they need—in connection with their desires, in connection with their environment, they always try to use the initiative within them. What is initiative within a person, what is it? Initiative is some creative faculty within you, a spark of that Infinite Creator within you.

America is a land of initiative in business, applied mechanism; India is a land of initiative in spirituality. What is this mysterious faculty? Examine a dozen minds; they all remind you of one horse-power engines. Most people are like that; the whole process, the whole activity of their life consists in waking ,eating, amusements and sleeping. What is the difference between yourself and the animals? One difference, psychologists say, is that man is a laughing animal. It is good to laugh. You need this consciousness of being human beings—if you cure yourself of your laugh, you lose one human evolution. Some people, day in and day out, take life seriously,—they don't enjoy life at all, are afraid to smile. One quality of human beings is to laugh. Another quality, the greatest of all qualities, is initiative.

Initiative means power of creation, the power of creating something nobody else has ever created. What have you ever done in this life, something nobody else has done? Initiative means trying to do things in new ways and trying to create new things. Initiative means creative ability, which is derived from your Creator directly. How many people try to use that ability? Weeks, months, years pass, and they are always the same, they have not changed, except in age. The man of initiative is like a shooting star—creating something from nothing, making the impossible possible by the great inventive power of the Spirit. There are three kinds of initiative people—the extraordinary class, the medium class and the common class, and in "no-man's land" are hundreds huddled together. Ask yourself this question—"Have I ever done anything new in life, have I ever done something new which nobody else ever did?" That is the starting point of your initiative, you must know that, before you can start at all. Some people think they have absolutely no power to act differently; they are walking in their sleep, affected by somnambulism. Their subconscious mind has suggested them into one horse-power people. In order to wake up, you must say: "I have man's greatest quality, every human being has some spark of power by which he can create something new which the world did not create before." How easily I could be deluded with the consciousness of the world, if I let myself be hypnotized by my environment! "Every line is crowded, why try at all?" That is why in every walk of life so many remain unsuccessful, because of lack of initiative, hypnotized by the consciousness of the world.

How to have initiative? The first quality of initiative is the common quality—the man with little initiative tries only to improve on others, somebody's else invention. And in spiritual things, many people just follow the same path,—they were born in some denomination and they die in that denomination. Or, "I was born a Baptist, but when I changed my residence, I happened to be near the Congregationalist Church, so I became a Congregationalist." You have a spark of Divinity within yourself, and you want to adapt yourself conscientiously according to its dictates.

My Master used to say, "Remember this, if you have that faith within you, and if there is something you desire which is not in the universe, it shall be created for you." And I had that peculiar belief in my own strength, in the strength of my will, and I found that some new lines were created to give me the things I wanted. The power of initiative within you remains undeveloped, unformed, unexploited, unused,— and that power is native to the soul, actually given to all of you, but you have not used it. You have lots of solar energy in you. Your first attempt is to try to improve on somebody else, if you have not developed the power to think for yourself, the initiative to have your own way.

The second quality of initiative, the medium quality, is shown by people who write a little new book, make some new inventions, something new, but small. That is the medium quality. The extraordinary quality of initiative is that which makes you stand in blazing fame before the world, like Burbank, Edison, men of initiative, spiritual initiative. Is God partial to these great men, that they had this particular greatness? Were they chosen by Divine will to take so much glory? Those who look for glory are never great,—in their inflated pride, they never receive the strength of God. Those who enjoy giving,—giving strength, courage, music,—they are great.

There is one way to be great, to have this extraordinary power of initiative, which not only gives you a medium quality, but can give you an extraordinary quality of initiative by which you can stand blazing before the eyes of the world. Most people who have become great have been subconsciously guided, have had a tinge of heredity which gave them the initial advantage,—and they used that in their life and thereby became extraordinary. Remember, if you have that extraordinary quality, you are led by unconscious forces of mind by which you change your environment, and in that new environment you can bring forth that great quality.

I believe, and I know, that great men can be made. By training and practice of Yogoda, they can develop that initiative quality and bring it into play. The ones who struggled long ago, see now the fruition of their activities. You must step out of that great horde who are just like automatons, step out and discover how much power you have, overcoming apparent impossibilities. At first, I was afraid to be a teacher—the name of teacher frightened me. You have to be a shock-absorber, love everybody and understand humanity. The moment you get disturbed, you are one with the one who has come to get help from you. You must always be ready to withstand the opinion of the world, in order to succeed. Stay away from one horse-power people; and then think differently, speak a little differently. And you must be untiring in your zeal. The man of extraordinary initiative swallows all difficulties, and says, "I am right." With unflinching steadiness march on your path, believing that the Infinite Creative Power is behind you. You must first get yourself in conscious contact with that Infinite Power. When you contact that Power, which is the source of all initiative, your subconscious mind becomes super-powerful. I used to be apprehensive that if I created a little initiative it might run out quickly under different tests. I know now that within myself is that great Infinite Principle, which is the source of all art, all music, all knowledge. If that is behind me, how can I fail? Whenever you want to create something wonderful, sit quietly and go deep. That Infinite Power, that inventive, creative power is within you. Try something new, and always be sure that that great creative principle is behind anything you do, and that creative principle will see you through. Every human being is guided by the great creative power of Spirit. You have choked your fountain—clear it out. Show infinite determination in everything you do.

People live in dead quotations, go on collecting ideas of others without ever showing themselves. Where are you? Where is the distinctiveness in you, where is the great distinctive power of God in you? You have not been using it. I made up my mind I would not lecture by

learning but by inspiration, believing that the Infinite Creative Power was behind my speech. In other things, too, I have utilized that, helping others in business, etc. I have used mortal mind to bring immortality. I did not say: "Father, do it," but "I want to do it! only, Father, You must guide me, You must inspire me, You must lead me on!"

Do little things in an extraordinary way, be the best one in your line. You must not let your life run in the ordinary way—you have got to do something which nobody else has done, which will dazzle the world, do something that will show that God's creative principle works in you! You may get the power of that great principle. Never mind the past. Errors as deep as the Atlantic Ocean cannot stop you, because the soul can never be darkened. Have unflinching determination to move on your path unhampered. Life may be dark, difficulties come, all chances may go, but never within yourself say—"I am gone, God has forsaken me." One cannot do anything for that kind of a person. Your family may forsake you, destiny seemingly forsake you, all the forces of nature be against you; but by that initiative quality you can go into paradise and defeat the invasions of fate created by your own wrong actions. I may be defeated one hundred times, but I am going to conquer! Defeat is not meant for eternity, defeat is a test for you. Disease, lack of prosperity, are not meant to crush you. Naturally, God wants to make you invincible, bringing into play the almighty power that is within you, so that on the stage of life you can fulfill your destiny. How are you going to find out what suits you! If we all want to be kings, who will be the servants? On the stage, king's and servant's parts are all the same if they play them well. Only remember, that is why we are sent into this world with various desires, various vocations. God meant the world to be a play, an entertainment, a huge show to entertain us. But we forget the Stage Manager and want to play our own parts. So on the stage of life, you are failing because you are trying to play a different part than the one designed for you. Tune yourself with Spirit, and in this earth-play play your part well! Sometimes, the buffoon attracts more attention than the king; so no matter how little your duty is, do it conscientiously.

The world is a stage wherein you are not meant to suffer—the ones who play the tragedy parts must know they are but play. Never mind, always strive to play your part well, in tune with the Stage Manager, so that your little play will dazzle the world. Play your part well, realizing that on the stage of the world the Infinite Power of the Spirit is there! Infinite Spirit creates new success! Infinite Spirit does not want you to be a mechanism! Tune yourself with Cosmic Power, and whether in the factory or the business world mixing with people, always say, "Infinite Creative Power is within me, I shall not go into the grave doing nothing. I am God-man, a rational animal; I am power of Spirit, dynamic source of soul; I shall create revelations in the world of business, in the world of thought, in the world of wisdom—I and my Father are One: what He can create, so can I!"

RECIPES April 1930

HEALTH RECIPE

Bathing Daily in God's Ocean of X-ray

When the sun shines everything seems to smile with its halo of golden rays. Gloomy, dark places seem to forsake their mystery-dreaded atmosphere. The sun seems to cheer the mind. It is the life of all Nature's living children, the trees, flowers, and human being.

We are proud of our sky scrapers and often remain there with seeming satisfaction, banished, imprisoned, and pigeon-holed, walking on velvet cushions, stuffed with rich food, without exercise and above all without the life-giving sunlight.

Scientists put some chickens in ordinary glass houses, and some others in small glass houses fitted with quartz glass. Within a month, the chickens in the quartz glass houses were twice as healthy as the chickens in the ordinary glass houses. The latter began to decline fast. Ordinary glass shuts out the ultra violet rays, whereas the quartz glass does not. The ultra violet rays are not only life-giving but they are the best killers of all forms of bacteria. How can we live safely in rooms fitted with ordinary glass? This is the reason that most indoor resorters, self-elected prisoners of darkness, business men and women, suffer from catarrh and colds and emaciation.

An ordinary bath cleans the body pores and keeps the sweat glands working properly, eliminating impurities. So the Hindu savants say that the person who bathes daily and keeps the pores of his body open, helps his increased body heat to escape through these pores.

Sunlight and ultra violet ray baths are also necessary to fill the tissues and pores with life-giving energy from without. They redden the hemoglobin of the blood, recharging it and making it richer and healthier. As an ordinary bath washes away and clears the bacteria and dirt from the human body, so also the ultra violet rays in the sunlight not only cleanse the body of bacteria but also destroy them. The ultra violet rays are the death rays which penetrate the homes of enemy bacteria hiding in the finger nails and body pores, and scorch them out.

By all means, if you have not time for a walk, open your glass windows and let your life-giving, soliciting friend, Sunlight, fall on you and bathe you all over. Keep on jumping up and down, if you are afraid of catching cold, but each morning do bathe in the ocean of X-Ray which God has created for you. Without a daily bath in God's sea of X-Ray, you cannot be healthy. And remember, only healthy persons are happy.

SPIRITUAL RECIPE

Beware of Jealousy, the Mental T. B.

People are afraid of decaying diseases which beset the body. But few seriously hunt for a cure when they contract the decaying psychological fell disease of jealousy. Shakespeare called it the canker eating at the roots of love. It is worse than that.

This jealousy epidemic seems to be raging in the minds of all nationalities. Jealousy is the matrimonial T. B. It eats into happy, healthy married life and utterly destroys it by suspicion hemorrhages. Continuous mutual nagging acts like bronchial outbursts, affecting the lungs of happiness. Get rid of it. Many youthful lovers have perished under its cruel stroke by exchanging bullets.

It is also the business T. B. when it enters into a business concern, the tissues of co-operation and unity, which are the life of an organization, begin to slowly or rapidly decay. It is this decaying disease of which all healthful political and religious organizations should beware.

This fell disease of jealousy consists of two kinds, the galloping kind and the slowly decaying kind. The first one speedily destroys organizations by wasting all their unifying power. The second one can gradually destroy the fibers of the most wonderful and powerful organization in the world. Unmarried lovers, happily married couples, political and religious organizations, beware! From the foils of jealousy guard your happiness.

ECHOES

My fresh-cut flowers
Of mental whispers of devotion,
I offered in my Temple of Silence.
Those blossoms of love
Droopingly spoke
Through their silent voice of fragrance,
Their love for Thee.
In the Temple of Peace,
At last Thy Light hovered over
And settled upon the altar of my prayers.
Thy invisible veil of secretiveness
Was burnt in the flames of wisdom.
And, lo: I behold thy glory!
Oh! Mutely shall I ever worship Thee,
With never whisper of complaint;
For I have found in Thee
All that I thought I had lost,
All I had so long sought in the Forest of Time.
Now, my roamings will cease,
—For in Thy Face of Nature and Inner Light,
All the beauties and dreams
Of my fulfilled ambitions of all incarnations,
I behold painted brightly there.
On the white altar of my love,
I shall ever keep for Thee
My fresh-cut flowers of devotion.

Paramhansa Yogananda

The silent song of their fragrance
Will eternally chant of Thee
To winging winds and storm-tossed seas,
—Until all creation shall ring
With the divine echoes of Thy Name.
From mountain peak to coral reef,
—From highest tree-top to sea-shell's heart,
—From East to West, and North to South:
My soul shall garner
And imprison on the altar of its prayers,
The fragrant echoes of one beloved Name . . .
Om! Om! Om!!!

GUESTS: GOOD AND BAD

Tied up, steeped in bad habits is mankind—and these bad habits are constantly being fed, while the good ones are starved. The undesirable guests have filled the seats in the auditorium of your mind, and the good ones are hardly granted an audience, so go away discouraged.

To develop good habits, you must nourish them with good actions; and to do this it is necessary to be in good company. Environment is very important, for it is stronger than will power.

Human beings are traveling matterward. The searchlight of the mind is constantly being thrown outside, whereas it should be thrown inside. People are running and running. But there is no place in the world where they can flee from themselves.

You must face yourself! If you pray for success, but have failure thoughts within, you are like a man who sends another on an errand and that one is attacked by robbers on the way. The thieves who take away your success are your own bad habits. You send your prayer-children to God without protection, and they are waylaid by robbers of restlessness on the way before they reach God. Of Course, God hears your prayers, for He is everywhere and all-knowing; but under certain conditions He does not answer those prayers.

Once there was a king who told one of his subjects that unless he could answer a certain question he would be hanged. The man said: "Tell me the question." The king then spoke as follows: "Where does God sit, and which way does He look—North, South, East, or West?" The man went home to think and told his servant that he would be killed unless he answered the king in a fortnight. The servant said to his master: "Let me go for you. I will answer the question." So the servant went to the king and said to him: "First, let me sit on your throne, because while I answer your question I am your master." The king surrendered his throne to the servant and then asked him: "Where does God sit, and which way does He look—North, South, East or West?" The servant on the throne made answer: "Bring me a cow." So a cow was brought. Then the servant said: "Where is the milk?" The king answered: "In the udder." "Nay, Sire," said the servant, "the milk is not only in the udder, but throughout the cow, for the milk is the essence of the cow."

Then the servant asked that a bowl of milk be brought; and when it was brought to him, said to the king: "Where is the butter?" The king said: "I see no butter." The servant answered: "The butter is throughout the milk. Just churn the milk and the butter will become separated from it. Thus, as the milk is all through the cow and the butter is throughout the milk, so is God everywhere." So did the wisdom of the servant save the life of his master, for the king received the correct answer to his question.

If you ask for yourself this same question, you will receive a like answer, for you must milk His Presence from all vast Nature, and you must churn Him from the diluted mind by power of inspiration.

God is not the monopoly of the Yogis or Swamis. He is in the heart and soul of every being. And when you open within yourself the secret temple in your heart, you shall read the book of life. Then, and then only, will you contact the living God. And then will you feel Him as the very essence of your being. Without this feeling in your heart, there will be no answer to your prayers.

When I was a child, I wrote a letter to God. I was so little I could hardly write, but I thought I told Him a great deal. I did not ask anything for myself. I asked to be told something about Himself. And every day I waited for the postman to bring me the answer to my letter, never doubting that it would come. And one day it did come. He came to me in a vision. I saw the answer of God written in letters of shining gold. I could scarcely read, but the meaning came to me. He said: "I am Life! I am Love! I am looking after you through your father and mother!" Then I understood. I felt God!

If your prayers reach God, it matters not if your sins be deeper than the ocean and higher than the Himalayas. He will destroy them. For a time, perhaps, you may sink underneath strata of darkness, but still you are a spark of an Eternal Flame. You can hide the spark, but you can never destroy it.

God is in everything. When you have Him, you have everything.

Whatever I wish for now comes to me immediately. So I must be careful in my wishing. First and last, I wish for God. But when I wish for others, I have to struggle, for I have to fight their Karmas. You must be careful though. You must not wish for God, while secretly wishing for something else, saying to yourself: "First, I will wish for God, and then surely I will get the automobile I want." That is not right. You cannot fool God.

We must seek unity of our consciousness with God's consciousness. When we have that, our prayers will not be waylaid. We are not beggars. We are sons of God.

Never pray for anything, unless you have first attained God. Do not fool yourself. Wake up and say to God: "I will forsake everything until I know Thee." Do not pray for anything in the world until you feel your identity with God. He knows what you need. Seek Him until you find Him, until your whole being throbs with His power and glory.

Ask Him to reveal Himself to you. Do not rest until He answers. Ask with all your heart, again and again: "Reveal Thyself! The stars may be shattered. The earth may be dissolved. Yet my soul shall cry unto Thee—'Reveal Thyself!'"

At last, like an invisible earthquake, He will suddenly make Himself manifest. The inertia of His silence will be broken by your steady, persistent hammering; the walls of silence will tremble and crumble, and you will feel that as a river you are flowing into the Mighty Ocean, and you will say to Him: "I am now one with Thee, whatever Thou hast, that same have I."

And then you will be consciously face to face with YOURSELF at last. The auditorium of your mind will be crowded to overflowing with the holy guests of your own divine thoughts. Beggars of grief and discord and pain will not be able to enter there and their wails and sighs will be drowned . . . in the harmony of an ever-singing and never-weary choir of happiness and peace.

Paramhansa Yogananda

LESSONS IN SPIRITUALITY

I have not come to you to give you intellectual sermons. I do not like to blindly give you the thoughts of others. You can read books for yourself. When I speak to you, I shall tell you what I feel of God. I shall tell you what I hear from God. It is my privilege to bring to you a message that will help you to realize God, and to develop yourselves harmoniously, physically, mentally and spiritually.

I have spoken to thousands, and aroused the feelings and emotions of the multitude. But now it is my desire to train a band of souls, who would not remain satisfied with intellectual reasonings and a superficial knowledge of God, but who would night and day make the effort to contact the God Whom I have found.

Why are your prayers not answered? Because of the evil seed elements in your subconscious mind, the bad habits of the past that stand between you and God. I wish you to read the Scientific Healing Affirmations daily, because health is not a permanent thing. There are destructive forces constantly lurking within you, as the result of past actions; therefore, you must be constantly watchful to counteract those forces. If you pray for success, but your subconscious mind is working against you, saying all the time: "I will not succeed," how can you succeed? How can you aspire to reach God with empty, dead prayers? Pray until you positively KNOW. Yogoda gives you the method whereby, through true and faithful application, you shall attain to God.

You must do away with the traditional ideas of your sinfulness and weakness, and insist fearlessly that you are a child of God. Always remember that. Release your mind from your countless matter-bound-desires; for until you let them go, you cannot see the flame of God.

In "Whispers From Eternity," I have laid, side by side, the feelings of the Great Masters. Let us take Moses. His was a martial spirit, such as befitted the time in which he lived. All great souls have met the need of a certain time. Goodness does not mean weakness. Goodness is a power that knows how to fight the forces of evil. If goodness has no stamina, it will be destroyed. Goodness must be harnessed with strength. Strength means power, and power is the ability to conquer. So the martial spirit of Moses was needed to meet the need of the time in which he lived.

One of the greatest contributions of the Jewish religion is the conception that there is only one God, but many prophets. No one should be put above God. Even though the waves and the ocean are one, still the ocean can never be taken for the wave. The ocean is the substance; the wave is one of the forms of the substance. The substance is the unchangeable; the forms are many and changeable. The substance is spirit; the forms are ever varying expressions of creation.

The greatest thing in the christian Bible is the statement that God made man in His Image. In this image lie all the qualities that are in the Spirit. In the drop are all the chemicals that are in the lake. We are made of spirit. It is false to say we are mortals, yet this mortal concept has grown so strong that it has become our second nature. We may know that we are made of spirit, but the consciousness of sin holds us in bondage.

Confession was a good thing; but it became, in certain cases, a mechanical affair. To recognize one's errors and discard them, is true repentance. And unless the spiritual doctor is told about the symptoms and spiritual troubles of his disciple patient, he cannot very well help him. But confession is meaningless and harmful when the spiritual advisor himself is not free from the disease he aspires to cure in others.

To make our prayer-demands effective, we must first find unity with God. These Lessons are given to you for that purpose only, to help you gain that unity with God.

Do not let wrong and discordant things of the world worry you. It is true that there are many bad things in existence. But if a thing is bad, why make it a part of yourself? You are your own greatest enemy; and you are your own greatest friend. It is in your power to choose that which you want to make a part of yourself. This applies to thoughts and feelings and desires, as well as deeds.

We must always remember and affirm: "Thou art the Father Who owns this universe, and because we are Thy children, we own it too." I can hear some of your say: "How is that possible?" The trouble is, we do not know how long we have been in bondage with weakness and wrong thoughts, and we have no realization of the depths of the mischief that has already been done by not being consciously identified with the Father.

Alight Publications (www.alightbooks.com)

Collected Works of Paramhansa Yogananda
The Essence Of Kriya Yoga
Practical Meditations
Balancing East-West

Books by Yogiraj Gurunath Siddhanath
Wings To Freedom
Earth Peace Through Self Peace
Dew Drops Of The Soul

Books by Rudra Shivananda
Chakra self-Healing By The Power Of Om
Breathe Like Your Life Depends On It
The Yoga of Purification and Transformation
In Light Of Kriya Yoga
Insight And Guidance For Spiritual Seekers

Books by Partap Singh
Time And The Human Condition
A Better Way

www.ingramcontent.com/pod-product-compliance
Lightning Source LLC
Chambersburg PA
CBHW071653160426
43195CB00012B/1451